THE LAST TUDOR KING

By the same author

★

Fiction

SHE SAW THEM GO BY
TO BE A KING
LONG DIVISION
I WILL BE GOOD
WORLDS APART
EVER THINE
FALLING STREAM
THE STONE LILY

Biography

GREAT VILLIERS
MARY II,
QUEEN OF ENGLAND
QUEEN ANNE'S SON

THE LAST TUDOR KING

A STUDY OF EDWARD VI

[OCTOBER 12TH, 1537 — JULY 6TH, 1553]

BY

HESTER W. CHAPMAN

JONATHAN CAPE
THIRTY BEDFORD SQUARE · LONDON

frontispiece: EDWARD AT 14½ YEARS

FIRST PUBLISHED 1958
© 1958 BY HESTER W. GRIFFIN

PRINTED IN GREAT BRITAIN IN THE CITY OF OXFORD
AT THE ALDEN PRESS
ON PAPER MADE BY JOHN DICKINSON & CO. LTD.
COLLOTYPE ILLUSTRATIONS BY L. VAN LEER & CO. N.V., AMSTERDAM
BOUND BY A. W. BAIN & CO. LTD., LONDON

CONTENTS

ILLUSTRATIONS

ACKNOWLEDGMENTS

THE two friends to whom the author is most deeply indebted are Miss Rosamond Lehmann and Mr Christopher Morris. Without the imaginative understanding and tireless sympathy of the one and the constructive, learned and meticulous criticisms of the other the difficulties of this first attempt at Tudor biography would have been immeasurably greater. Such help is of the kind that can only be assessed in recollection.

Grateful acknowledgments are due to Her Majesty the Queen for permission to reproduce the full-length portrait of Edward VI at Hampton Court Palace; to Lord Brabourne, for the reproduction of the painting of Admiral Seymour of Sudeley; to the Right Honourable the Viscount de Lisle, v.c., for that of the Duke of Northumberland; to Sir Harry Verney, BT, for that of the Duke of Somerset; to the National Portrait Gallery for those of the profile of Edward, the head of Jane Seymour and the drawing of the Princess Mary; to the Washington Art Gallery for that of the portrait of Edward in infancy; to the Trustees of the British Museum for leave to reproduce an enlarged print of Henry VIII from the painting in his Psalter; to the Master and Benchers of the Inner Temple for permission to photograph Edward's Device for the Succession. Finally, for their invaluable advice, help and co-operation thanks are offered to Mr H. G. Groves, Miss Patience and Miss Constance Hoare, Mrs Nelson-Smith, the Reverend Maurice Ryan, Mr George Rylands, Mrs F. W. Thomas and the Staffs of the London Library and the British Museum.

HENRY V m. Katherine of France m. Owen Tudor
1387–1422

Edmund Tudor m. Margaret Beaufort

HENRY VII m. Elizabeth of York
1457–1509

Arthur m. Katherine of Aragon   HENRY VIII
d. 1502   1491–1547
                                    m.

(1)	(2)	(3)	(4)	(5)	(6)
Katherine of Aragon	Anne Boleyn	Jane Seymour	Anne of Cleves	Katherine Howard	Katherine Parr
	x 1536			x 1542	

MARY
1516–58

ELIZABETH I
1533–1603

EDWARD VI
1537–53

GENEALOGICAL TABLE

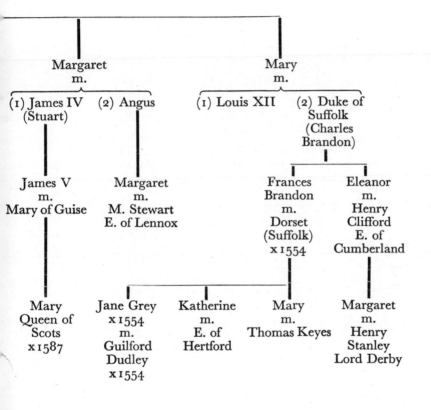

To

PATRICK FILMER-SANKEY

THE LAST TUDOR KING

But the Lord said unto me, Say not, I am a child: for thou shalt go to all that I shall send thee, and whatsoever I command thee, thou shalt speak ... See, I have this day set thee over the nations and over the kingdoms, to root out and to pull down, and to destroy, and to throw down, to build and to plant ...

Jeremiah I. 7–10

FOREWORD

EDWARD VI, the youngest child and only surviving son of Henry VIII, was born in 1537, the twenty-ninth year of his father's reign. He succeeded at the age of nine and died in 1553, three months before his sixteenth birthday. Inevitably he has been and will no doubt remain overshadowed by the longer-lived members of his dynasty. Yet although the grandson of Henry VII and the half-brother of Mary and Elizabeth I must sink into the background of the Tudor panorama, an account of his temperament and circumstances may show him, potentially at least, as remarkable as any of his race. This boy king who died young was, in fact, a more formidable and less pathetic — perhaps even a rather less appealing — figure, than such a phrase implies. His reign produced one of the most chaotic and disastrous upheavals in our history; two of the politicians who staked their lives and fortunes on its fluctuations were as masterful, as brilliant and as unusual as he promised to be; and their struggles to subjugate him and break one another forced his character into a startling and singular maturity. It is therefore arguable that Edward was not the sickly, helpless creature pitied and relegated by most historians, but an intelligent, vigorous, high-spirited boy who, born to despotism and reared in splendour, was destroyed by the Furies that he himself helped to conjure up from the gulfs and chasms of the English Reformation. In the light of this suggestion — for to theorize would be unseemly and tedious — the story of the last Tudor king is presented.

※

THE TUDORS AND THE SEYMOURS

O N September 16th, 1537, Jane Seymour, third wife of Henry VIII, moved into the Palace of Hampton Court for the birth of her child. Proclaimed — but not crowned — Queen of England eighteen months earlier, this self-possessed young woman of twenty-eight was reaching the apotheosis of a career for which a highly developed social poise, a cool temperament and a placid comeliness were largely responsible. She could now contemplate a past of perfect respectability and a future for which all the omens were propitious. The months of her pregnancy had gone smoothly by; the physicians and soothsayers assured her of a son;[1] and the King's adoring care surrounded her movements, forestalled her wants and provided for her most trivial caprices. Wherever she walked or ate or slept, in presence-chamber and gallery, in chapel, banqueting-hall and state bed-room, she could see her arms and initials intertwined with those of the Tudors in medallions of gilded carving and crude colour. In this time of contented expectancy and penultimate triumph — while the quails for which she longed turned on the spits of the fine new kitchens;[2] while tournaments, masques and feasts succeeded one another; while Henry maintained his routine of jousts, hunting-parties, daily Masses and council meetings; while the congregations of a thousand churches poured out their hearts in prayer for the safe delivery of a prince — her supremacy seemed permanent and the power of the Seymours irrevocably established. There is no indication that it ever occurred to her or to any of those about her that a few weeks later she would be carried out of Hampton Court in her coffin.

The family raised by Jane Seymour to wealth and greatness was ancient, prosperous and undistinguished. According to Elizabethan genealogists, the St Maur who founded it followed William the Conqueror into England and fought at Hastings;[3] possibly William de St Maur, first heard of in 1240 as Master of

Woundy and Penhow in Monmouthshire, was one of the many landowners who bribed the monks of Battle to insert his name in the Abbey Roll. Some two hundred years later his descendant, Roger de Seymour, acquired the property of Wolf Hall in Wiltshire, where he established his line, becoming Bailiff and Guardian of Savernake Forest; his badge of office — a huge hunting-horn tipped with silver[4] — was still in the possession of Jane's father, Sir John Seymour, when he was knighted and made Sheriff of Wiltshire, Dorset and Somerset in 1518, some twelve years after his marriage to Margery Wentworth, daughter of Sir Henry Wentworth of Nettlested in Suffolk. This lady, who could trace her descent from Lionel, Duke of Clarence, and thus from Edward III, had ten children — six sons and four daughters. Jane, the eldest, was born at Wolf Hall in 1509. Little is known of her early years beyond the fact that she was well educated and the possibility that she accompanied her eldest brother, Edward, to the Court of Francis I in 1528, remaining there in the service of Queen Claude. She met Henry VIII for the first time when he stayed at Wolf Hall in 1535.[5] A few weeks later her father obtained for her the post of lady-in-waiting to Anne Boleyn, who had then been Queen of England for three years and was approaching her hideous but not unexpected end. By the time Jane Seymour entered her service, Anne's hold over the King had been fatally weakened and she was in a state of nervous tension that alternated between hysteria and collapse. Having failed to produce a male heir — the birth of the Princess Elizabeth in 1533 was regarded not only as a national disappointment but as a portent of her mother's ruin — she knew herself, although pregnant again, unloved and the symbol, in her husband's eyes, of a sin that must be expiated as soon as a suitable opportunity arose.

The new lady-in-waiting's character and appearance — more important still, her grasp of the situation — were all that was needed to bring on a crisis and loosen such restraint as Henry had been able to exercise over his revulsion from the woman he had idolized for eleven years. With the installation of Jane Seymour the contrast between her and her mistress became a favourite topic amongst those whose acumen had formerly guided them out of Katherine of Aragon's circle into that of the Boleyns. It was at once observed that this small, fair, composed creature had a greater dignity and beauty than the overwrought, ailing, black-eyed 'night crow'[6] whom she served: also that she was 'of a more even and constant temper'. Another historian has said that 'the richer she was in clothes the fairer she appeared: but that the Other, the richer she was apparelled, the worse she looked'.[7] Finally, while Jane Seymour showed 'a pleasing sprightliness' on all social occasions, her response to the King's advances was noted to be discreet to the point of prudery.[8]

Within a few weeks of Jane Seymour's arrival at the Palace of Westminster Henry began his courtship, combining a traditional and romantic approach with crude attempts to break down the respectful humility of her rebuffs by offers of money and jewels. She refused all these, but accepted and put on a locket containing his portrait. By one of his gentlemen he then sent her a purse of gold pieces. She knelt and kissed it, saying: 'There is nothing I value so much as my honour. If the King's Grace wisheth to send me a present of money, I humbly ask him to reserve it for such a time as God will be pleased to send me an advantageous marriage.'[9]

Henry did not act on this practical suggestion; it may be that even then he visualized Jane Seymour rather as a consort than as a mistress and foresaw the destruction of Anne Boleyn. His prescience in human affairs amounted to genius; it was the result of a sleepless sensitivity to the fluctuation of temperament in others and a knowledge of the varying range of his own powers that had long been instinctive. Concealed by the urbane, forthright yet dominating address of a potentate whose supremacy has never been in question, his response to every situation was at the same time subtle and creative. He now blandly accepted the part of the rejected aspirant in order to further a process controlled by himself, in which the influences of Jane and Edward Seymour — Edward was by this time Master of the Horse and Baron Seymour — were subsidiary; Henry, therefore, made no objection to the young man's chaperonage of his sister during most of their interviews.[10] Edward Seymour, adaptable yet resolute, accomplished, graceful and bold, was the perfect type of the 'new' great noble, and high in Henry's favour before, during and after his wooing of Jane, who seems to have collaborated with her brother in her presentation of an unassuming but inviolable chastity that yet allowed the King to take her on his knee in the Queen's ante-chamber. Here Anne found them; as soon as she and Henry were alone she burst into furious and tearful reproaches, of which the fate of the child she carried was the practical theme. 'Be at peace, sweetheart, and all shall go well for thee,' said Henry soothingly.[11] A day or two later Anne drew the obvious conclusion from Jane's new locket and tore it from her neck so violently that in the struggle she wounded her hand. The result was another fit of hysterics; on January 29th, 1536, she was delivered of a dead boy. When Henry came to scold her for the loss of self-control that had caused this disaster, Anne roused herself to reply with the fiery resilience that had once so entranced him: 'You have none but yourself to blame for this disappointment', adding some bitter comments on 'that wench, Jane Seymour'. Henry replied: 'You shall have no more boys by me', and walked out of the bed-chamber.[12]

Jane Seymour was far too astute to remain in attendance on the now piteous figure of the woman she had supplanted. Escorted by her brother, she retired to Wolf Hall, thus making it clear to Henry what he was missing, and might even lose.[13] The stakes were high; and she had to wait four months before Anne Boleyn reached the block by a route in which the accusations of adultery and high treason and the verdict of a packed court made milestones that were to recur in Henry's matrimonial progress. By this time his affection for Jane Seymour had become common knowledge. Hastily subscribing to the vision of herself that she and her brother had set before him, he punished such tale-bearers as could be traced, and wrote to her in the gently chivalrous strain that their circumstances required: 'My dear Friend and Mistress, The bearer of these few lines from thy entirely devoted servant will deliver into thy fair hands a token of my true affection for thee, hoping you will keep it for ever in your sincere love for me. Advertising you that there is a ballad made lately of great derision against us, which if it go abroad and is seen by you, I pray you to pay no manner of regard to it. I am not at present informed who is the setter forth of this malignant writing; but if he is found out, he shall be straitly punished for it. For the things ye lacked, I have minded my lord [Treasurer] to supply them to you as soon as he could buy them. Thus hoping shortly to receive you in these arms, I end for the present, Your own loving servant and sovereign, H.R.'[14]

During the weeks of Anne's imprisonment Jane Seymour returned to London, but not to Court; with her parents she remained in their house overlooking the river, where Henry visited her — still under the supervision of her brother and father.[15] So the image of a modest and virtuous queen consort was created in the public mind.

Within a few hours of Anne Boleyn's condemnation Jane and Edward Seymour moved to Hampton Court where they were joined by the King, and on the day of her execution — May 19th — the betrothal was announced to the Privy Council. The Seymours then withdrew to Wolf Hall for a week, returning to London for the marriage, privately performed and granted a special licence by Cranmer, Archbishop of Canterbury, in the Palace of Westminster. On the 29th Jane was proclaimed Queen and the plans for her coronation were set in hand. In June she held her first official reception in honour of Eustace Chapuys, Ambassador to the Emperor Charles V. This acute and critical observer was disappointed at first; he found her appearance unremarkable and her response to his master's fulsome messages of congratulation inadequate. Henry apologized for her shyness. 'You are the first Ambassador to whom she hath spoken', he said. Later on, when they were able to converse more informally, Chapuys found the new Queen very intelligent and noted that she was not to be drawn into discussions on religion or politics, adding that she bore her honours with dignity.[16]

Indeed, it seems as if Jane Seymour had been training herself rather for years than for months to replace the reckless termagant whose pride and violence had precipitated her death. Before taking his bride on the round of hunting-parties and progresses that was to make her known to the people, Henry settled the matter of her arms. The three lions of England were quartered with those of the Seymours, and a personal badge designed for the redecoration of Jane's apartments. This was a circular castle, issuing red and white Tudor roses, flames and a phoenix, the whole surrounded with the motto chosen by herself — 'Bound to Obey and Serve' — that in the course of a few days was substituted for Anne Boleyn's white falcon; in the larger area of Hampton Court the workmen

21

were so pressed that they had to superimpose the J.S.s over the A.B.s.[17] The dedication of Coverdale's Bible, then reprinting at Zürich, was similarly treated; the frontispiece enshrining the late Queen's initials had been set up during the last months of her life and there was no time to recast it.[18]

There followed a happy time, perhaps the happiest of Jane Seymour's short life. She and Henry progressed in state by water from Greenwich to Westminster — their magnificent new barge was copied from the Venetian Bucentaur — and attended High Mass in the Abbey. Then a water fête was held which the King stopped when in a mock fight between two galleys one overturned and a competitor was drowned; they returned to watch a tournament in Whitehall from the Holbein gateway. In the winter Jane was the centre of a procession from Westminster to St Paul's; and when the Thames froze the people crowded the banks to see Their Graces ride over the ice on their way to Greenwich, followed by a train of courtiers and yeomen of the guard. As soon as the Christmas festivities were at an end, the King and Queen visited Canterbury and inspected the new pier at Dover.[19] Everywhere the slight, blonde girl and the bulky, ageing man were cheered and blessed; not even the patient and obstinate Katherine of Aragon seems to have been as popular as the most self-contained of Henry's queens.

During the summer and autumn of 1536 Jane Seymour established the surviving members of her family. Three of her brothers were dead and her sisters married. Her fourth brother, Henry, turned away from Court life; having received his knighthood and some grants of land, he remained quietly in the country until his death in 1578; he survived to see the ruin of all the Seymours. Edward became Viscount Beauchamp of Hache, Chancellor of North Wales and Lord Chamberlain to the King. The sixth brother, Thomas, a handsome, shallow and supremely egotistical young man, was given property and made Gentleman of the Privy Chamber. He considered this treatment, compared with that of Edward, shabby; the result was a bitter and violent jealousy of which his nephew received the full impact on his accession ten years later.

Naturally there was much grumbling among the longer established courtiers and statesmen about these favoured country squires, as being too recently ennobled to deserve honours and power. Jane and Edward Seymour might have replied, if they had not been as circumspect as they were determined, that their lineage was of a far higher degree than that of the Tudors. Henry VIII's great-grandfather, Owen Tudor, had started life as Clerk of the Wardrobe to Katherine de Valois, widow of Henry V, whom he married secretly not long before his execution during the Wars of the Roses; his elder son, Edmund, Henry VIII's grandfather, restored the family status by his marriage with Margaret Beaufort, the great-great-grand-daughter of Edward III. Thus the son of Jane and Henry descended from that monarch through both parents, but on the distaff side only; in fact, it had long been tacitly acknowledged that Henry VII's claim to the throne rested rather on his victory at Bosworth Field (although he had dated his reign from the day before it), than on his Plantagenet ancestry.

Jane Seymour's coronation was now postponed, first on account of a fresh outbreak of plague in London and then by the early stages of the Northern rising. In March 1537, her pregnancy put any such ceremony out of the question; she was not carrying her child easily, and seemed low-spirited and nervous. In a letter to the Duke of Norfolk, the King gave her state as the reason for his decision not to preside over the newly formed Council of York. 'Being but a woman,' he explained, 'upon some sudden and displeasant rumours and bruits that might by foolish or light persons be allowed abroad in our absence ... she might take ... such impressions as might engender no little danger or displeasure to the infant.'[20]

Henry and Jane were happy together in spite of her bouts of depression and her failure to influence his policy over the repercussions of the rebellion. When she begged him on her knees to restore the Abbey lands of the North — those acquired by the Seymours were, presumably, another matter — he told her, quite kindly, to get up and not meddle in his affairs as her predecessor had done.[21] In her efforts to reconcile him with the Princess Mary, then aged twenty, she was more successful. Mary's refusal to acknowledge her father as Supreme Head of the English Catholic Church had not only estranged them but brought her into grave danger. Mary, who appears to have continued to love Henry in spite of his grossly brutal treatment of her mother and herself, had been made very miserable by his displeasure. Their reconciliation and her return to Court were effected by one of Jane's more agreeable machinations. 'Why, darling, how happeneth it you are no merrier?' asked the King on one occasion. 'Now it hath pleased Your Grace to make me your wife, there are none but my inferiors to make merry withal, Your Grace excepted — unless it would please you that we might enjoy the company of the Lady Mary's Grace at Court. I would make merry with her.' 'We will have her here, darling, if she will make thee merry,' said Henry, and the Princess was sent for. She appeared from her semi-imprisonment at Hunsdon in Hertfordshire, splendidly dressed, with all her ladies. As soon as she entered the Presence-Chamber, where the King and Queen surrounded by the Court awaited her, she made a low curtsy; then, falling on her knees, she asked her father's blessing.

Henry raised, kissed and blessed her; he led her up to the Queen who embraced her and bade her welcome. With the malicious pleasure that he sometimes took in confounding sycophants and toadies, Henry turned to the lords and said: 'Some of you were desirous that I should put this jewel to death.' Mary began to tremble, and the Queen intervened. 'That had been great pity, to have lost your chiefest jewel of England.' 'Nay, nay,' said Henry, with a return to his famous bluffness, 'Edward ... Edward ... ' clapping the Queen on the belly.

At this point the Princess's nerve began to give way; she was almost fainting when Henry took her by the arm and walked her up and down till she recovered. [22] Later, the rumour went round that he had said to Mary: 'She who did you so much harm and prevented me from seeing you for so long hath paid the penalty.' [23] Thereafter she was given presents of jewels and money, rooms at Court and constantly visited by himself and the Queen; the order went forth that she was to regain her original title of Lady Princess.

Mary's half-sister, who was sharing her household, was not so well treated. On her mother's disgrace and execution, her father had declared Elizabeth illegitimate; as soon as Jane Seymour became pregnant and Mary was again received, he commanded that Elizabeth should be known simply as the Lady Elizabeth. When the Governor of her household, Sir Francis Bryan, solemnly announced this decision to the four-year-old princess, he got a severe reception. 'Why, Governor,' said this very sharp child, 'how hap it yesterday Lady Princess, and today but Lady Elizabeth?' Sir Francis Bryan's reply has not been recorded.[24]

A rumour was put about by Chapuys that the Queen had influenced her husband to degrade the daughter of Anne Boleyn. This is unlikely; Jane Seymour had sense enough to realize that if her child were a boy both Mary and Elizabeth must be relegated; and it was the business as well as the pleasure of herself and her brother to be friendly with all the members of the family on which they depended, even with the most insignificant; also the peaceful, domestic atmosphere created by Jane Seymour's kindness to his daughters strengthened her hold over the King.

As if she were beginning to enjoy her power, the new Queen now set forth her rules for the dress of her ladies-in-waiting. There was, naturally, great competition to enter the household before the birth of her child; afterwards, the establishment of another royal nursery would produce more and better Court posts. One impoverished peeress managed to 'place' two daughters, after sending quails, weekly, and a supplementary present of lap-dogs, with one of which, a white poodle, Jane had her portrait painted. When the girls appeared at Hampton Court in the French hoods and plain dresses that were all they had for best, the Queen pointed out that their head-dresses must conform to the accepted English style and their girdles be set with pearls, according to custom.[25] A hundred and twenty pearls — all she could afford — were collected and sent off by the eager mother, only to cause further criticism; these were not enough to create the effect ordained by the fashion. The Queen was so kind as to put up with the inadequacy for the time being: but at the christening, the young ladies were told, they would not be allowed to appear unless properly dressed.[26]

As the time for that ceremony came nearer, tension centred in the new wing on the east front of Hampton Court Palace and radiated outwards to the remotest districts of the countryside. What if this child of many prayers were another daughter, or stillborn, as four of Henry's children by his first wife and one by his second had been? He was now in his forty-sixth year — past middle age, by the standards of that day — and his splendid health and tireless physical energy had begun to fail. He could no longer hunt all day and dance all night; nor could his physicians find a cure for the ulcer on his leg or the increasing weight that made his movements those of an old and tired man. Since the legitimacy of the two princesses had been as irremediably smirched by Henry himself as by his enemies, this baby might well be the sole, frail heir to the inheritance that only once, four hundred years before, had fallen to a woman, whose attempted rule had resulted in civil war. The faith of those in the King's immediate circle — 'Look daily for a Prince', wrote one statesman to another[27] — and the unshakeable optimism with which Henry ordered a Garter stall to be made ready for 'the Prince hoped for in due season', were not shared by all his people. There were indeed many to whom it had been revealed that he would have a son whose birth would bring in 'a golden world'.[28] But from others, to whom the ruined abbeys and broken images remained symbols of an unforgivable sin, there came premonitions, prophecies, warnings of God's vengeance on the dynasty. Out of the mists and mountains of Wales, from the very place where the handsome and penniless Owen Tudor had ventured to seek his fortune, the primeval voices rose — Merlin's above the rest — and were echoed by those of the local magicians. '*E. shall succeed H. and wear the crown of England and there shall be more murderers and traitors in his time than in his father's*', and '*There shall never be a King of England crowned after this King*'. So the sayings multiplied. No threat, no punishment could stop them; as soon as one wizard was burnt or hanged another took his place.[29]

Naturally these forebodings were kept from the Queen; and the King had no doubt at all that God was on his side — had he not put away two wives to that end? Coming out of the Queen's Presence-Chamber to wash before rejoining her for supper, he greeted a group of his gentlemen with the frank gaiety that sometimes made him irresistible, and spoke again of her coronation, adding that he had resolved not to travel more than sixty miles from the palace until she was delivered. They found him 'well and merry', and showing no sign of anxiety or suspense.[30]

And then at last the hour came. On the afternoon of October 9th, 1537, Jane Seymour began her labour. As soon as the heralds reached London with the news, bells rang and Masses were sung in every parish; the crowds who could not get into the churches accompanied the processions of priests and monks from St Paul's to the Abbey.[31]

Perhaps the God of the Church of England — the deity that Henry VIII had himself created out of his peculiar brand of theology and expediency — was still on his side; but it seemed as if those older and more terrible gods, whose warnings he had ignored, were revenging themselves on his wife. After a labour lasting three days and two nights, their son, a healthy normal child, was born. By two o'clock in the morning of October 12th, St Edward's Eve, Jane Seymour's work was done and her final triumph achieved. At eight the news reached London; and rejoicings poured over the city. Bells clashed and pealed; banners streamed out in a wild fantasia of lions, greyhounds, dragons, crowns and roses; doors and balconies glowed with garlands and hangings; two thousand salvoes sounded from the arsenal of the Tower; a representative gathering of the remaining orders of monks and friars assembled at St Paul's in their best copes carrying jewelled candlesticks. While the bishops feasted the people at the doors, the foreign ambassadors and Court officials crowded in for High Mass. All that afternoon and evening and through the night and the next day bonfires glittered and roared, while the Mayor and the aldermen rode through the crowded streets calling on the citizens to give thanks to God. It was perhaps necessary that they should be so reminded; for every conduit gushed ale or wine, and families sat round them on empty hogsheads, eating, drinking, lurching up to dance and kiss each other, crying, laughing, bawling out choruses from the broadsheets that had been printed weeks before:

> God save King Henry with all his power,
> And Prince Edward, that goodly flower,
> With all his lords of great honour —
> Sing on, troll away, sing, troll on away,
> Heave and how, rumbelow, troll on away —

and while they shouted and jigged, the pickpockets and the vagrants were the busiest and happiest of any, sure of the general pardon that would be part of His Grace's loving-kindness to his people.[32] As the news spread over England, every town and village

27

rocked and blazed: as it reached the Continent, secretaries hurried to compose royal assurances of goodwill.

The absence of any report on Jane Seymour's state during the next few days is typical of the contemporary attitude towards childbirth. She had survived a hideous ordeal, produced a son who seemed likely to live and was now available for further breeding. In any case, those about her were too much occupied with plans for the christening — which took place three days after the birth — to see beyond their share in the intricate ceremonial that the occasion required. The King began by curtailing the number to be admitted: for many of the nobles and officials now making the cross-country journey from London to attend it had been in or near the plague areas. Proclamations were issued forbidding persons from Croydon to come at all; no duke was to bring more than six gentlemen, no marquess more than five, and no bishop more than three chaplains. The gathering collected in the ante-rooms to the state bedchamber for the procession to the chapel — newly decorated for the last time in Henry's reign — must nevertheless have comprised between three and four hundred persons.[33] The 'ordinances' originally set out by the King's grandmother, Lady Margaret Beaufort, included the formal reception of all these guests by the Queen, who was lifted on to a state pallet, or sofa, decorated with the Royal Arms. Wrapped in velvet and fur, with Henry at her side, she remained seated during the next five or six hours. The outgoing procession — in which, according to the ancient etiquette, neither parent took part — was headed by gentlemen of the household carrying torches. The choir and the Dean preceded pairs of abbots, chaplains, bishops, privy councillors and noblemen; the Lord Treasurer and the Controller of the Household headed the foreign ambassadors, the Lord Chamberlain, the Lord Privy Seal (Thomas Cromwell) and the Lord Chancellor. Then came the godfathers — the Dukes of Norfolk and Suffolk and the Archbishop of Canterbury. The Earls of Sussex and Montagu (carrying silver basins), of Wiltshire (a wax taper), and Essex (a gold salt-cellar) were next. The honour of bearing the jewelled chrysome was given to the little Princess Elizabeth; as it was extremely heavy, she herself was carried by Edward Seymour. Finally the Prince appeared, in the arms of Lady Exeter, under a canopy supported by three marchionesses, of whom the principal was Lady Dorset, Governess of His Highness's household; she was attended by a group of nobles, two of whom held up the long folds of her robe. The end of the procession was formed by the wet-nurse and midwife under a canopy carried by six more noblemen, one being Thomas Seymour — not a very distinguished position — and another party of gentlemen with wax tapers, the Princess Mary and her ladies.

As soon as all these personages had been conducted to their places the trumpets sounded and the baptism was performed by Cranmer from the new silver-gilt font; on one side of it was a curtained space containing basins of perfumed water on warming-pans of hot coals for the washing of the Prince.

After the blessing the trumpets blared out again. Then Garter-King-of-Arms stepped forward and proclaimed: 'God of His Almighty and infinite grace give and grant good life and long to the right high, right excellent and noble Prince, Prince Edward, Duke of Cornwall and Earl of Chester, most dear and most entirely beloved son to our most dread and gracious Lord, King Henry VIII. Largesse, largesse, largesse!'[34] It was now midnight. The procession re-formed, returning through passages lined by men-at-arms to the state apartments, where Edward was presented to and blessed by the King and Queen. By this time the illuminations 'were so many', according to one observer, 'that it seemed like day'. As Henry took his son in his arms the tears ran down his face.[35]

Once more the trumpets rang out. Then the Duchess of Suffolk carried the Prince, his personal entourage of four hundred persons following them, to his apartments on the other side of the palace. Again, no comment on Jane Seymour's appearance is extant; no doubt it was in the correct tradition of gracious composure.

Celebrations were resumed next day, and the mood of almost hysterical thankfulness continued. Latimer, then Bishop of Worcester, whose attitude towards his betters was rather censorious than cringing, wrote to Cromwell: 'Here is no less rejoicing at the birth of our Prince, whom we hungered for so long, than there was at the birth of John the Baptist ... God give us grace to be thankful ... We have now the stop of vain trusts ... and the stay of vain expectations.'[36]

Before this letter reached the Lord Privy Seal, the Queen's

weakness — euphemistically described as 'natural' by those about her — had resulted in fever, delirium and collapse. These symptoms became apparent on October 18th, three days after the christening. Henry had intended to leave for Esher, to hunt; now he decided that, if she did not improve, he should remain at Hampton Court. Next day, early in the morning, she saw her confessor and received the last sacraments; but though her condition, that of puerperal fever, seemed desperate, she held her own. Five days later she was at the crisis, and the doctors told Henry that if she survived the next few hours she would recover. She died at two o'clock on the morning of October 25th.[37]

Henry was with her till the end. Then he left the palace for Windsor, too broken to be able to consider the arrangements for the lying-in-state, or the funeral. He ignored — he may not even have heard — the inevitable rumours that his wife had been sacrificed to his son, that the doctors had been careless, that the child had been torn from the womb at his command. All he could do now was to order Masses to be said for her soul, and leave the rest to the Privy Council.[38]

For three weeks the Queen lay in the Presence-Chamber at Hampton Court Palace in a robe of gold tissue, jewelled and crowned, her long hair framing her face, more impressive, perhaps, in death than she had been in life. On November 12th the funeral procession left for Windsor. The coffin, covered with black velvet, was drawn by six horses. Preceded by the Princess Mary as chief mourner, the whole Court followed, all, according to the new fashion, wearing black instead of purple. After the funeral a Requiem Mass was sung at Windsor and a dirge at St Paul's. In all the churches the bells tolled from midday until six in the evening. Twelve hundred Masses were said in the city of London alone. Henry 'kept himself close', according to one chronicler, 'for a long while'. In his reply to Francis I's congratulations on Edward's birth he wrote simply of 'the Divine Providence who hath mingled my joy with the bitterness of the death of her who brought me this happiness'. Those who knew him best were surprised that he refused to consider remarrying immediately — 'though His Grace taketh this chance', Cromwell noted, 'reasonably'; he was able to tell his master that the Prince was well 'and sucketh like a child of his puissance', subjoining to this report a list of suitable consorts.[39] Presently the King roused himself to organize his son's household.

Henry's ideas of hygiene were considerably in advance of his age, and his care for the minutest details in the management of Edward's nurseries is shown by the records of Hampton Court. Here — and at Havering-atte-Bowe, Enfield, Woking and half a dozen other country palaces — the most perfect cleanliness was ordained under pain of imprisonment for disobedience. Courts, galleries and passages were to be scrubbed and swept twice daily; no dirty dishes left about; dogs, with the exception of the ladies' pets, kept in their kennels; and the medieval, hugger-mugger custom of the whole household eating together discontinued. Though water had to be carried up by hand from the outside conduits, all the principal apartments had lavatories; in the servants' quarters there were fifteen jakes; and, in the royal and private rooms, baths. The most detailed precautions against murder and infection were set out in the King's own hand. No outsider was to touch or approach anything used by Edward's attendants; every article of clothing, cutlery or pottery with which he had contact was to be washed after use; all food must be tasted; none of his suite were to come near or speak to anyone from London or the countryside; beggars and sick persons were to receive alms from beyond the outermost gates of the palace. Waste was as severely punished as neglect of these commandments; and every soul, from the Lady Governess to the youngest scullion, was bound by oath to keep them, as long as they remained in the service of 'His Majesty's most noble jewel'.[40]

Either these ordinances, or Edward's natural robustness, or their combination, had excellent results. The baby whom the people called England's Treasure continued healthy and vigorous, even a little in advance of his age, judging by the comments of the critical and sometimes hostile ambassadors who visited him during the first months of his life. Henry was congratulated on his son's progress, and became as popular as at any time during his reign.

Yet Edward's apparently unassailable inheritance was already disputed, not only by the potentates of Europe, but in the hidden cells of rebellion in his own country. Within a few weeks of his birth the Catholic powers issued a solemn and irrevocable denial of his right to the English throne. His father had broken with the

Holy See; still daring to call himself a Catholic, he had flouted the Vicar of Christ and put away his first and only lawful wife for a concubine and her bastard, thereafter crowning this defiance by his marriage to Edward's mother under laws not recognized by the Vatican. His younger children were thus both illegitimate. Mary was the heir.

Henry might — and indeed did — ignore the repercussions from the Continent; within the area of his own jurisdiction, absolute though it was, he had to eliminate revolt before his son succeeded to the Supremacy over Church and State that he had moulded out of chaos and revolution into an intensely personal and ingenious autocracy.

NOTES TO CHAPTER I

[1] *Letters and Papers of Henry VIII*, vol. XII, part 1: 196.
[2] Ibid., 494.
[3] Collins, *Peerage*, vol. I, p. 141.
[4] Ibid.
[5] St Maur, *Annals of the Seymours*, p. 24.
[6] Cavendish, *Life of Cardinal Wolsey*, p. 203.
[7] Heylyn, *History of the Reformation*, p. 15.
[8] Ibid., p. 5.
[9] *Cal. Span. P.*, vol. V, part 2, p. 54.
[10] Ibid.
[11] George Wyatt, *Memoir of Queen Anne Boleyn*, p. 443.
[12] Heylyn, p. 5.
[13] St Maur, p. 28.
[14] Halliwell-Philipps, *Letters of the Kings of England*, vol. I, p. 350.
[15] *Cal. Span. P.*, vol. V, part 2, p. 106.
[16] Ibid., p. 157.
[17] Gairdner, *History of the English Church in the Sixteenth Century*, p. 192.
[18] Ibid., p. 192.
[19] *Cal. Span. P.*, vol. V, part 2, p. 182.
[20] *L. & P.*, vol. XII, part 1: 839.
[21] Ibid., 994.
[22] H.M.C. Rutland MSS, vol. I, p. 310.
[23] *Chronicle of Henry VIII* (ed. Hume), p. 72.
[24] Rutland MSS, vol. I, p. 310.
[25] *L. & P.*, vol. XII, part 2: 1267.
[26] Ibid.
[27] Ibid.
[28] Pollard, *Tudor Tracts*, p. 17.
[29] *L. & P.*, vol. XIV, part 2: 11; Fabyan, *Chronicle*, p. 702.
[30] *L. & P.*, vol. XIV, part 2: 11.
[31] Wriothesley, *Chronicle of England*, vol. I, pp. 66-70.
[32] *L. & P.*, vol. XII, part 2: 894.
[33] Ibid.
[34] Hume, p. 74; *L. & P.*, vol. XII, part 2: 894.
[35] Hume, p. 74.
[36] *L. & P.*, vol. XII, part 2: 894.
[37] Ibid., 1012.
[38] Ibid.
[39] *L. & P.*, vol. XIII, part 2: 953.
[40] Ibid., vol. XII, part 2: 894; Nichols, *Literary Remains of Edward VI*, vol. I, p. xxviii.

※

CHAPTER TWO

THE INHERITANCE

B Y the time Edward was three months old the plague scare
had died down, and he was visited daily by a number of
persons, some of whom, as they favoured Princess Mary's
cause, hoped, and indeed tried to persuade themselves, that he
would not survive. This made them all the more eager to obtain
one of the most distinguished courtesies Henry could bestow — a
personal invitation to see his son. In the fourth month of Edward's
life Chapuys reported that 'the King has invited my colleague and
myself to a banquet at Antoncurt [sic] to see the Prince'. A month
later he was writing jubilantly that Edward was dead; two years
after that that he was slightly ill; and three years later still that he
had a weak constitution. The French Ambassador suited his
accounts to the situation. During Edward's fifth year, when his
marriage with one of the daughters of Francis I was in question, he
described him as 'handsome, strong, and marvellously big for his
age'. When the negotiations seemed likely to fail he said that
Edward had 'a natural weakness' that would make him the victim
of any disease; and in the following year he sent news that he
could not possibly live much longer. Whether hostile or loyal, all
the reports agree on one point; Edward was a beautiful child.[1]

It is doubtful whether he would be considered so today. He was
white-faced, very fair, grey-eyed and, during infancy, rather large
for his age. Extreme pallor of skin and hair — what might now be
thought of as a colourless insipidity — was the especial admiration
of the Renaissance connoisseur in both sexes and at all ages. As a
very young man, Henry VIII's light auburn beard and the trans-
parency of his complexion were his chief claims to a beauty that
his courtiers envied and tried to emulate by artificial means. The
effect most sought after was that created by the violent contrast of
heavily jewelled, slashed and embroidered garments cut on lines
that caricatured or disguised the body and an unshadowed delicacy that was sometimes enhanced by dyeing or plucking eyebrows

PARVVLE PATRISSA, PATRIÆ VIRTVTIS ET HÆRES
  ESTO, NIHIL MAIVS MAXIMVS ORBIS HABET.
GNATVM VIX POSSVNT COELVM ET NATVRA DEDISSE,
  HVIVS QVEM PATRIS, VICTVS HONORET HONOS.
ÆQVATO TANTVM, TANTI TV FACTA PARENTIS,
  VOTA HOMINVM, VIX QVO PROGREDIANTVR, HABENT
VINCITO, VICISTI. QVOT REGES PRISCVS ADORAT
  ORBIS, NEC TE QVI VINCERE POSSIT, ERIT.

EDWARD AT 2½ YEARS

and eyelashes. In Edward's case, the almost perfect uniformity of what might be described as a white-gold surface was emphasized by his proportions; from Holbein's portrait his contemporaries would therefore have received the impression of an ideal type: to a modern observer he may well appear fat, pasty and, as is usual with babies forced to sit still, of a rather sullen temper. The standards of those whose early accounts of him are extant required that a prince should be 'merry' — that is, quietly amiable — solid, and smoothly blond. Dark hair and rosy cheeks were thought plebeian; and vigour, from the earliest age, must be instinct with dignity. So Chapuys describes him as 'one of the prettiest children that could be seen anywhere', and a Spanish merchant as 'most beautiful'.[2] The English courtiers were naturally more effusive. Edward was nearly a year old when Sir Thomas Audley wrote that he never saw 'so goodly a child of his age, so merry, so pleasant, so good and loving countenance, and so earnest an eye, as it were a sage judgement towards every person that repaireth to his Grace'.[3]

While it was therefore impossible for the Catholic envoys to criticize Edward's looks, they continued to seize on all the rumours of his sickliness, aware that the unpleasant fact of his existence could only be swallowed in the hope that it would be brief; for, from the moment of his birth, the religious and economic conflict in which their countries were involved was connected with this child's inheritance. It fluctuated very little; until Henry's iron grasp relaxed in death the three parties into which England was divided would remain more or less static and difficult to exploit. It was because they knew this that the Venetian, French and Spanish Ambassadors sustained their masters with the belief that the Prince would die before the King: only so could Henry's achievements be undone and the party they supported regain its ancient power. This section, that of the 'Roman' Catholics, desired the return of the papal jurisdiction and the abolition of the Royal Supremacy. The reforming party had split into two sections — that of the Moderates, sometimes described as the Henricians, and that of the Extreme Protestants. The leaders of the Henricians were Bishop Bonner, Bishop Gardiner and Thomas Wriothesley, the Lord Chancellor. This party was Catholic in doctrine, but supported the Royal Supremacy and had been in favour of the divorce of Katherine of Aragon and the dissolution of the monasteries. Its members continued to call themselves Catholics.

Among the Extremists, Cranmer and Cromwell were the most influential; after Cromwell's execution in 1540, Lord Hertford, Latimer, Hooper and Ridley were allied with Cranmer as its sincerest and most powerful supporters. This party was gradually to affiliate itself with the post-Lutheran, Continental Protestantism of Zwingli (1484–1531) and Calvin (1509–64). Until Henry died, their doctrines were, of course, regarded as heretical, and their adherents punished accordingly: but the number of these adherents was rising.

In the years immediately following Edward's birth the main struggle in England was between the Extreme Protestants and the Henrician Moderates. Henry, while in favour of a few of the alterations advocated by the Extremists, identified himself with the orthodoxy of the Moderates; in this attitude he seems to have been supported by the middle classes and the 'new' nobility and gentry who had bought or been given the monastic lands, and were gradually acquiring political power.

Easy of access though he was, Henry stood apart and alone. None of his circle had his subtlety of mind, nor his interest in and knowledge of the finer points of theological controversy; nor did they ever quite grasp all his mental processes ('If I thought that my cap knew what I was thinking,' he said once, 'I would throw it in the fire'),[4] nor attain his understanding of the connection between European politics and religious divisions at home; but they realized that Henry's victory over the Northern Catholics of the Pilgrimage of Grace in the year of Edward's birth had so strengthened his personal authority, and as it were coloured his legend, that his supremacy was not only royal but semi-divine; and they approached him accordingly. (Cranmer, pleading with Henry for Cromwell, spoke of the fallen Minister as 'one whose surety was only by Your Majesty, who loved Your Majesty, as I ever thought, no less than God'.)[5] During the first nine years of Edward's life this power, while not absolutely corrupting, so swayed Henry's judgment that at times cruelty and caprice took the place of the intellectual suppleness and administrative genius that had made him a great king and England a strong and independent kingdom.

In fact, Henry VIII's position in the 1530s and 1540s was rather like that of a skilled exponent of the *haute école*, who, directing three horses at high speed in a small area, yet keeps them on a level and himself in control. No one but Henry would have expected — and planned — to perpetuate this process by the gradual substitution of his son for himself. Yet he did visualize this impossible feat; and his attempts to effect it illuminate every point and every scene in Edward's upbringing, from infancy to boyhood.

Below and around the pyramidal structure of King, Church and State ebbed and flowed the ceaseless turbulence of the English people, whom no threat of torture or execution, however prolonged and ghastly, could silence or subdue. Theologians, brawlers and high livers; at the same time recklessly open-handed and grossly calculating; arrogant, treacherous and bold, greedy, pious and excitable, they alarmed while often fascinating those resident foreigners whose business it was to assess their capacities and foretell their reactions. Naturally these expatriate merchants and envoys were apt to generalize too wildly in reports that, necessarily superficial and sometimes absurd, are yet convincing and vivid. Over a gulf of four hundred years, their contrasting accounts of the masses that Edward was to govern make an extraordinary yet startlingly familiar panorama, at once impressive, comical and bizarre.

Then, as now, the idleness and frivolity of the English people staggered these serious, frugal and hard-working persons, who were at first appalled and then won over by the improvident hospitality they received from all classes except the poorest. 'They never save,' says one visitor, 'they eat a great deal, and sit three or four hours over a meal, not so much to eat, however, as to go on talking to the ladies, without whose company no banquet is ever given.'[6] Too lazy to sow enough corn to base their diet on bread, the English consumed enormous quantities of meat — 'which is of excellent quality and much varied' — with pudding *and* cheese (an extravagant but enjoyable habit) at every meal.[7] The Venetian Ambassador, Soranzo, equally pained by this particular self-indulgence, came to the conclusion that it partly accounted for the native ferocity and insubordination, adding that when the English went to war they took more trouble about stocks of provisions than of arms. 'They are interested neither in war nor in literature', he complained, after five years' residence. 'They fight bravely, but eat too much.'⁸ Cardano, the Paduan philosopher and mathe-matician, said it was better to get out of the way when the English got angry, although he enjoyed his visit, being especially struck by the high standard of looks and the rich clothes that, rather negligently worn, enhanced the fairness of the women, and the stature of the men whom he found 'much like the Italians, but whiter, more ruddy and broad-chested'.⁹ 'The women', says Ubaldini, 'are as beautiful as the most beautiful Italians — even the Sienese.' Their delicacy of complexion was due, he adds, to their custom of being bled two or three times a year instead of painting themselves, as the Italians did; and Soranzo writes admiringly of their light (*bianchi*) eyes, but he thought their expenditure on clothes pretentious and absurd, and the lower classes far too well dressed for their station; although they sensibly wore black for best, they drew attention to themselves by trim-mings of coloured ribbons and caps of fur or white cloth (the upper-class women wore hats, of French design) in open defiance of the laws that forbade them the use of more expensive materials.¹⁰ On the whole, the Italian fashions were more popular than the French. 'When I rode about London', says Cardano, 'I felt as if I were in Italy.'

One of the most trying characteristics of the English was their exuberant vanity. 'They think no other race their equal', says one traveller. 'Whenever they see a handsome foreigner, they say: "He looks like an Englishman." ' 'Thinking no country can be com-pared with their own', he goes on, 'they are suspicious of foreigners, proud, obstinate and quick to take offence.' 'The men', says another, 'are not amorous. But', he adds complacently, 'the women are violent in their passions.' The lower classes, according to Soranzo, 'treat foreigners with great arrogance and rudeness'.¹¹ Worse still, 'they distrust and criticize their rulers, and are very suspicious of those in authority. The nobles think themselves no less noble than their King'. He notes that this class showed great courtesy to foreigners — their habit of remaining uncovered during the whole course of a conversation he found especially winning — although they were secretive and reserved at meals, which in private houses were generally eaten in silence. At the taverns, Ubaldini reports a great deal of talk, mostly of sport and theology, in which the women took as large a share as the men: but he thought both rather mean about spending money on wine: their great swillings of ale and beer could not be healthy.

The most startling feature of social life in the taverns — which were fairly clean, with a large choice of dishes — was the freedom of manner in the women, who, casually getting off their horses or mules on arrival, thought nothing of showing their legs, kissed strangers of both sexes on introduction and would dine unchaperoned with their husbands' male acquaintances. If the husband happened to come in, 'not only does he not take it amiss, but will shake hands ... returning thanks for the invitation to his wife'. Easy-going and boisterous, this strange race 'has no idea of the point of honour. When they do fight, it is for some caprice, and after exchanging two or three stabs with a knife, even when they wound each other, they will make peace instantly, and go away and drink together'.[12]

This deplorable indifference to convention contrasted oddly with the English snobbery about birth that took pride in any family records of execution for the most fashionable crime — high treason. A Venetian, thinking to please an English friend by asking him if any of his relations had been beheaded, was amazed to hear him say: No — upon which another Englishman, taking him aside, whispered: 'Don't be surprised. He is not a gentleman.'[13]

And yet this seriousness about social position alternated with a wild and shocking levity. Any mention of the Pope (now too often referred to as the Bishop of Rome), the sight of a foreigner, or of someone in the stocks — even, sometimes, of the celebration of Mass — might be greeted with peals of laughter, bawdy comments, stone-throwing and curses.[14] No one was respected. The Lord Privy Seal was made fun of because he was a blacksmith's son and did not dress finely; and Latimer's suggestion, during one of his sermons at Paul's Cross, that it was more desirable to go to church than to have a holiday in remembrance of Robin Hood and his men, was received with shrieks of mockery.[15]

As for the English climate, it was, quite simply, ridiculous. There was no spring; great heat succeeded icy cold without the least warning, so that many people wore fur all the year round; the fogs were terrible; the fine weather was damp and steamy — and yet these islanders reiterated that there was nothing like it, it had made them what they were: one Englishman, a Parisian envoy was told, was a match for six Frenchmen; the proof being that England held Calais and Boulogne without difficulty, and that several of their kings had been crowned in Rheims.[16]

Visitors found it useless to criticize our dirty habits or the squalor in which the common people seemed content to live. It was forbidden, for instance, to kill kites, crows or ravens, because they ate up the refuse thrown into the streets, with the result that 'the raven croaks at his pleasure, for no one heeds the omen', often snatching from the children's hands the bread that was 'smeared with butter ... and given them by their mothers'. And not only did these mothers and fathers allow their children to eat unsuitable food; they treated them with the utmost coldness and brutality, forbidding them to sit or speak in the presence of their elders, punishing them for trifles and sending them away at the age of seven or so, for eight or nine years, to be boarded out, in order — this was the excuse — to learn the manners that they did not trouble to teach them at home. Very often, Ubaldini observed, the poor little creatures never saw their parents again, for the girls were married off and the boys apprenticed, even in the upper classes.[17]

Over this people Henry VIII exercised the watchful and terrifying fatherliness that Edward was being educated to inherit; his training began before he could walk or speak plainly. In one respect Henry broke away from tradition; when his children were not under his displeasure — and Edward never was — his personal relationship with them was highly unconventional. After the formalities had been observed he would pet and play with them, delighting to show off their gifts and graces to visitors. Within a few weeks of Queen Jane's death he returned to Hampton Court so as to see Edward every day, instructing the Princess Mary to visit him when he himself had to be elsewhere.[18] Edward's first Christmas was spent with all the Court, at Greenwich. When he was seven months old Henry took him to his hunting-lodge at Royston; there the King spent the greater part of a whole day in the nursery, while the townsfolk crowded to watch, 'with much mirth and joy, dallying with the Prince in his arms a long space, and so holding him in a window to the sight and comfort of all the people'.[19] A few days later, in May 1538, the King paid £6500 into Edward's account, and with a view, presumably, to economizing, promoted

Lady Bryan, who had been in charge of Elizabeth's household, to the command of his son's as well. By this time both children were installed at Havering-atte-Bowe, in Essex, as being healthier during the summer months than Hampton Court. Here Henry seems to have found fault with Edward's wardrobe as not fine enough: for in reply to the criticisms passed on by Cromwell, Lady Bryan wrote in protest and self-justification that she would obey His Majesty's desires 'with such things as is here to do it withal', when he came again; but it was difficult. 'The best coat my lord Prince has is tinsel, and that he shall have on at that time. He hath never a good jewel to set in his cap. But I shall order all for my lord's honour the best I can, and Master Vice-Chamberlain and Master Cofferer will do their best.' Lady Bryan kept the important news for the end. 'My lord Prince is in good health and merry. His Grace hath four teeth, three full out, and the fourth appearing.'[20]

Lady Bryan's early reports indicate that Edward had few teething troubles and that he was unaffected by his nursery being moved from Havering to Waltham, thence to Ashridge and back to Enfield or Richmond. He was so healthy that if he had not been the sole heir Henry might have remained unmarried. But the death from consumption of the Duke of Richmond — Henry's eighteen-year-old son by Elizabeth Blount — in 1536, and the Princess Mary's delicacy, gave the King and his advisers the impression that this or some other disease might recur in his family; he must therefore delay no longer in finding a fourth queen; and during the spring and summer of 1538 various alliances were considered.

Henry's wide culture, intellectual power and range of accomplishments were combined with a fastidiousness that shows him as rather selective than gross in his relations with women. Now, urged on by Cromwell, whose influence and power appeared unassailable, he prepared to contract a marriage that would strengthen his ties with the Lutheran states and that the temporary alignment of the Emperor and Francis I seemed to make imperative. Throughout the negotiations, which occupied the first two years of Edward's life, those ambassadors whose masters wished to ally themselves with England were much concerned with him, not only from courtesy, but in order to be sure that Henry had produced a healthy son. The results were fairly satisfactory, even when Edward was not on his best behaviour; he was, of course, still teething. But that was negligible; so long as he appeared reasonably strong he must be shown, reported on, moved to another hunting-box or palace for change of air, again inspected and again described, by all who saw him. Access must be a matter of privilege and compliment, but not of mystery or intrigue. He was the central point, the dynastic symbol, of Henry's autocracy. His conduct and appearance were primarily the responsibility of Lady Bryan (Lady Dorset's post of Governess of the Household was honorary), and in a lesser degree of his wet-nurse Sibylla Penn, his rockers, and the chamberlains, cofferers and groom-porters in charge of his setting. His chief physician, Dr George Owen, was directly responsible to the King.

Lady Bryan carried her burden with what now seems an amazing coolness and optimism; from the tone of her letters it is clear that she loved Edward. A warm-hearted, efficient yet easy-going woman, she was fully conscious of her own interests, but enjoyed her position as much for itself as for the power and influence it brought her. Within a few months of her installation she had placed various relations in Edward's service and obtained grants of land for her husband. Everything of that kind had to be arranged through Thomas Cromwell; it was he who settled the cost of provisions, of tasters' fees, cradles and baby-clothes, the pay of Edward's musicians and assessed the value of the presents he received.

Cromwell decided who should see Edward; and his secret police were so organized that much of the private correspondence relating to these visits fell into his hands and was sometimes passed on to the King. It may have been with this knowledge in her mind that the lady who had manœuvred two daughters into the late Queen's service wrote to her husband that Edward was 'the goodliest babe that ever I set mine eye upon. I pray God make him an old man, for I should never be weary of looking upon him'.[21] When the Lord Mayor with six aldermen and two sheriffs called, their compliments were taken for granted: any criticisms or complaints of Edward's having supplanted his elder sister were kept and used against the speakers, however insignificant they might be. One of the humbler instruments of Cromwell's system, an itinerant tinker working between London and Essex, who eked out his existence by eavesdropping at taverns, reported some scraps of talk at the Bell Inn on Tower Hill; from the Lord Privy Seal's memoranda the beery voices and the clink of tankards rise in confused and grumbling reverberation.

A mariner repeated the old prophecy that the Prince would be as great a murderer as his father, adding: 'He must be a murderer by kind, for he murdered his mother at birth.' 'He is to live in Ireland', another man put in. 'God forbid he should go thither till he is crowned king', said the innkeeper. Merlin's prophecy that 'E. should succeed H.' was again recalled, and he went on: 'The same prophesier said to me, "O thou child that murdered thy mother in her womb, thou shalt have so much treason wrought in thy time — more than ever thy father had — and yet shalt thou prosper and go forth".' 'That prophet is very cunning, and the best in England', said someone else — and then the mutterings die away till the innkeeper is taken and 'examined': whether under the threat or use of the rack, is not recorded. [22]

A few days later another visitor wrote to Cromwell that he thought Edward, whose first birthday was approaching, slightly thinner. 'Yet', he added hastily, 'albeit a little His Grace's flesh decayeth, he shooteth out in length and waxeth firm and stiff, and would advance himself to move and go if they would suffer him.' No reflections on Lady Bryan were implied. 'They do best, considering His Grace is yet tender, that he should not strain himself, as his own courage would serve him, till he come above a year of age.' It was a good plan, this painstaking courtier went on, that the Prince should leave Havering, as that palace was not warm enough for the winter months. [23] Without comment Cromwell added this report to his dossier, paid in £5000 to his young master's account and a few days later told another correspondent that the King and Prince were both 'merry and in good health'. Next month there was a report from a spy operating in Oxford that a waxen image with two pins stuck into it was meant for His Highness; its owner had been traced from one of the colleges as far as London. That particular scare came to nothing; the image-maker was never found. [24]

Although Henry could afford to disregard the creators of such trivialities as this, he decided to dramatize the destruction of two other images that for many generations had commanded the reverence of those still looking towards the past. Orders went out, first to Kent and then to the Marches of Wales, for the removal to London of the Rood of Boxley, and of Darvell Gadarn. The crucified Christ of Boxley was no ordinary remembrance of the Passion, but a miracle-working figure that sometimes answered the prayers of the faithful by noddings of the head, eyes that rolled and lips that moved in warning or benediction. Darvell Gadarn, a huge wooden idol of primeval structure, had a longer, darker history, a more terrible grandeur that derived, as it now seems, from an age when the old gods of fertility and revenge ruled with a moody despotism that not even a Tudor dared emulate; for he could drag souls out of hell, if adequately propitiated. [25]

In wild excitement — and perhaps with some secret atavistic pangs — the people of London saw the Rood of Boxley taken to pieces, its mechanism laid bare, the strings that worked it torn away and the whole creation burnt to ashes. Three months later Darvell Gadarn, with a friar who had denied the Royal Supremacy, also perished in the flames of Smithfield. Friar Forrest's grisly end — too horrible, in its refinements of torture, to be described — was a secondary feature in the double lesson of which the Boxley Rood and Darvell Gadarn symbolized the antique, doomed way of life and thought that was to burst out again in bitter defiance and desperate fury at the beginning of Edward's reign. [26]

This ceremonial holocaust was one of the preliminaries to the Lutheran alliance. By the beginning of 1539 negotiations for Henry's marriage to the sister of the Duke of Cleves were going forward, and the younger Hans Holbein was commissioned to paint her for the King; at about the same time his first portrait of Edward was sent to Germany. For this, the Prince, holding a golden rattle, was dressed in a red velvet coat with sleeves of gold brocade and a gilt-tagged red hat. Underneath this likeness the Latin inscription composed by Sir Richard Morrison, one of Henry's envoys, may be roughly translated as 'Little one, imitate your father and be the heir of his virtue, the world contains nothing greater. Heaven and Nature could scarcely give a son whose glory should surpass that of such a father. You only equal the acts of your parents, the wishes of men cannot go beyond this. Surpass him and you will have surpassed all the kings the world ever worshipped, and none will ever surpass you'. Shortly after the portrait was dispatched the Duke's ambassadors made their state visit and were received at Hampton Court. As soon as they had seen the King they were conducted to the Prince's apartments; and a detailed account of Edward's behaviour during this official occasion survives. It must be admitted that at the age of eighteen months, with plenty of similar experiences behind him, he does not come out very well. Perhaps his teeth were troubling him.

The envoys were shown into the Prince's Presence-Chamber. He appeared in the arms of Sibylla Penn (he had been weaned six months earlier, and she now held the post of dry-nurse) with Lady Bryan and some of the nursery staff. Several of his father's courtiers were in attendance, among them Bishop Gardiner and the aged Earl of Essex, both Henricians and Church-and-King men of the old-fashioned sort, who had done all they could to stop this association between England and the heretical states. In silent disapproval they watched the bearded, oddly dressed Germans approach Mother Jack, as Edward called the dry-nurse, bow and wait for His Highness to hold out his hand.[27]

Alas! Not only did the Prince refuse to do this; he hid his face in Mrs Penn's shoulder and would not even look at them. Lady Bryan intervened, 'cheering and flattering' her charge; he took no notice. Lady Bryan then removed him from the nurse and with much soothing and coaxing urged him to behave in the proper manner. She could not prevail; he snatched his hand away and remained with his face buried; again pressed, he burst into roars of anger and disgust.

This embarrassing scene continued for some time. Nothing — no persuasion, dandling or petting — could break Edward's resolution not to treat with his father's new allies, who, obtaining 'none other sight of my Lord Prince, for all the labour taken', according to Gardiner, withdrew from the Presence-Chamber.

As soon as they had gone, Essex, unable to contain his exultation at this proof of His Highness's perspicacity and at the snub the Germans had received, came up to him and, assuming 'a stern countenance', thrust his own 'great rough beard' into the child's face, taking his hand. At once Edward stopped crying, smiled, thrust his fingers into his old friend's whiskers, 'took pleasure, and was merry'. Heedless of etiquette, Essex burst out: 'Now, full well knowest thou that I am thy father's true man and thine, and these others be false knaves!'

Gardiner was more discreet; but he never forgot the scene, and years afterwards described it to a friend, adding: 'Such speech escaped the old Bowser [his nickname for Essex, who was a Bourchier] suddenly, for which perchance he might have been blamed of some.' But, he went on, those who knew the Prince — God save him! — knew also that he had all his father's genial charm. 'Thereupon,' he concluded triumphantly, 'a man might say was caused in my Lord Prince *an alienation in nature* from the Germans — for I never saw the King's Highness himself had any affection for them.'[28]

Gardiner's sly hit at Henry's distaste for Anne of Cleves was part of his wisdom after the disastrous event of the King's fourth marriage. A year after the ambassadors' visit the wedding took place and next morning Henry, who had recoiled at the first sight of his bride, angrily complained to Cromwell that she was 'nothing fair, and had very ill smells about her'. Nor did he believe her to be a virgin: though he was sufficiently cautious — or fastidious — not to treat her as a wife in anything but courtesy. Anne, unaware of the split between Francis I and Charles V that had made Henry's sacrifice pointless, continued to tell her ladies how much she liked him: 'Every night he saith "Good night, darling", and in the morning, "Farewell, sweetheart",' she confided to Lady Rochford, who smartly replied: 'There must be more than this, madam, if we are to see a Duke of York.'[29] A divorce was arranged from Anne; she expressed a preference for living in England, was dowered, honoured and became the friend of the Tudor family. Cromwell, whose failure over the alliance had hurried on his fall, was executed. Meanwhile Edward had been sent back to Hunsdon to be with the Princess Elizabeth, where he continued, says Lady Bryan, in one of her last letters to the Lord Privy Seal, 'in good health and merry. I would to God', she goes on, 'the King's Grace and your lordship had seen him yesternight — for His Grace was marvellously pleasantly disposed. The musicians played, and His Grace danced and played so wantonly that he could not stand still, and was as full of pretty toys as ever I saw a child in my life'.[30]

With this flash of gaiety the second year of Edward's life concludes. But for his unfortunate lapse with the German envoys, all his days up to now seem cloudless, bringing toys, compliments, treats and presents: from the King gold plate, a golden bell and whistle from one courtier, a feathered bonnet from another, oxen and sheep from a third.[31] Princess Mary's presents were the most carefully thought out; whenever she visited Edward at Hampton Court — generally coming by water from Richmond, where she was now established as first lady of the kingdom in a household of her own — she brought something elegant and rare; a gold brooch enclosing a figure of John the Baptist, an embroidered crimson satin coat. She did not in the least care that Edward's existence had sent down the value of her dowry; money never troubled her: she spent freely, losing a good deal at betting and cards.[32] The six-year-old Elizabeth already showed that gift for economy that was to become one of her most admired characteristics. Year after year she sent her half-brother (for whose wardrobe £100 a month was allowed) a cambric shirt of her own making. She was a pretty child, and Edward seemed very fond of her.[33]

The happy time was coming to an end. At three, Edward was to begin his first lessons. Already conjectures about Henry's plans for his education were rising, and the Extreme Protestant party were throwing out hints about sufficiently advanced instructors in the faith. And with these signs of a more serious way of life came harder tests of character — ailments, discipline, punishments and reprimands.

NOTES TO CHAPTER II

[1] *Cal. Span. P.*, vol. V, part 3, p. 509.
[2] Ibid.; Hume, p. 73.
[3] *L. & P.*, vol. XIII, part 2: 306.
[4] Cavendish, p. 397.
[5] Strype, *Life of Cranmer*, vol. I, p. 59.
[6] Von Raumer, *History of the Sixteenth and Seventeenth Centuries*, vol. II, pp. 72-5.
[7] Ibid., p. 73.
[8] *Cal. Venetian State Papers*, vol. IV, p. 1672.
[9] Morley, *Life of Cardano*, vol. II, p. 130.
[10] Von Raumer, vol. II, p. 73.
[11] Sneyd (trans.), *Relazione d'Inghilterra*, pp. 20-5.
[12] Perlin, *Antiquarian Repertory*, vol. IV, pp. 504-14.
[13] *Ven. S.P.*, vol. IV, p. 1672.
[14] Ibid.
[15] *Sermons*, p. 79.
[16] Carloix, *Mémoires du Sire de Vielleville*, pp. 48-52.
[17] Sneyd, p. 22.
[18] *L. & P.*, vol. XVII, part 2: 254.
[19] Ibid., vol. XIII, part 1: 1011.
[20] Ibid.
[21] Ibid., part 2: 898.
[22] Ibid., 11.
[23] Ibid., vol. XIV, part 2: 12.
[24] Ibid.
[25] Constant, *The Reformation in England*, vol. I, p. 303.
[26] Ibid., p. 304.
[27] *L. & P.*, vol. XIX, part 2: 871.
[28] Ibid.
[29] Ibid., vol. XV: 850.
[30] Ibid., vol. XVI: 380.
[31] Ibid.
[32] Madden, *Expenses of Princess Mary*, p. 43.
[33] *L. & P.*, vol. XVI: 333; *Cal. Span. P.*, vol. V, part 3, p. 509.

❀

CHAPTER THREE

THE EDUCATION OF A PRINCE

RECOCITY, a word long used in a pejorative sense, has been welded on to the character of Edward VI by almost every historian of the nineteenth and twentieth centuries, with the result that misapprehension has obscured his circumstances and distorted his personality. More recently, this practice has been mechanized by the automatic connection of 'priggishness' to the original attribute, thus blocking with a catch-phrase — apparently for ever — the way back into the past.

If any of those responsible for Edward's training had been able to grasp what is meant by these two substantives, they would almost certainly have perceived in their combination an ideal product; for the scholars and innovators of his day did not see children as beings to be played with and cosseted, guarded from responsibility or kept in ignorance of cruelty, horror and despair. Apart from the affection his tutors and governors felt for Edward, their attitude was unsentimental and respectful, but omnipotent and static; their aims were unalterably fixed from the moment they took charge. Speed in development, depth rather than range of knowledge, and the multiplicity rather than the specialization of talent formed the central motif of a culture based on the classic past and looking forward to a revolutionary future; the whole instinct with a highly articulate piety and an elaborate code of rules for every detail of dress, relaxation, social intercourse and public duty.

These were the standards set for every boy of the ruling class. The record of Edward's progress in lessons, pastimes and general behaviour from his fourth to his tenth year shows him as an intelligent, 'average' child, neither more nor less advanced than the majority of his contemporaries. After that, the pressure caused by his succession — in circumstances without parallel in English history — so affected his outlook and temperament as to isolate him, morally and intellectually; they so heightened the strength and rapidity of his spiritual growth that he did become, in some respects, a phenomenon. Starting as a clever but not a brilliant boy, he might have turned into a first-class administrator, if he had not been forced into the mould of a saviour and a genius, while being treated as a cat's-paw. He died in the process — possibly because of it.

In this connection, the inscription composed by Sir Richard Morrison for Holbein's portrait may be used as a summary of what was expected of Edward, and as a definition of his status and potentialities. The standards it comprised were set up for him long before he could consciously take them in; implicit and permanent, they were as much a part of his existence as food and sleep, light and darkness. 'Imitate your father, the greatest man in the world. Surpass him, and none will surpass you.' These directions informed the attitude of every single person in contact with Edward, from the King himself down to the pages and grooms of the household. It is by their light that his development during the first ten years of his life can be most clearly seen and understood. A more detailed picture is provided by the theories of Elyot and Ascham in their books on education.

Sir Thomas Elyot, who died the year before Edward's accession, had published his *Book of the Governor* in 1531, a handbook for the training of the upper classes, that opens with an attack on the medieval idea that 'to a great gentleman it is a notable reproach to be well learned'. Elyot believed that the aristocrat should take all learning for his province, throwing in the arts as well. We now live at so slow an intellectual pace that it is hard to grasp the rush of sixteenth-century life in that respect, or the carefree manner in which pupils embarked on courses of study, using the oral method for Greek and Latin, so that they spoke and understood both languages before they could read or write; this period usually covered the fourth to the seventh year. Edward was 'taken out of the hands of the women', as he himself afterwards put it,[1] when he was six; till then his education followed the lines laid down by Elyot and later elaborated by Ascham. His first tutor was Richard Cox (Provost of Eton and Canon of Westminster) and his attendants were selected from the educated class, so that through them as well as through his tutors he acquired a clear and grammatical way of expressing himself in English, Greek and Latin before he knew his alphabet, on Ascham's principle that 'no learning ought to be learnt with bondage ... Whatsoever the mind doth learn unwillingly, with fear, the same it doth quickly forget'.[2] When he began reading, it was from a horn-book, in which the letters were illustrated in colour. Writing, a much more complicated business, came later; he learnt first with Vannes, an Italian, and continued with Ascham.[3] It was then the custom to teach upper-class children two kinds of handwriting, first the 'Roman' hand, which resembled printing and was used for ordinary correspondence, and then the 'engrossing' style that entailed so many convolutions and flourishes that it took several years to perfect; to learn it at all was like learning to draw; it was impossible for all but the most accomplished to use easily or rapidly. Edward never became an adept at it, because he soon fell into the habit of putting his thoughts on paper, and was rather concerned with content and clarity than with decorative effects.

The preparatory stage of Edward's education had just begun when, a few days after his fourth birthday, he fell sick of a quartan fever (malaria) while at Hampton Court with his father and his second stepmother, Katherine Howard, the eighteen-year-old cousin of Anne Boleyn who, although much censured for her haughty yet volatile manners and her coldness towards the princesses, seems to have taken Jane Seymour's place in Henry's affections.[4]

The King and Queen had just returned from a happy and triumphal progress in the North when the double blow of his son's illness and his wife's adultery fell on Henry. At first he refused to believe either Dr Owen's diagnosis, or the evidence of Katherine's having renewed one relationship with a youth who had seduced her at the age of fourteen and begun another with a gentleman of the household. Only the day before, when they had taken the sacrament together, Henry had publicly given thanks that 'after so many strange accidents that have befallen my marriages', God had given him a 'jewel of womanhood, and perfect love'.[5] He made great efforts to control his grief, desiring Cranmer — who alone had dared to bring him the news of Katherine's deceptions — to substantiate all the charges, past and present, against her, at the same time convening the best physicians in the country to report on Edward. There was no escape. Edward was dangerously ill; and the proofs of Katherine's unfaithfulness, as of her former conduct, were incontrovertible. She was imprisoned in her rooms at Hampton Court and then at Sion House. A few days later the doctors told Henry that Edward's inherent strength would probably save him; but one secretly informed the French Ambassador that the Prince's chances were poor, adding: 'He is so fat, unhealthy and overfed that he cannot live long.'[6] For many weeks, while the depositions of the Queen's relatives and attendants were taken down and collated with her frenzied outbursts of denial and confession, Edward's state was critical; he was not sinking; neither was he on the mend. When at last it became clear that the illness had been arrested, Henry went to hunt at Oatlands. As his child slowly fought his way back to life, the threads of his wife's destiny ravelled and broke. By the end of November 1541 Edward, although weak, was progressing, and the Princess Mary was sent for to keep an eye on him. By the time he had begun his convalescence at Ashridge their stepmother had taken her last look at the world of the living from Tower Green.

Henry remained 'sad, and disinclined for feasting'.[7] Lonely, embittered and anxious, in constant pain from the ulcer on his leg, he could only hope that his own physician, Dr Butts, was not too optimistic in the reports he sent to Edward Seymour, now Lord Hertford, about Edward's recovery.

Dr Butts's visits were necessarily frequent and prolonged, his manner over-solicitous; he began to get on Edward's nerves. Soon he was able to tell Hertford that 'the Prince's Grace proceedeth in amending daily'. Edward longed for solid food, meat above all, instead of broths and messes; he had become very lively again, and was beginning to play and run about, 'so that now', the doctor went on, 'I think shall be no less business to dissuade him from taking of meats than hitherto to move him to take anything'. He slept soundly all night, only rousing himself to drink. At last the coveted dish of meat was allowed and had no ill effects. Best of all, when the anxious physician pestered him with inquiries as to whether he felt 'any disposition to vomit', Edward's reply was reassuring, if rude: 'Go away, fool.' 'If I tarry till he call me knave,' Butts joyfully concluded, 'I shall say *Nunc Dimittis*.'[8]

So at last the pleasant routine of life in the country palaces that Edward generally shared with his sisters was resumed, without lessons for a time. When they were separated he sent them presents — a gilt chalice for Mary, and for Elizabeth a necklace and a pair of stockings embroidered in silk and gold thread; on another occasion he sent Mary a basket of artichokes — then a new and rare delicacy — from Greenwich, and another piece of plate, receiving in return a clock from her and the usual home-made shirt from the younger sister. A few months later, when he and Elizabeth were together at Havering, Mary brought him a book, no doubt devotional, bound in gold; his musicians played for them, and Mary gave them a present of money.[9]

Edward spent most of the early part of 1543 at Ashridge, where his lessons with Dr Cox were resumed; sometimes he worked with Elizabeth under Ascham's direction; but her exceptional brilliance and her four years' seniority made her less of a companion for him than Jane Dormer, the grand-daughter of his Chamberlain, Sir William Sidney; she was three months younger than himself. This friendship was encouraged, and many years afterwards, when Jane had married a Spanish nobleman and was living in Madrid, she recalled how she and her governess would come to spend the day at Ashridge, because the Prince's Grace so much 'desired her company'. They would look at books together; then the musicians were sent for, and they danced; tiring of that, they sat down to cards; when she lost, Edward would say: 'Now, Jane, your king is gone, I shall be enough for you.' All her life, although she deplored everything that he later represented, she remembered his generosity: how he would call her 'my Jane': and she recollected also that then, and afterwards, he preferred the Lady Mary's company to that of the Lady Elizabeth, in spite of the twenty years' gap between them.[10] Edward's fondness for Jane encouraged Sir William Sidney to bring his fourteen-year-old son Henry to Ashridge; the Prince took such a liking to the handsome, intelligent boy that Henry Sidney later became his cup-bearer and one of his closest friends.[11]

In the summer of 1543 this informal, comparatively quiet life came to an end. With Mary and Elizabeth, Edward was summoned to Hampton Court to meet his father's sixth wife, Katherine Parr, the most satisfactory of his stepmothers. Twice widowed and now in her thirty-first year, the new Queen reunited Henry with all his children and gave them their first experience of undisturbed, sheltered family life. Beautiful, affectionate and highly cultured, she leaned towards the Protestant party: but she was far too intelligent to press her views, or to interfere with the fervour, already inclining to bigotry, of her elder step-daughter's loyalty to the old faith. Edward and his half-sisters soon became very fond of her; for a time, at least, she re-created the intimacy with their father that all three had once enjoyed and still desired.

Neither Henry's monstrous egoism, nor his calculated outbursts of rage, nor his unfathomable caprice, nor the increasing burden of his work destroyed the fascination he could exercise when he chose to make much of his children. Throughout their stiff correctness and exaggerated subservience, their letters to him reveal their half-fearful delight in his company. When was he coming? How soon might they visit him? It was long since they had waited for a meeting. Their need of him was probably enhanced by the growing uncertainty, the cataclysmic force of his incalculable moods. And, by their standards, his super-eminence was not only that of a father and a king, but of a man who could set hand and mind to anything. If he had been cast down from his high place with empty pockets, Henry VIII could have earned a living and gained a reputation as a musician, a composer, a poet (his Mass is still sung, and his poems remain in more than one anthology), an engineer, or a man-at-arms. He was a skilled and subtle theologian and diplomat: he had been a writer and translator, a fine athlete, a graceful dancer, a great huntsman. He played four instruments, spoke five languages and had a fair knowledge of the arts and sciences; above all, he was a master of statecraft, and could see into men's hearts and minds as clearly as if he had created them. Knowing while yet deceiving himself, his sense of drama was sometimes expressed with ringing eloquence, sometimes in a terse, harsh phrase that held the memory and struck the imagination. 'I never spared man in my anger nor woman in my lust', one courtier heard him say;[12] and another, remembering his declaration that as 'God's appointed Vicar and High Minister' he could 'see divisions extinct and enormities corrected', recalled also how that assurance had been acclaimed with tears when he added to it the promise that love should never be dissolved between himself and his people.[13]

To a man who could so dominate — by personal care and

mystical paternalism, as much as by terror, cruelty and the strong hand — the subjugation of his impressionable and sensitive children was automatic and, in a sense, lasting; while he lived, and long, long afterwards, from beyond the grave, the peculiar and frightening genius of Henry VIII was reproduced, again and again, in their public and private utterances, as in their mannerisms and tone of voice; in their strength and weakness; in their cold withdrawals; in their outbursts of passion, piety or despair. Consciously or not, Mary, Elizabeth and Edward Tudor modelled themselves in their father's image; it is impossible to visualize even the greatest of the three without becoming aware of that tremendous shadow behind her.

The trouble was that during the last four years of Henry's life — from Edward's point of view, the most important — his contact with his family gave way to the pressure of illness, anxiety and disappointment. He had loved Edward, not only for himself, but for what he represented and was going to be; yet it appears that he was no longer capable of expressing that love, or even, perhaps, of feeling it, as he had before the tragedy of Katherine Howard, the death of Richmond, or the rebellious and — as it seemed to him — ungrateful obstinacy and wrong-headedness of the men and women who, falling upon the English Bible that had been his greatest gift to them, drew from one passage after another nonsensical or blasphemous interpretations of their own. Henry's principal griefs were two: the realization that he would not live to see his son's majority; and that a few dissentients among the people he had brought out of the wilderness of papal tyranny and medieval credulity should have paused by the wayside to worship strange gods set up by themselves. *He knew* what was best for his loving subjects; none of them must dispute his decrees. So the bitterness resulting from his intensely possessive attitude towards the nation affected that towards the children of his flesh and blood. After his sixth marriage he was with them often, but no longer, as before, part of them. There is no single record of his interest in and care for Edward stretching beyond the limits of forethought and responsibility. For some time these had included plans for Edward's marriage to the infant Mary Queen of Scots, whose ambassadors had visited him at Enfield 'greatly rejoicing to behold so goodly and towardly an imp'.[14] Their interview with Henry was not so happy; his terms were hard. Within two years the Scots Queen must be handed over to him: 'I look on her as my own daughter', he added. When the envoys demurred, he flared up. 'Such a marriage is to be desired for the daughter of any King in Christendom', he exclaimed. He went on to say that Mary Stuart must be brought up under his care, in order to acquire 'the fashion and nurture of English ways' although she would of course be allowed to bring her own attendants with her.[15] On these terms the treaty of peace and marriage was eventually signed; but the Queen Regent, Mary of Guise, and her chief minister, Cardinal Beaton, were playing for time, in view of a French alliance; they had no intention of delivering Mary Stuart into the hands of the English, or of marrying her to Edward, if they could do better elsewhere — as Henry well knew; although he also appeared to consider the matter settled, he instructed Hertford to prepare for the invasion of Scotland.

To such a task Hertford's military experience and talent for organization rose easily; he found it much harder to appease his brother, Thomas Seymour, now back from foreign service and bitterly jealous of his senior's high position and favour with the King. Hertford had real affection for the conceited and pushing young man; but he knew better than to impose him on his royal brother-in-law. So Thomas again resumed his post of Gentleman of the Bedchamber; he became increasingly resentful and more determined than ever to find power for himself.

Henry faced the prospect of war on two fronts — for it was becoming clear that he would soon have to besiege Boulogne in order to prevent the French sending help to Scotland — with equanimity, resuming his custom of 'feasting the ladies' at Hampton Court, as in Katherine Howard's time. In this, Edward's fifth year, most of which was spent at Hampton Court, the day began at six, when the King got up, followed by Mass at seven and then a ride, or shooting at the butts in the great orchard, or, in wet weather, a game of bowls in one of the galleries, till ten. Then came dinner, the principal meal of the day, served with elaborate and splendid formality. When the cloth had been laid, the Lord High Steward saw that the salts were placed with mathematical exactness. Towels, basins and ewers of scented water were brought in and held ready by servants standing in line behind the table.

To the sound of trumpets the royal family, each leading a guest by the hand, entered the Banqueting Hall, and the bread was ceremoniously removed from the table for the saying of grace. As soon as it was replaced everyone sat down and the carving began. The first course was generally brawn, with mustard, and white wine; then came soup, then the main dish — for which geese, stuffed swans, beef, mutton and venison were presented — and after a change of plates, game pies. Officially, these dishes concluded the meal; breadcrumbs were swept away, a fresh cloth laid and the serving-men stepped forward with their towels and basins, the Tudors being served on the knee by those persons in whose families this privilege was hereditary. Cheese, fresh fruit, sweets, biscuits and cakes appeared on trays, followed by further washing and the final removal of the cloth. The King then led the way out of the Hall and transacted business, either privately or in committee, till four, the supper hour. If this was made the occasion for a banquet, followed by a masque, games or a concert, it was usual to provide a choice of six dishes for the first course (serving meat and fish simultaneously) and from fourteen to twenty-four dishes for the second. Music was played throughout, so that the business of eating was not interrupted by too much conversation, while the greatest noblemen in the realm stood behind the chairs of the King and his family, occasionally putting in a word when they caught His Majesty's eye, the entry of each course being marked by the sound of trumpets. The whole procedure was directed by the Lord High Steward from a dais at the end of the Banqueting Hall, below the musicians' gallery; the dishes were carried in as it were from the wings, at the upper end.[16]

Edward's share in this and other rituals was curtailed only by a simpler diet, lessons and the fact that on certain occasions he received visitors independently of his father and stepmother. His later letters and the diary that he kept from his fourteenth to his sixteenth year show that he was always aware of Henry's plans for his future, and co-operative in feeling if not in practice. The prospect of a permanent peace with Scotland through his marriage with Mary Stuart was present in his mind from 1543 to the last year of his life, and he attached increasing importance to it as his political consciousness matured. So his uncle Hertford's departure to the Border in March 1544 to enforce the marriage contract and the delivery of Mary Stuart with the threat of 'fire and sword', and Henry's subsequent declaration that Beaton and the Queen Regent had 'dishonourably swerved' from their promises through the 'sinister enticements' of their French allies, made an impression that was fully expressed when he became king, three years later.[17]

By the end of 1543 the delicacy arising out of his first serious illness had disappeared and his natural vigour was stimulated — it seems pleasantly — by Cox and the masters who taught him music, dancing and outdoor sports and games. A year later his understanding of spoken Latin and Greek was good enough for him easily to translate and compose from and in both languages and to learn Latin grammar and syntax; his English reading was mostly confined to the Bible at this time. In his play hours he studied singing, musical composition and the lute — and probably other instruments — under a Fleming, Philip van Wilder.[18] He also began to acquire a simplified knowledge of tilting, running at the ring, hawking, tennis and one or two indoor games, such as cards, chess and backgammon. (Cards and chess were later discouraged by Ascham, because they were an incentive to betting, a favourite pursuit of Henry VIII.) Dancing, far the most important accomplishment, became a means of instruction in the art of symbolism. 'The first moving in every dance', according to Elyot, 'is called Honour, which is a reverent inclination or curtsy, with a long deliberation or pause, and is but one motion, comprehending the other three motions, or setting forth of the foot. By that may be signified that at the beginning of all our acts we should do due honour to God ... which honour is compact of ... fear, love and reverence ... By the second motion ... may be signified celerity and slowness, which two, albeit they seem to discord ... may well be resembled to the *bransle* [brawl, or altercation] in dancing.' Elyot then clears up his apparent contradiction by describing this discord as Maturity, or 'a mean between two extremities'. The third motion, walking, he goes on, symbolizes Prudence and Industry; the fourth motion, stepping backwards, Circumspection, the sixth, seventh and eighth Judgment, Modesty and Experience, respectively.[19] It is clear that Edward literally took much of this portentousness in his stride, for subsequent records show that he preferred music, dancing and running at the ring to all other pastimes; he became passionately addicted to this last, giving up hawking and tennis for it as soon as he was in a position to choose his relaxations for himself.[20]

Edward's training was set on a new basis by Henry before he left for France in the summer of 1544. The Prince was six and a half years old: his nursery days were over. Sir Francis and Lady Bryan and all those working under them were therefore pensioned off or given other posts, and another and larger establishment formed; this was supervised by Katherine Parr, who acted as Regent till Henry's return in the autumn. Some ten years earlier, he had had to settle innumerable squabbles and intrigues in the forming of a similar household for the Duke of Richmond. This was partly the reason for his dismissal of everyone employed in Edward's, except Dr Cox, who was relegated to the post of Almoner.[21] Cox, an affectionate and sensible man, had no objection, having probably always known that at this point the Prince's education would be taken out of his hands; he only desired to remain in his service. At the end of the year he sent a full report of his pupil's behaviour and progress to Sir William Paget, writing informally, as to an intimate friend, but presumably on the assumption that his letter would be passed on to the King.

The retiring tutor had been amused by the gay and ready manner in which Edward replied to the rather heavy teasing of one of his chaplains, Dr Bill. Unfortunately the part of Cox's letter that relates this dialogue has been damaged; a fragment remains, Bill said: 'I desire you to have the Fox ... in conditions [i.e. under control] in all your house.' Edward replied: 'Doctor, I see what ye mean, well enough. I see by you, ye would have the Fox yourself.' This answer, although no more than a pert *tu quoque*, was so roundly given out that Cox felt it worth recording. No clue as to who the Fox really was, exists; it was one of the nicknames given to Eustace Chapuys, who was extremely unpopular with Henry's courtiers.

Cox had several suggestions to make about Edward's charities. A certain sum — His Majesty would perhaps decide how much — should be set aside every month for His Grace's alms. If the King objected to this, the next best thing would be for the Prince to administer a portion of the £20 allotted by the Treasury for the poor of Hampton Court. Edward's ideas about alms-giving were too vague, and this plan would bring him into closer contact with his future subjects. Cox then turned to the question of the Prince's lessons.

'As concerning my lord and dear scholar,' he says, 'he is not much behind in his feats. He hath expugned and utterly conquered the captains of ignorance.' He then explains how he had induced Edward to concentrate on his studies by presenting them, in what might be called the Ascham-Elyot method, as military objectives. Naturally, Edward was deeply concerned with his father's capture of Boulogne from England's ancient enemies; so Cox based his teaching on the pretence that Edward first besieged and then took by assault the duller portions of learning. The eight parts of speech were the defenders; as soon as they surrendered and became His Grace's 'subjects and servants', he must tear down the outworks of the Latin nouns and verbs; this done, he must build them up again, 'like as the King's Majesty framed up Boulogne after he had beaten it down'.

At first Edward took to this game with enthusiasm; the result was that he could 'frame well his concords of grammar', and had already produced some eleven or twelve short proses, described by Cox as 'pretty Latins'. He was therefore primed to conquer the new territory of Cato, Aesop and any other 'wholesome and godly lessons' that Cox's successor might devise for him. So, for a time, he enjoyed both his Latin excercises and his Bible readings; then his tutor's insistence on the daily learning by heart of Solomon's Proverbs became irksome; he wearied of the Jewish monarch's admonitions about discipline, the Commandments and filial obedience. Cox could not make it out; he was even more taken aback when his own lectures on the danger of frequenting 'strange and wanton women' and being grateful to those who told His Highness of his faults were received with inattention, boredom and, finally, open revolt. He returned to his first method. His Grace was faced with a great enemy, 'Captain Will', who must be defeated before further progress could be made.

Edward remained unmoved. The military game had lost its charm. Cox persisted. Captain Will, he tells Paget, 'was an ungracious fellow, whom to conquer I was almost in despair'. He tried coaxing, then threats: both were unavailing — what was to be done? Cox did not want to punish his pupil; that was the old-fashioned way, and a sign of defeat besides. So his threats became more severe. Edward stood aloof and uninterested; he had heard a hundred times what would happen if he did not try harder, and did not believe it. 'He thought my meaning to be nothing but dalliance', Cox explained. The tutor uttered a last, unheeded warning. His 'morrice-pike' (whether by this he means the rod, or the flat of his hand, is not clear) would be used, and sharply, if Captain Will was not subdued. An interval followed. Then, the occasion arising as he had thought it would, Dr Cox hit Edward very hard indeed.

It was a shock — and a victory for the tutor. 'At Will I went', he pursues, 'and gave him such a wound that he wist not what to do, but picked [himself] privately out of the place, [so] that I never saw him since. Methought it the luckiest day that ever I had in battle. I think', he triumphantly concludes, 'that only [one] wound shall be enough for me to daunt both Will and all his fellows.'

After this, the substitution of a tournament for a siege analogy had greater success. When Cox told Edward that 'there was another cumbrous captain, called Captain Oblivion, that appeareth out of his pavilion', the child's response was satisfactory. 'By labour and continuance of exercise', Oblivion was chased away.

Cox wound up his report in a burst of love and pride. His dear lord was 'a vessel apt to receive all goodness and learning, witty, sharp and pleasant'. He could relinquish his position with a clear conscience, and a very natural complacency.[22]

So this child's life rushed on, fast, faster, in a deepening channel, to its apotheosis. As the small, dancing figure adoringly watched by Lady Bryan and her posse of nurses and rockers gave way to the rather recalcitrant conqueror of Captain Will and cumbrous Oblivion, that shape in its turn diminished before the prototype of the Renaissance patrician, vigorous yet disciplined, tireless, accomplished, graceful and serene. In the ten years that remained to him Edward was to know other pleasures, interests and excitements — but always consciously. All learning, all experience, all delight was to be assessed, savoured and so fitted into the grand design for present development and future greatness.

NOTES TO CHAPTER III

[1] *Lit. Rem.*, vol. II, p. 209.
[2] Ascham, *The Schoolmaster*, p. 198.
[3] *Lit. Rem.*, vol. I, p. 210.
[4] *L. & P.*, vol. XVI: 1334.
[5] Herbert, *Life of Henry VIII*, p. 534.
[6] De Marillac, *Correspondence Politique*, p. 89.
[7] *L. & P.*, vol. XVIII, part 1: 904.
[8] *D.S.P. Addenda*, vol. I, part 2.
[9] Madden, p. 47.
[10] Clifford, *Jane Dormer, Duchess of Feria*, p. 59.
[11] Collins, *Letters and Memorials of State*, p. 82.
[12] Cavendish, p. 100.
[13] Hall, *Chronicle*, pp. 864-6.
[14] Holinshed, *Chronicle*, p. 816.
[15] *L. & P.*, vol. XVII: 1221, 1233.
[16] Law, *History of Hampton Court Palace*, vol. I, p. 67; Thomas, *The Pilgrim*, p. 28.
[17] *Lit. Rem.*, vol. II, pp. 319, 325, 334.
[18] Ibid., vol. I, p. 45.
[19] *The Governor*, pp. 280-3.
[20] *Lit. Rem.*, vol. I, p. xlv.
[21] *L. & P.*, vol. XIX, part 2: 726.
[22] Ibid.

※

CHAPTER FOUR

THE ACCESSION

HENRY VIII had long been accustomed to keep in touch with the most promising University scholars through Dr Butts, who in the spring of 1544 advised him to replace Dr Cox by John Cheke, a fellow of St John's, Cambridge; Cheke was said 'to have laid the very foundations of the [new] learning in that college'.[1]

At thirty Cheke had already made his name as a scholastic innovator and revolutionary, not only through his affiliation with the Protestant groups in the University and at Court, but by his methods of teaching, and his victory, after a series of dramatic contests with the authorities, for the wider study and different pronunciation of Greek. In his immensely popular lectures he had exploded the medieval traditions and theories on this subject, thus obtaining a Greek lectureship from the King, who then sent him on a Continental tour. Among his pupils was a number of brilliant and ambitious young men: Ascham; Sir Thomas Smith, who later became one of Edward's Secretaries of State; and William Cecil, whose career began with the secretaryship in Hertford's household that Cheke obtained for him, and with his marriage to Cheke's sister, Mary.

Cheke's intellectual powers were of the highest order and his writings much admired; but it was as a teacher and a friend that he was chiefly remembered. Warm-hearted, outspoken, sensitive and witty, he infected his pupils with an enthusiasm that made each lecture an event and his talk a stimulating memory. From Edward's seventh to his fourteenth year, Cheke's influence was paramount, partly because his outlook was rather that of the scholar-companion than of the courtier, and partly because he gave his whole heart and mind to his pupil, for whom he was ambitious, watchful, sometimes critical and demanding, but never harshly so. It was partly through his talks with Cheke that Ascham had evolved his own system of insinuating knowledge and culture,

The humdrum, laborious methods of Cox would have been in-comprehensible — comparatively enlightened though they were — to Cheke, who taught as if he himself were discovering his subject for the first time and sharing, rather than doling out, its pleasures and rewards.

Most teachers of Cheke's generation, however exceptional, had been influenced by the precepts of *The Governor*. Elyot's warnings against overstrain and his schemes for relaxation became part of the new tutor's system from the moment that he entered Edward's service. The habit of relaxing, according to Elyot, was rather to be acquired than fallen into, and one of the easiest and pleasantest ways of doing this was through music of all kinds — except that of communal singing, which he considered undignified for young gentlemen of breeding. (Painting and carving, he adds, are also desirable, as long as the pupil is not encouraged to get messy, or to appear looking like a professional.)[2] Edward had little or no interest in the visual arts — unless his love of jewels, beautiful clothes and all kinds of pageantry may be taken as a sign of this — but he had his father's passion for music, although he would never have equalled Henry's technical and creative proficiency.

Naturally, Edward soon acquired a simplified form of Henry's skill and pleasure in theological debate, although he never seems to have been puzzled by the fact that the father who lived and died a Catholic had put his son's education in charge of Extreme Protestant tutors. This apparent inconsistency bears out the belief of Henry's intimates that during his last years he was preparing to accept, remould and dominate the new religion, stamping it with his own image and superscription, as he had the old. Henry must have perceived what the next phase of the English Reformation was going to be, and visualized all the aspects of its control and direction; the best he could do for Edward was to train him to master it through such tutors as Cheke and Ascham.

Learning, Ascham says, in a book written some years after Edward's death, is more valuable than knowledge of the world; and he goes on: 'If King Edward had lived a little longer, his only example had bred such a race of worthy and learned gentlemen as this realm never yet did afford.'[3] Here Ascham's ideal and Cheke's practice necessarily diverged. Edward had always been a leading figure in the world of Courts and embassies; now the time had come for him to meet men of distinction in other walks of life. Shortly after Cheke's installation, when he and Edward were at Enfield, the tutor heard that Dr Haddon, a fellow of King's and a friend and contemporary of his own, was staying in the neighbourhood; he had a letter of introduction to the Prince from Dr Cox but was shy of presenting it. Cheke insisted on his appearance, himself firmly taking the letter from his friend's hand and giving it to Edward. The Prince read it and asked Haddon how his old tutor was. Some further conversation seems to have been attempted; but neither Cheke nor his pupil could break down Haddon's reserve. He was not accustomed to courts, and was overcome by the impact of royalty. When Edward had walked on through the Presence-Chamber and was out of hearing, Cheke urged Haddon to stay till the Prince returned. Haddon refused: he had to get back to Cambridge, he said; but the picture of Edward's gaiety and kindness remained with him. [4]

Edward was now at the age when the companionship of other boys was desirable. What might be described as a small private school of some eight or ten children was therefore set up within the Court, supervised by Cheke, who directed the staff of chaplains, physicians, visiting masters and attendants in the intervals of his private lessons with the Prince. These boys were selected by the King, and their numbers and ages so varied that Edward never became the centre of a static group. His companions, all but a few, came and went; and he plunged into the delights of shared games, sports and lessons with the energy that informed everything he did.

Although this new existence was eventful and stimulating, liberty, as the word is now understood, was unknown, and would have been looked on as time-wasting licence by those responsible for Edward's training. As in Elyot's elaborate dance symbolism, the most trivial activity had to be related to the conduct of life as a whole. Every facet in the daily routine was cut and polished for that purpose, and no single pursuit independently visualized. To stand in the correct posture — the forefinger of one hand slipped into the waistband, the other at the side, one foot slightly in advance of the other — to bow, to kneel, to walk with long, slow steps that must not be strides: to know when to uncover and how long to wait before replacing one's cap: to determine the moment

E   65

for ending an interview or changing the subject: to acknowledge and interchange courtesies according to the rules of rank and precedence: to make the slight, graceful gestures that permitted one person to rise, another to withdraw and a third to approach: to feel rather than to decide the time for holding out one's hand to be kissed: to assess the variations of tone for formal conversation and private talk; all these minutiae were part of a ritual that embraced games, meals, lessons, getting up, going to church or to bed, even walking from one room to another, and that practice turned into a series of reflex actions, with the result that Edward's dignity and his sense of what was fitting became instinctive before he was seven years old. His natural exuberance was rather enhanced than curbed by being directed into a traditional pattern designed to please and impress. The responsibility of having to decide how to behave on any given occasion — one of the heaviest burdens that can be laid on a child — did not arise until after his accession, and not often then. His freedom was, therefore, of that highly developed, eminently sensible kind that no longer exists, and that even in his day could only be created by experts: freedom to exercise his faculties without the regrets and conflicts that come from facing a choice.

The three years that preceded Edward's accession were the happiest of his life, partly because of the 'sweetness and easiness' of Cheke's methods.[5] He got through his first Latin grammar — a thick, rather grubby volume, now in the British Museum — within two years. Time was saved by translating the portions of Scripture that he had first learnt by heart into Latin, and then parsing them.[6] Once a week he composed a short letter in the same language to someone who would so answer it as to give this rather artificial correspondence a personal touch. These formal notes, addressed to the King, the Queen, the Princesses, Cox, Hertford and Archbishop Cranmer respectively, have also been preserved.[7] Those to Hertford, Cranmer and Elizabeth are the briefest and least informative; in those to Cox the writer's instinct to please is shown by the classical or scriptural allusions in which the ex-tutor delighted, with inquiries about his recent illness and hopes for his return. From the rest, a more definite impression of Edward's development emerges. His affections are centred on Mary, whom he would like to see more often, and his father. He fears to trouble the King with too many letters: he knows how busy he is: if only a peace could be concluded, they would meet sooner. Henry replied with presents — a gold chain, rings set with precious stones, a jewelled collar, brooches and new clothes; these last seem to have given more pleasure than anything else. To Mary, Edward says: 'Although I do not write more often, you must not think me ungrateful, for just as I seldom put on my best clothes, yet I love them more than the others.' While he was at Enfield with Ascham, Cheke and Elizabeth, and Mary remained at Hampton Court with the Queen, rumours of the Princess's dancing, card-playing and betting appear to have reached him in an exaggerated form. (Ascham's disapproval of gaming, always strongly expressed, was one of the themes in his book on archery, which he commended as the best relaxation for young people and an antidote to cards and other undesirable indoor games.)[8] Edward therefore urged the Queen to beg his half-sister to 'attend no longer to foreign dances and merriments, which do not become a Christian Princess'.[9]

Modern historians have acclaimed this message as the proof of Edward's priggishness; and from a modern standpoint it is, of course, odious. Allowances must be made for the heady effects of Ascham's prejudices and Cheke's Protestantism on an eight-year-old enthusiast; historically, this letter is interesting, for it is one of the first signs of the struggle between Mary and the Extreme Protestant party, who were beginning to use Edward as a weapon, thus poisoning — although they never destroyed — the love and sympathy that this brother and sister had for one another. Katherine Parr was a highly influential figure in this group; now she was trying to draw her elder step-daughter into her circle of intellectual Protestant ladies. Edward shared in Katherine's hopes for Mary; the possibility of her conversion was put into his mind at this time and remained with him till he died. His growing concern with this and other religious questions was that of any intelligent boy in similar circumstances; as theological controversy had long been of paramount interest to all those about him, so he pondered its problems in accordance with his increasing awareness of the responsibilities that he was to inherit; and, by this time, the moment of his accession must have seemed nearer than it really was.

Shortly after Henry VIII returned from the campaign of 1544 his health deteriorated further; he walked with great difficulty: stairs were beyond him; a 'machine' was therefore devised to move him from one floor to another.[10] Sometimes the pain in his leg became so acute as to make him speechless and black in the face; he was nearly always in a state of suppressed or violent irritation.[11] These and other symptoms of his succumbing to an undiagnosed disease of many years' standing could not possibly have been concealed from Edward, however little they saw of one another; and as Henry's power and fame derived mainly from his achievements in the early stages of the English Reformation since his personal authority was bound up with those achievements, so Edward must have begun to feel the peculiarities of his own position, and the tremendous labours demanded by a half-finished revolution about which no two parties had yet agreed. It was therefore inevitable that at a very early age he should become obsessed with the — to him — dangerous opinions and habits of Mary (whether shown by her addiction to 'foreign dances and merriments', or by her loyalty to the old faith), not only because she was next in line to the succession, but because he loved her.

In one respect Edward's training may have been inadequate. Neither Cheke nor Ascham had much interest in the imaginative and romantic aspects of literature. Naturally, they advocated the learning and appreciation of poetry, but as an exercise, a means to an end, at best a relaxation from more strenuous tasks. For fantasy and story-telling they had less use than Dr Cox, with his analogies of captains and sieges. In the record of Edward's library there is no mention, for instance, of Malory or of Chaucer. (Ascham, in fact, strongly objected to any young person reading about King Arthur's savage and sensuous paladins; and the effect on the immature mind of that deplorable business of Lancelot and Guinevere was not to be thought of)[12] while Cheke's sophisticated and classic taste rejected the primitive and haunting magic of such books as *Huon of Bordeux*, *Reynard the Fox*, or *Valentine and Orson*. So it was inevitable that Edward's intellect, although acute and highly powered, should remain literal, unimaginative and absolutely uncompromising in all matters of faith. Indeed, this rigidity might rather have increased than diminished if he had lived to grow up. Most children see all issues, practical or moral, in black and white; in this sense Edward was what is sometimes called an ordinary, 'normal' child; his outlook and attitude were no doubt crystallized by the daily companionship of a set of boys of his own calibre.

In the list of those who were known as the King's children are two names that in the 1540s were comparatively obscure — Barnaby Fitzpatrick, eldest son of the Baron of Upper Ossory, and Robert Dudley, afterwards Earl of Leicester. Both were four years older than Edward. With Henry Sidney, Barnaby shared the first place in the Prince's affections. Edward's relations with Robert Dudley were fleeting and casual; those with his father, John Dudley, Viscount Lisle — now Privy Councillor, Knight of the Garter and Lord High Admiral — were to follow the pattern of three generations of Tudors with three generations of Dudleys. For a corresponding period — from the early 1500s till 1588 — the name of Dudley was connected, in the minds of the English people, with a sinister, mysterious and tainted power.

John Dudley's father, Edmund, beginning his career as a lawyer at Gray's Inn, had been one of Henry VII's chief ministers; with Empson, another Crown official, he continued, during the last part of his master's reign, to raise money for him through fines imposed for breaches of the law; for these services he received a large percentage and the wardship of an heiress, Elizabeth Grey, the daughter of Viscount de Lisle, whose title and arms he assumed after their marriage. When Henry VIII succeeded, those who had suffered at Dudley's hands appealed for redress; in 1510 he was attainted and executed and his wife and children were ruined. His eldest son John, aged nine, was adopted by Sir Richard Guilford, who, two years later, persuaded the King to reverse the act of attainder and restore the Dudley property; he then married John to his daughter Jane, who bore five sons and two daughters. By 1538 John Dudley had fulfilled all Guilford's hopes, mainly through his naval and military services abroad; he was Governor of Calais and high in Henry's favour. His outstanding administrative ability, energy and physical courage were set off by great charm of manner. Tall, dark, vital and bold — as ready and acute in the council chamber as he was skilful and brilliant in the tilt-yard and the tennis-court — he carried most situations and people before him, and could afford to ignore the furious contempt and spiteful censure of those he had surpassed; for it was noticeable that whenever he set himself to win over any member of the old nobility, he generally did so; courtiers who had complained of or mocked at this upstart, climbing son of a disgraced and low-bred father were, in the end, ready to swallow family pride and forget personal jealousies when they were given the chance of allying themselves with him. His bravery, openhandedness and gift for the common touch made him popular with the soldiers, sailors and country people. He was not, perhaps, markedly pious: but the Catholic party seem to have looked on him as reassuringly orthodox, while the Protestants were beguiled by his sympathetic attitude and enlightened views.

Such a man could not fail to appeal to Edward, into whose notice he began to insinuate himself unobtrusively and at secondhand by placing Robert, the best-looking of his sons, in a privileged circle that, besides Barnaby Fitzpatrick and Henry Sidney, included Edward Seymour — Hertford's eldest son — the Duke of Suffolk, the Earl of Maltravers, Lord Talbot, Lord Fitzwarren and Lord Strange. Of these, Suffolk and Sidney were the most gifted and intellectual; Barnaby the poorest and most agreeable; and Robert Dudley the most athletic and dashing. He and the Princess Elizabeth were exactly of an age: they saw a good deal of one another at this time; Robert's father encouraged the friendship, although discreetly and without appearing to push his son forward. With Hertford, Lisle was on the happiest and most intimate terms; shortly after Robert's entry into the Prince's household the two noblemen began to consider a match between Hertford's daughter Anne and John, Lisle's eldest son. Rather inexplicably Lisle, the lesser power, hung back; from year to year he postponed the betrothal. It does not seem to have occurred to the magnificent, high-minded and supremely confident Hertford that his fellow-councillor might have been holding up the arrangements for purposes of his own. Lisle, having established his family (the marriage of his daughter Mary with Henry Sidney was now under discussion but not celebrated till 1551) returned to his duties at Calais. It is possible that his great scheme of domination had already taken shape; for he was one who, planning far ahead and ever revolving a series of alternatives, was accustomed to wait upon events with a watchful patience masked by the agreeable manners that few could resist. In the three years preceding Henry's death he made no attempt to obtain anything more for himself and did his work admirably, with the result that he was trusted by most people, feared by none, and had a number of allies at Court who kept him informed of the King's health and of the political and religious influences prevailing in Edward's household.

Here, the pleasant routine of games, lessons and mild festivities continued undisturbed. Edward and his companions, absorbed in pursuits for which fencing-masters, huntsmen and professors of modern languages were responsible, were waited on by a body of 'henchmen' — boys of gentle birth, also under the control of Cheke and his staff.[13] Jean Belmaine, Edward's French tutor, came to him every day; his resident chaplains, Dr Aire and Dr Tony, conducted services in English, for which Thomas Sternhold later provided a metrical version of the Psalms. His tailors and laundresses, who each received sixpence a day, were also part of the household; and John Allen, Yeoman of the Prince's Beasts, took orders for the staging of fights between mastiffs and bears once a month.[14] In theory, the household was permanently established at Westminster or Hampton Court; whenever the plague broke out Edward removed to Copthall or Ashridge, where with Cheke and a skeleton staff he and Elizabeth shared their lessons.[15] Dr Cox, who saw the Prince at intervals, felt that he might be over-disciplined. 'I trust', he wrote to Paget, 'the Prince's Grace will content his father's expectations hereafter. We suffered him hitherto to grow up according to his own wish.'[16] But although Cheke saw to it that, as in the case of every grammar-school boy of his age, Edward's repertoire of passages from Cato, Aesop, Cicero and the Old and New Testaments increased weekly, he encouraged a number of outside interests to which Cox would not have had access. Other Cambridge friends besides Haddon were brought to see his pupil; and in 1545 Cheke summoned the great antiquary, John Leland, to talk to the Prince about the investigations that had taken him all over the country for the famous *Itinerary* that was published in 1549.

Until the autumn of 1546, Edward's official appearances had taken place within the precincts of his father's palaces, and the general public had hardly seen him. Now they were to do so because the political situation made it necessary. Henry, having determined to show the Courts of Europe that he could drive a wedge between the Scots and the French, began by renewing his negotiations for the marriage of Edward and Mary Stuart, hinting that he might go so far as to allow the Prince to live in Scotland for a time. Here his judgment erred; no one believed for a moment that he would give up his son. He then put forward suggestions for two different alliances, one between the Duke of Orleans and the Princess Elizabeth and the other between Edward and the Emperor's niece. Chapuys, summoned to state his master's terms for the Spanish dowry, mentioned the sum of 100,000 crowns. Henry exclaimed: 'That is an affront to my son — a future King!' and when Chapuys began to talk of a compromise he refused to discuss it. 'There is no more to be said', he declared, adding that he was surprised and hurt by such a paltry offer. 'I cannot proceed,' he went on, 'unless the Prince's bride be as well dowered as the Duke of Orleans will be if he marries the Princess Elizabeth.' Chapuys received this shaft imperturbably; he continued to urge the Spanish marriage on Henry, who burst into one of his appalling rages, shouting: 'Your people are supporting the Scots, my enemies!' Chapuys, seeing him as convulsed with pain as with anger, left the Presence-Chamber; in his report to the Emperor he added that as negotiations for the Scottish marriage were still going on, there was no point in further discussion of a Spanish alliance.[17]

The proof of Henry's attachment to France had now to be publicly demonstrated. Peace between the two countries was signed in June 1546. In the following September, Claude d'Annebault, Governor of Normandy and Admiral of France, whose attempted invasion of England had been defeated by Lisle in the summer of 1545, arrived for a state visit to Hampton Court. Henry decided that the first stages of the reception should be his son's responsibility. Edward, who had only just begun to learn French, wrote to his stepmother about his greeting — did she think the Admiral would understand Latin?[18] Obviously he was not eager to try out a new language on an occasion of such moment. The Queen's reply has not survived; but whatever tongue he used, Edward's share in the ceremony was well performed, although his letter to Katherine Parr indicates that he was rather nervous.

Riding abreast with Cranmer, his uncle Hertford and his cousin the Earl of Huntingdon, Edward proceeded three miles beyond the gates of the palace, attended by his schoolfellows, their henchmen, his gentlemen of the bedchamber and eight hundred yeomen of the guard. D'Annebault and his suite were awaiting them on the river bank at Hounslow, having come by water from the Tower. Edward wore a crimson and white satin doublet sewn with jewels; his gentlemen and yeomen were dressed in cloth of gold. At the riverside Edward dismounted and bowed very low; the Admiral then advanced and kissed his hand; Edward kissed him on both cheeks, and made a short speech of welcome. He had never before spoken in front of so large an audience or in the open air. His voice carried over the heads of the French and English courtiers to the crowds beyond, who 'much marvelled', according to an eye-witness, at His Grace's 'high wit and great audacity'.[19]

The bearded, elderly warrior and the eight-year-old boy re-mounted, d'Annebault putting his right hand under Edward's left; so linked, they rode back, their respective suites following them in order of precedence, to the main gates of the palace, where the Lord Chancellor and the Council awaited them bare-headed. Edward's control of his horse was perfectly sustained, his bearing high and serene.[20] When they had all dismounted again the procession re-formed, and the Prince, his hand still resting on the Admiral's, conducted him through forecourts, passages and galleries to his apartments, where refreshments were served on the knee, further compliments interchanged, introductions made and the first instalment of the King's presents — gold and silver plate — brought forward and given by Edward to his guest. It was not until many hours later, possibly the next day, that Henry came into the picture, of which Edward remained the centre during the week of masques, banquets and jousts that followed. The profile portrait by an unknown artist shows him as he then appeared — fair, delicately featured, with reddish-gold hair, long-lashed grey eyes, clearly marked eyebrows and a keen yet considering expression — a figure of princely dignity and unselfconscious grace.

Henry's plans for his son's minority were now put forward. Neither his capacity for hard work nor his eye for detail had been affected by disease; and his arrangements for the Regency combined a superb disregard of others' potentialities with a refusal to admit the inefficacy of the dead hand that was the final proof of a transcendental egoism. He did not fear death; indeed, he welcomed it: with the tranquil assurance of one simply moving on to rule from a higher sphere, he divided his power amongst a set of men he had trained and dominated but never, with the exception of Cranmer, inspired. The sixteen Councillors of the Regency were appointed, and their respective duties ordained. It did not occur to their master that any of his creatures might rise to tamper with the machine he had devised and set in motion, and that he alone could control. It is characteristic of Henry that he was never more supremely confident than in the last year of his life, when he treated his legatees as a team whose only strength was in their unity and their subservience to his decrees. Of these, Edward was, of course, the centre, and the official, if not the actual, mainspring of power; and Edward alone kept, or tried to keep, his place in the design.

The principal virtue of that design was its fluidity — a point Edward could only have grasped if he had lived to grow up, and that his ministers ignored or despised. Like an underground river, the course of the English Reformation was now to disappear until the genius of Elizabeth conjured it out of darkness into a twisted yet broadening channel. In 1539, her father's less highly developed talent for compromise had taken the form of a temporary retreat from what seem to have been his original aims; this was set out in his *Act for the Abolishing of Diversity of Opinions*, later known as 'the bloody Act of the Six Articles', or 'the whip with six strings'. In this, belief in the Real Presence in the sacrament, Communion in one kind, celibacy of the clergy, auricular confession and prayers for the dead were re-enforced; the services were still to be read in English; but in 1542 permission to read the Bible in that tongue was confined to the educated classes. Both Acts received the support of the middle class, and that of the ancient and new nobility, and both were, naturally, a blow to the Protestant party. But this party was still a small one; most of Henry's subjects rated security higher than freedom; the risk of civil war, and the foreign invasion that might have followed it, appeared far more dreadful to them than the stake, the rope and the disemboweller's knife. His persecutions never interfered with their paramount interests — making money and enjoying the resultant comfort and display; therefore they remained loyal to him: passionately so. His personality typified the national ideals of force, prosperity, independence and ostentation.

Nevertheless, between 1539 and 1547 Henry's unavailing efforts to establish religious uniformity resulted in a harsher tyranny and further confusion and revolt in the minds of the unsophisticated minority, who, enraged by this capricious removal of their right to read the Scriptures 'in high and loud voices', or to enjoy 'disputation, argument or exposition of the mysteries of the Mass' whenever and however they chose,[21] expressed their disgust in such conversations as the following:

The scene is, naturally, an ale-house. Two peasants, Cook and Baker, are arguing over their drink. Cook, something of a firebrand, is deriding Baker's orthodoxy. 'What availeth,' he exclaims, 'to pray for them that be departed? You will never leave your beggarly ceremonies for your advantage! What availeth your babbling and your singing at matins? By God's blood, no more worth than Tacker's wife's cow to low, or else that my bitch should take Richard Tacker's sow by the ear!' Baker discreetly rejoins: 'The King and the Council and all his clergy hath mitted [given] us matins to sing and to say', and Cook goes on: 'What availeth it to me, without it be said or sung in English?' to which Baker answers resignedly: 'If Christ suffer his passion, we must believe as the Church teacheth us.' No doubt Cook had a clinching argument on the tip of his tongue; but at this point a priest and another man came in, and 'bid them hold their peace'.[22]

The opposing point of view was more forcibly expressed by the Vicar of Tower Hill, 'a strong, stout, popish prelate', who, dispossessed for refusing to conduct the services in English, remained in his parish and, as soon as prayers began, rang the bell, so that nothing else could be heard, breaking off to bawl in the choir or to challenge the preacher in the pulpit, with the result that the congregation joined in the argument and a free fight sometimes ensued.[23] For such offences Henry's peculiar line of demarcation was enforced by punishments that his victims took for granted: they saw nothing grotesque or horrible in the destruction, on one day, of six persons; three men hanged for denying the Royal

Supremacy, and three burnt for heresy; nor could they perceive the connection between this severity and the incipient spiritual chaos that by the end of 1547 resulted in mules and horses being stabled in one church, ornaments stolen from another, gibberish that was supposed to be Latin mumbled in a third, and dogs held up in imitation of the lifting of the Host; in a few ale-houses amateur theologians bandied sacred names in the intervals of berating or falling upon one another and abusing those set in authority over them.

Only Cranmer's attitude was one of leniency tinged with humour. To a priest who had appealed to him for help, he observed: 'It is told me that you be imprisoned in the Fleet for calling me an hostler, and reporting that I have no more learning than a gosling. Did you ever see me before this day?' 'No, for-sooth.' Cranmer pursued: 'What mean you, then, to call me an hostler, and so to deface me among your neighbours?' 'I was over-seen with drink', replied the priest. 'Well,' Cranmer went on, 'now ye be come, you may oppose me to know what learning I have. Begin in grammar, if you will, or else in philosophy, or other sciences, or divinity.' 'I beseech your Grace, pardon me, I have no manner of learning in the Latin tongue, but altogether in English.' 'Well, then, if you will not oppose me, I will oppose you. Are you not wont to read the Bible?' 'Yes, that we do daily.' 'I pray you, tell me then, who was David's father?' There was a pause — then: 'I cannot surely tell your lordship.' 'If you cannot tell me that, yet declare unto me who was Solomon's father.' After another silence the reply came sullenly: 'Surely, I am nothing at all seen in these genealogies.' The lecture that followed was extremely mild. Cranmer said: 'Then I perceive, however you have reported to me that I had no learning, I can now bear you witness that you have none at all. There are such a sort of you in this realm that know nothing, nor will know nothing, but sit upon your ale-bench, and slander all honest and learned men ... God amend you, and get you home to your cure, and from henceforth learn to be an honest man, or at least a reasonable man.'[24]

Naturally, such an appeal was incomprehensible to those it saved from a horrible death: as were Henry's comparatively gentle censures of 'fantasies, abuses and naughty opinions',[25] his sterner warnings and his final revenges. A very small minority, of whom

Hertford was one, was sickened by the barbarity of this iron age; and Hertford alone imagined that it could be ameliorated.

These dissensions added to the burden of Henry's work; his private and domestic life continued its usual course. At Hampton Court he was able to enjoy a little fishing, the last outdoor sport that remained to him. Within the palace he solaced himself with music, playing his own compositions or accompanying his fool, Will Somers. An illustration in the King's psalter shows him white-haired, wrinkled and irascible, sitting at his lute, while Somers, a hunchback, stands at a distance singing with all his might and looking rather uneasy.[26]

Edward had no share in these pursuits; he was at Ashridge, Enfield, or Woking, never at Hampton Court and does not seem to have visited the King during his last months at Whitehall. Here, Henry took final measures for the safety of the succession that was now suddenly menaced by two of the leaders of the Catholic party.

On December 12th, 1546, the Duke of Norfolk and his elder son, the Earl of Surrey, were arrested and sent to the Tower for conspiring to seize the Regency and murder the Council. The whole extent of their guilt will never be known; but it is clear that there was some truth in the description of Surrey, a crypto-Protestant, a brilliant poet and a recklessly courageous soldier as 'the most foolish proud boy that ever was in England'[27] — for he had quartered the royal arms with his own, suggested to his sister (Richmond's widow) that she should become the King's mistress, and been often in trouble for window-breaking, brawling and hooliganism generally. Norfolk confessed that he had concealed, if not abetted, Surrey's attempts to seize the guardianship of Edward by a *coup d'état*; these may be illustrated by a conversation between Sir George Blagge, one of Henry's gentlemen, and this wild and prepotent young man. Blagge, afterwards a member of the Regency Council, warned Surrey against trying to overset the King's arrangements, adding: 'Then the Prince should be but evil taught — rather than that it should come to pass that the Prince should be under the government of your father or you, I would bide the adventure to thrust this dagger in you.' To which Surrey replied: 'You are very hasty — God sends a shrewd cow short horns.' When Blagge answered, 'Yea, my lord, and I trust your horns also shall be kept so short as ye shall not be able to do any hurt with them', Surrey immediately offered to fight him, and presently was heard boasting of his schemes to gain complete control of Edward. [28]

On January 13th, 1547, a special commission found Surrey guilty of high treason; he was beheaded a week later. On the 18th, Parliament met to discuss Norfolk's attainder and execution, and the investiture of Edward as Prince of Wales. By the 24th, the bill of attainder was prepared, and on the 27th the King's assent to it was conveyed to the Houses by the Lord Chancellor. In the Tower, Norfolk waited for death — as did Henry VIII in his Palace of Westminster. The warrant remained unsigned; the hand that had 'made heads fly', as Henry once put it, was powerless at last; the King could no longer see, or hold a pen.

During the night of the 27th physicians and ministers came and went through Henry's bedchamber and the ante-rooms beyond it in terror and perplexity. He was dying fast: but it seemed that he did not know it; and who should dare to tell him? To speak of his death was high treason by Act of Parliament. Yet to let him perish without giving him the chance to repent was a greater crime.

At last, at about eleven o'clock, Sir Anthony Denny, Chief Gentleman of the Bedchamber, resolved to risk his life for his master's soul. He approached the bedside, and said: 'In man's judgment, Your Majesty is not like to live. I beseech Your Majesty to prepare yourself for death, and to consider the sins of your life past.' There was a pause. Then Henry replied calmly: 'The mercy of Christ is able to pardon me all my sins, though they were greater than they be.' 'Shall I send for any learned man for Your Majesty to confer withal?' Denny asked. Henry said: 'With no other but with Archbishop Cranmer — and not with him, as yet. I will first repose myself a little, and then, as I find myself, I will determine accordingly.'

He slept for half an hour and, waking to find himself much weaker, desired Denny to send for Cranmer, who arrived at midnight. By now Henry was speechless. He stretched out his hand to Cranmer, who, holding it fast, implored him to give some sign of his trust in Jesus Christ. The King gripped Cranmer's hand and wrung it. As his hold relaxed he sank into unconsciousness. For two more hours doctors and councillors watched and listened. At two o'clock on the morning of January 28th, Edward Tudor became King of England.[29]

All this time, the two principal members of the Council — Sir William Paget and Lord Hertford — had remained outside the death-chamber, walking up and down the long gallery. By the time Henry was dead, they had agreed on the subversion of his Will, and how best to turn that subversion to their common advantage.

NOTES TO CHAPTER IV

[1] Strype, *Life of Sir John Cheke*, p. 20.
[2] *The Governor*, pp. 43-8.
[3] *Lit. Rem.*, vol. I, p. cxxxvi.
[4] Ibid., p. lxxix.
[5] Strype, *Life of Sir John Cheke*, p. 22.
[6] Baldwin, *Shakespeare's Small Latin and Less Greek*, pp. 200-56.
[7] *Lit. Rem.*, vol. I, pp. 12-50.
[8] *Toxophilus*, p. 217.
[9] *Lit. Rem.*, vol. I, p. 16.
[10] Burnet, *History of the Reformation*, vol. I, part 1, p. 539.
[11] *Cal. Span. P.*, vol. VIII, p. 332.
[12] *The Schoolmaster*, p. 231.
[13] *Lit. Rem.*, vol. I, p. xli.
[14] *L. & P.*, vol. XXI, part 2: 814; *Lit. Rem.*, vol. II, p. 383.
[15] Ibid., vol. XX, part 2: 726.
[16] Ibid.
[17] *Cal. Span. P.*, vol. VIII, p. 332.
[18] *Lit. Rem.*, vol. I, p. 2.
[19] Hall, p. 867; Holinshed, p. 859.
[20] Hall, p. 867; Holinshed, p. 859.
[21] Hayward, *Life of Edward VI*, p. 28.
[22] *L. & P.*, vol. XV, part 2: p. 821.
[23] Strype, *Ecclesiastical Memorials*, vol. III, part 1, p. 344.
[24] Strype, *Life of Cranmer*, vol. I, pp. 628-9.
[25] Hayward, p. 79.
[26] Law, vol. I, p. 69.
[27] *L. & P.*, vol. XIV, part 2: 141.
[28] Ibid., vol. XXI, part 2: 1383.
[29] Godwin, *Annals of England*, p. 207.

✠

CHAPTER FIVE

THE SUPREME HEAD

AT three o'clock on the morning of January 28th, Lord Hertford left London for Ashridge to break the news of Henry's death to Edward. Paget then discovered that he had taken with him the key to the safe in which the late King's Will was deposited, and sent a messenger after him to bring it back. In returning the key, Hertford wrote to Paget to remind him of their agreement to keep the contents of the Will secret for the present.[1] Then his thoughts seem to have turned from his own schemes to Edward's feelings. Instead of telling him at once of his father's death, Hertford removed his nephew from Ashridge to Enfield, where Elizabeth was, so that the brother and sister should be together when they heard the news. Sir Anthony Browne, Henry's Master of the Horse, accompanied them. During the rest of that day Edward and Elizabeth remained in ignorance, as did everyone else in their respective households, of what had happened. On the 29th they were in the Presence-Chamber with their attendants when Hertford and Browne asked to be received and, kneeling, told the nine-year-old boy that he was King of England.[2]

A portion of the Presence-Chamber — all that remains of the Palace of Enfield — can still be seen, much as it was on that Sunday morning, four hundred years ago. It can never have been a large or formal room. The walls are oak-panelled in a geometrical pattern, the plaster ceiling is decorated with roses, fleur-de-lis and small pendants, the leaded windows are framed in strap-work. The great stone chimney-piece is the centre of a design in which coronets, portcullises and roses surround the griffins supporting the Royal Arms. In the wide hearth a fire must have been blazing when Edward received his first homage as king. He may have suspected or been told that Henry was dying: certainly Elizabeth would have become aware, during these last weeks, what the situation was. In any case, the news came as a shock, if not as a

JANE SEYMOUR

ENRY VIII AND WILL SOMERS

surprise, to both children. They burst into a passion of sobs and clung, weeping, to one another, while Hertford and Browne seem to have stood watching them in silence. 'Never', says Edward's first biographer, 'was sorrow more sweetly set forth, their faces seeming to beautify their sorrow ... The most iron eyes ... were drawn thereby into the society of their tears.'[3]

This description is rather romantic than perceptive. Somerset was tender-hearted and easily moved; Browne had been deeply attached to Henry; the personal attendants of all the Tudors remained devoted to them, whatever the circumstances; to Edward and Elizabeth, the death of Henry VIII must have seemed cataclysmic, the rolling up of a scroll; and as to weep communally and in public was customary, and on this occasion proper, no doubt they all cried together for a considerable time.

Hertford then decided that Edward should spend the rest of that day and the following night quietly at Enfield, setting off at eleven o'clock next morning for the Tower, where, according to custom, he would remain until his coronation three weeks later. They hoped, he wrote to the Council, to be in the city by three in the afternoon of the 30th.[4] He said nothing more about the late King's Will; in fact, Paget had already prepared the doctored version that was to be put before the Council. Further concealment of the Will was now out of the question, nor indeed was it necessary: all Hertford and Paget had to do was to carry the Council with them; their plan for doing so was admirably simple.

Henry had decided that in the event of Edward dying without issue, the crown was to come to Mary and her heirs, then to Elizabeth and hers, provided they married in accordance with the wishes of their brother and his advisers. If all three died childless, the Scottish branch — the descendants of Henry's elder sister Margaret, grandmother of Mary Stuart — was to be passed over, and the daughters of his second sister, Mary, Duchess of Suffolk, would succeed; these were Frances, Marchioness of Dorset, and Eleanor, Countess of Brandon. Frances's three daughters were to succeed her. Thus eight women were in line for the throne.

As there seemed, at that time, every hope of Edward's living to continue the Tudor dynasty (preferably by marrying Mary Stuart, who was five when he succeeded) this part of the Will was not debatable; that for the Regency — equal shares in the

F   81

executive power by the principal members of the Council — was overthrown within forty-eight hours of Henry's death, to the disgust and rage of those whom Paget and Hertford had out-stripped during the last hours of their master's life. During the first part of Edward's reign the most influential Councillors were Hertford, Cranmer, Lisle and Paget: this nobleman's plan of becoming the power behind all powers was that of the subtle, brilliant and unscrupulous politician, so eager to better himself that he relegates those to whom he has given his allegiance. Paget, using Hertford, was himself to be used by a more cunning and ruthless intriguer than himself — Lisle, whom he underrated. Already, Cranmer's ability had raised him above all Henry's Ministers to the unique and unassailable position that he held until his martyrdom in Mary's reign. Cranmer had genuine care for the religious settlement that Henry had not lived to perfect, and that he had intended to continue step by step, until the laws of uniformity laid down in the Six Articles gave way to the Protestantism into which the English people were to be guided rather than driven. Hertford, a first-class soldier and a sincerely religious man, also thought of himself as dedicated to the progress of this second phase in the Reformation: he would have been horrified at the idea of grasping at power for its own sake; yet he trusted no one but himself to carry through the religious and political reforms that were too far in advance of the age to be effected by any but an administrative genius. And Hertford was no genius. He was a visionary, with a streak of monomania.

The fall of the Howard faction (Norfolk was still in prison) had made Hertford very powerful before the death of Henry; such rivals as he had were in a minority. He and Paget had therefore rightly assumed that to substitute a Protectorate for a Regency would be a matter of proposal and acceptance. On the morning of January 31st, while Edward and Hertford were on their way to London, Paget approached the Council and after some objec-tions from Wriothesley, the Lord Chancellor, they agreed on this major reversal of Henry's decrees. Before the uncle and nephew reached the Tower a fresh commission had been drawn up, in which it was announced that 'some special man ... should be preferred in name and place ... to whom, as to the head of the rest ... all might have access', and that this man should be the

Earl of Hertford under the title of Lord Protector.[5] Certain minor conditions were added, limiting his jurisdiction; it was not long before these were unobtrusively eliminated. Then, in order to invest what was in fact the dictatorship of a single nobleman with the aura of regality, it was declared that a king's authority was in no sense affected by his age. Edward VI inherited the autocracy of Henry VIII without a single reservation but that of deferring to the Protector's advice. His prerogative was officially that of an adult. 'A king', said Gardiner, a year or two later, 'is as much a king at four as he is at forty years of age.'[6]

The effect of Edward himself of this view — the creed and propaganda of his government — may be imagined. He was, and knew himself to be, in a unique position; for the minorities of Henry III, Henry VI and Edward V were in no way comparable with his. He was absolute monarch and ruler of his people, responsible for their souls and bodies. He took up the burden consciously, aware that he must answer to God and before the Bar of history for any mistakes that might be made. He had been trained to carry it, and he was in his own mind prepared, in fact eager, to do so.

Until this moment, and during the first months of his reign, Edward's relations with Hertford were excellent. His elder uncle represented the ideal at which he had been taught to aim — that of the pious, high-minded, great gentleman of many accomplishments, combining the knowledge of the scholar with the grace and dash of the athlete and the soldier. Edward had no idea, until two years later, of the insuperable difficulties confronting Hertford — a debased currency, incipient economic chaos and a discontented and divided kingdom, directed by a corrupt and self-seeking ministry. Indeed, it seems as if Hertford himself underrated the enormous complications of the task that was made harder for him by the behaviour of his second wife, Anne Stanhope, at whose demand he had disinherited both his children by his first, Catherine Fillol. By the time Edward became king the second Lady Hertford had borne her husband nine children, six daughters and three sons, and was supposed by those who knew her best to dominate his private life.[7] The extent to which she really did so is indefinable; there is no doubt that she was an arrogant, predatory and pushing woman, totally uninterested in her husband's political and religious schemes, and bent only on grasping power and wealth for herself and her children. Any chance of Hertford's retaining such popularity as he still had among his equals was destroyed by her attitude and conduct; she appears to have been behind his most tactless and unwise actions. The Princess Mary was fond of her; otherwise she was universally disliked. Hertford, now in his forty-second year, was admired and loved by the common people; he kept their affection long after that of Edward had sunk away.

The loyalty felt throughout the country for the King and the Protector was epitomized in the ecstatic welcome of the crowds awaiting them outside the Tower on the afternoon of January 31st. Officially, the city was mourning Henry, and his son had not been proclaimed. Yet there he was, at last — 'an image so high, of so great hope and promise ... a right Briton, both bred and born'[8] — the idol of a nation who saw in the small, stately figure the symbol of their golden world. Edward was radiant. His spirits rose above the shock and terror of the last twenty-four hours to meet his people's wild acclaim with an excitement that matched their rapture. 'His eyes', says one historian, 'seemed to have a starry liveliness and lustre.'[9]

At the outer bastion of the fortress — the Red Bulwark — Hertford and Sir Anthony Browne, who had been on either side of him, reined in their horses to let him ride on, alone. At the great gates he was met by the Constable of the Tower. As he dismounted, Archbishop Cranmer and the Lords of the Council came forward and knelt before him. Hertford on one side and the Constable on the other, the Council preceding them, he was led into his Presence-Chamber, newly hung with cloth of gold. Sitting there under his canopy of state, he received the homage of the nobles; he was then conducted to his private apartments to change his clothes. While the guns thundered on, the peers held a short conference on the Will, afterwards dispersing, some to their rooms within the Tower, others to lodgings near by.

At three o'clock the next morning Edward sat in council. He was asked if he were willing that his uncle should be proclaimed Lord Protector of the realm and Governor of his person during his minority. Three years later, writing his 'chronicle', he remembered that 'all the gentlemen and Lords did agree, because he was the King's uncle on his mother's side'.[10] One by one, Hertford taking precedence, the peers knelt to kiss his hand, saying 'God save Your Grace!' Hertford then stepped forward and promised that with their help he would do his duty. The Lords replied with an assurance of loyalty — to the Protector first, and then to his nephew — concluding with a shout of 'God save the noble King Edward!'

Edward stood up. He took off his cap. Then he said: 'We heartily thank you, my lords all. And hereinafter, to all that you shall have to do with us, for any suits or causes, you shall be heartily welcome to us.'[11]

The next few days were spent by the Lords in private conference. On February 14th Hertford went to Westminster Hall to take the oaths as Lord Treasurer and Earl Marshal of England, relinquishing the post of Lord Chamberlain to Lisle, who in return handed over the command of the Navy to Thomas Seymour. On the morning of February 16th, Edward, wearing his purple velvet robe and cap and a mourning-stole, invested the Lord Mayor and the Lord Chief Justice with the Order of the Garter.[12] On the 17th the funeral of Henry VIII took place at Windsor. Edward was not present; his brief description of the ceremony shows that he received an account of it from someone who was. He had never been quite clear about his father's last illness — 'a dropsy, as it was thought', he wrote later — but certain aspects of Henry's burial remained in his mind: the white staves of the household officers, for instance, that they broke 'with much solemnity ... hurling them into the grave'. How was it, he seems to wonder, that these 'were restored to them again, when they came to the Tower'?[13] The trivial questions that children brood over in secret are apt to linger on when more significant incidents have been forgotten. If the story of Henry's cerements bursting open and dripping blood ever reached Edward, he did not record it: nor the proclamation of his own titles over his father's open grave, nor the fact that sixteen of the strongest yeomen of the guard were needed to lower the huge coffin into the vault beside his mother's.[14] His recollection moved from the broken staves of office to the new titles that he bestowed on February 18th. Lisle was made Earl of Warwick, Thomas Seymour became Baron Seymour of Sudeley, and Hertford received the dukedom of Somerset. This last creation was effected with a much more elaborate ritual than was custom-

ary, as if to emphasize the semi-regal omnipotence of the Lord
Protector. During the long process of the other investitures —
sixteen in all — the new Duke stood alone beside Edward, a
dominating, splendid figure, handsome still in middle age; full-
lipped, fresh-coloured, aquiline, his face has a melancholic
distinction; is not that of a man who takes life easily.

Somerset's temperament was in marked contrast to that of his
younger brother. Thomas Seymour was brilliantly good-looking.
He had only to enter a room for everyone to stop talking and turn
to stare at him, however familiar his height and elegance might
already be.[15] 'He was fierce in courage,' says a Protestant historian,
'courtly in fashion, in personage stately, in voice magnificent, but
somewhat empty in matter.'[16] In fact, the new Lord Admiral
could charm people of both sexes and all ages whenever he so
desired — which he did simply with a view to his own interests.
As soon as this became apparent to those he subjugated, they
found him even shallower and more foolish than he really was, so
startling was the disillusionment caused by his peculiar and re-
current sequence of vigour, gaiety, arrogance and recklessness that
culminated in outbursts of spiteful bad temper when he did not
get what he wanted. During the three weeks that elapsed between
the death of Henry and the coronation of Edward, Seymour spent
most of his time at the Tower, making himself extremely agreeable
to everyone and laying plans for a career that had begun well —
though not nearly well enough, he considered — with his barony,
Warwick's presentation of the Admiraltyship and many large
grants of land. Though he was secretly disgusted at his brother's
seizure of power, Seymour suppressed the chagrin that in a lesser
degree was shared by the Queen and Bishop Gardiner, neither of
whom had been left any part in Henry's arrangements for
Edward's minority. Katherine Parr was sensible enough to settle
for the comforts of private life on a large income and the writing
of a pamphlet — *The Lamentations of a Sinner*, with a preface by
Cecil — that remained popular for many years after its publication.[17] In any case, Edward was so much attached to her that she
could count on his support, as on that of her step-daughters, so
long as she kept out of palace intrigues.

Gardiner, who had done his utmost to prevent Somerset's
nomination as Protector, was no longer a member of the Council,

and was already in conflict with him over the alteration of Henry's plans for the gradual relaxation of the Six Articles; now he found that all that was allowed him was the organization (and even that under Cranmer's jurisdiction) of the mourning for their late master. Proud, intractable, yet with a substratum of prudence and cunning, Gardiner submitted to his relegation, rather unfairly working off his resentment on the Earl of Oxford, whose private company of actors were planning to show their sense of the public grief in 'a solemn play, with music'. It was brought home to Gardiner how utterly powerless he had become when these despised creatures ignored his ban on their performance, and the city magistrates declared themselves unable to support him; finally, one of them told the enraged prelate that though he could not stop the play being acted, he could forbid anyone to go to it; and with this Gardiner had to be contented.[18]

During the days immediately preceding his coronation Edward was busy with his correspondence, still using the Roman hand, as there was no time for the more suitable, engrossing style; even then his letters were as short as courtesy allowed. It seems as if Cheke had joined him at the Tower by this time, for his notes exchanging condolences with the Princesses, Queen Katherine, the Emperor and Francis I are all in perfectly phrased, if rather platitudinous, Latin.[19] Any lessons, however simple or short, must have been hard to concentrate on in the week that led up to the most splendid and triumphant two days of his life, those on which his accession and his coronation were respectively celebrated.

From the public point of view, the first — his progress from the Tower to the Palace of Westminster — was by far the more thrilling and memorable; for his coronation was a private rite that only the higher clergy and nobility were permitted to attend. It was on the day before that of his enthronement in the Abbey that Edward made his public and official entry among his people as their ruler; the varying phases of this dramatic and elaborate display were so planned as to give every citizen, of whatever grade, the chance of looking at him closely — even, here and there, at length — and thus achieving direct contact with the magic of kingship and the almost divine power of the dynasty. To Edward was assigned the principal part in a semi-religious, semi-mythological panorama that lasted some five hours without a break, and that called for a perfectly sustained display of grace, poise and amiability. He rose to the occasion with no difficulty and little sign of strain or self-will. Those who designed the contrasting effects of this progress assumed, as he did, that at nine years old a well-educated and intelligent boy can be counted on to behave with the desired combination of propriety, courtesy and charm.

On the morning of February 19th, Edward was dressed in a gown of cloth of silver embroidered in gold with a belt of silver filigree set with rubies, diamonds and true lovers' knots of pearls; this fell away to show his doublet and buskins of white velvet, similarly worked; his white velvet cap was so thickly set with diamonds and pearls as to make a dazzling halo, worn at an angle that outlined his profile. Just before one o'clock he came out of the main courtyard of the Tower, where his horse, caparisoned in crimson satin sewn with gold damask and pearls, was waiting under a canopy carried by six mounted noblemen. It then became clear that, thus surrounded, he would be entirely hidden; it was therefore arranged that he should ride a few feet in advance of these attendants, while Somerset rode on his left, a little beyond. So the glittering white and golden figure of the child stood out alone against the tall armoured horsemen, in their surcoats of blue, purple, scarlet and green.

This central part of the cavalcade was preceded by a concourse of courtiers, clergy, statesmen and foreign ambassadors, riding in pairs or quartets and numbering some hundreds of personages. The Marquis of Dorset appeared immediately before the King, carrying the Sword of State. The procession concluded with several thousand men-at-arms, yeomen of the guard, halberdiers and grooms of the Privy Chamber, marching in sections. As the King entered Mark Lane — the City frontier — a peal of cannon sounded from the arsenal of the Tower.

All along the route the streets were sprinkled with gravel and railed off. Against the steely winter sky, the grey and white buildings and the black woodwork, windows and balconies dripped arras and cloth of gold. Order was ensured by the gentlemen-pensioners and tipstaffs on horseback and foot who kept the delirious crowds from breaking through the first row of spectators — the aldermen, craftsmen, priests and clerks of the City, with their families. The first pause was at Fenchurch Street, where a choir standing on an ornamental scaffold was giving a recital of sacred music: this was momentary. The point of the procession began at the conduit in Cornhill, already running with white wine and surrounded by a troupe of children, two of whom stepped forward and addressed Edward in a rhyme that opened with:

> Hail, noble Edward, our King and Sovereign,
> Hail, the chief comfort of your commonalty,
> Hail, redolent rose, whose sweetness to retain
> Ye unto us all such great commodity ...

the rest making up in fervour for what it lacked in syntax and precision.

Thereafter, love and loyalty were poured out as fast as the claret that gushed from the conduits of Cheapside, St Paul's, St George's and Fleet Street. Symbolism ran riot: in verses from Valentine and Orson, one wreathed in moss and ivy and carrying a knotted club, the other in gilded armour ('All those that be enemies to Edward the King, I shall them clout with great confusion'); in rockeries painted with roses and carnations, from which little boys issued as Grace, Nature, Fortune and Charity, while ladies appeared as the Seven Liberal Sciences (Logic, Rhetoric, Arithmetic, Grammar, Music, Geometry and Astronomy); in fights of phoenixes and crowned lions who defeated serpents belching fire; in parties of angels leading garlanded lambs; in dialogues between little girls representing England, Regality, Justice, Mercy and Truth — all in a phantasmagoria of colour, movement and music, all ceaselessly reciting, while at each stage the enraptured audience drowned the actors' lines with roars of 'God save the King!'

After some three hours the procession halted at the Cross in Cheapside, where the Mayor and aldermen were waiting. Here a different note was struck. Allegory was abandoned. The Mayor stepped forward, and, kneeling, presented Edward with a purse containing a thousand crowns — 'the which,' says the official chronicler, 'His Grace received, and gave them thanks'.[20]

According to an eye-witness, this sudden change from fantasy to reality caused the first hitch in Edward's reception of homage. It is unlikely that he had ever before seen such a quantity of money, or handled more than the few coins necessary for scattering largesse. Bewildered, he turned to the Protector, and said: 'Why do they give me this?' 'It is the custom of the City', Somerset replied. Edward had leaned down to take the purse. It was large, and of considerable weight; he could not hold it, and the reins, and go on raising his cap to the people for the rest of his progress. Somerset told him to give it to the Captain of the Guard. The anonymous observer, adding that this solution seemed to cause offence, sums up the incident with unconscious and prophetic irony. 'It was too heavy', he says, 'for him to hold.'[21]

The next tribute reaffirmed the symbolical theme by a presentation of Edward the Confessor, St George on horseback, a mechanical lion whose head moved to and fro, 'and a fair maiden holding a lamb in a string'. At this point a child was to have made an oration in Latin, and St George a speech in English; but the procession had already outrun its schedule. The cavalcade moved on to St George's church.

Here, for the first time since his accession, Edward asserted himself and stopped the proceedings; for he was faced with an enthralling spectacle, unlike any that had gone before. From the church steeple to the ground a rope — 'as great as the cable of a ship' — had been stretched, fastened by an anchor to the gate of the Dean's house. 'And when His Majesty proceeded near the same, there came a man, a stranger (being a native of Aragon) lying on the same rope, his head forward, casting his legs and arms abroad, running on his breast on the same rope, from the said battlements to the ground, as it had been an arrow out of a bow ... Then he came up to the King's Majesty and kissed his foot, and so, after certain words to His Highness, departed from him again, and went upwards upon the said rope, till he was come over the midst of the said churchyard, where ... he played certain masteries ... as, tumbling and casting himself from one leg to another ... which stayed the King's Majesty, with all the train, a good space of time ... '

Eventually Edward tore himself away to the great conduit of Fleet Street, where he was once more confronted by Faith, Justice and Truth ('I, ancient Truth, that long time was suppressed ... '), thence to Temple Bar, and so, at last, to his Palace of Westminster. During the latter half of his progress the ballad that was sung

throughout his reign echoed the refrain that still carries with it the
love and hope of the humble and the obscure —

> Sing up, heart, sing up, heart, and sing no more down,
> For joy of King Edward, that weareth the crown!
>
> Your song in time past hath been down-a-down,
> And long it hath lasted in town and town.
> To very much metre Down hath been added,
> But Up is now sweeter, to make our hearts gladded.
>
> Ye children of England, for joy of the same,
> Take bow and shaft in hand, learn shootage to frame,
> That you another day may so do your parts,
> As to serve your King as well with hands as with hearts.
>
> Ye children that are towards, sing up and down,
> And never play the cowards to him that weareth the crown,
> But always do your cure his pleasure to fulfill,
> Then shall you keep right sure the honour of England still.
>
> Sing up, heart, sing up, heart, and sing no more down,
> For joy of King Edward, that weareth the crown!

And so they sang, up and down, all the rest of that day, and the
night, until morning, while King Edward VI slept in the great
bedchamber where his father had died holding Cranmer's hand.
He was woken very early, for his coronation.

It had been decided that this ceremony should be cut down from
its usual length of eleven or twelve hours, to seven, in view of
Edward's age. As soon as he was robed in his surcoat, train and
gown of crimson velvet embroidered in gold and furred with
miniver, and his black velvet cap had been put on, he, Somerset
and a train of nobles took the state barge from Westminster,
landing at the Privy Stair of Whitehall where the scarlet-clad
pensioners with their gilt axes were lined up, and proceeded
through the open courts of the Palace to Westminster Hall. Here
the procession formed, Somerset carrying the crown, Suffolk the
orb, Dorset the sceptre and Warwick the King's train. Behind
them walked his school-fellows, each bearing some part of the

regalia, till they reached the door of the Abbey. There, preceded by the Dean and the choir, they went up the aisle, taking their places on either side. Edward moved on alone to St Edward's Chair. As soon as he was seated, Cranmer, who had been awaiting him at the altar rails, turned to the great concourse of nobles and clergy and proclaimed: 'Sirs, here present is Edward, rightful and undoubted inheritor by the laws of God and man to the crown and royal dignity of this realm. Whereupon ye shall understand that this day is prefixed and appointed by all the peers of the realm for the consecration, enunction and coronation of the said most excellent Prince Edward. Will ye serve at this time, and give your wills and consents to the same consecration, enunction and coronation?'

The reply came resonantly and formally. 'Yea! Yea! Yea! God save King Edward!'

Edward was then conducted to the high altar, where Cranmer was kneeling. After a short pause Edward lay on his face below the steps while the Archbishop repeated the *Veni Creator Spiritus* to the accompaniment of the choir and the organ. While the Litany was said, Edward remained prostrate. Then he was led into a side-chapel, where he changed into a coat of crimson satin, buttoned in front and at the side; his black cap was exchanged for one of gold cloth. Meanwhile a general pardon to those the late King had condemned was declared, with the exception, among others, of the Duke of Norfolk.

Edward then approached the altar, where his surcoat was un-buttoned for the anointing of arms, breast, back, forehead and hands. When Cranmer had wiped away the oil and refastened this garment, his coronation robes were put on over it. The sword was offered to the altar, and redeemed for a hundred shillings.

Once more Edward took his seat in the Confessor's Chair. He was then crowned by Cranmer with three crowns — with that of St Edward, an antique gilt circlet: with the Crown Imperial of the realm, which, too sacred to be altered, was held over his head: and finally with a smaller reproduction of it that had been made to fit him. Between each crowning the trumpets sounded. The marriage ring was placed on his finger, and his vows made; after that he was invested with the orb, the sceptre, the staff, bracelets and spurs. He received the homage of his peers, of whom Somerset was the first to kneel before him, kissing his right foot and his cheek, and the Mass of the Holy Ghost was sung. Then Edward was carried in his chair to the four corners of the dais and presented to the peers.[22] Cranmer came to the foot of the dais. He turned to the crowned child in the Confessor's Chair, speaking to him alone, but loud enough for everyone in the Abbey to hear.

'Most dread and royal Sovereign,' he began, 'the promises Your Majesty hath made here, at your coronation, [are] to forsake the devil and all his works ...' He then gave a brief account of Henry VIII's split with the Papacy, and went on: 'The Bishops of Canterbury, for the most part, have crowned your predecessors and anointed them Kings of this land; yet it was not in their power to receive or reject them; neither did it give them authority to prescribe or to leave them conditions to take or leave their crowns ...'

After a brief exposition of the subservience of the Church to the Monarchy, Cranmer paused. Then he resumed: 'Therefore, not from the Bishop of Rome, but as a messenger from my Saviour Jesus Christ, I shall most humbly admonish Your Royal Majesty what things Your Highness is to perform. *Your Majesty is God's Vice-Regent and Christ's Vicar within your own dominions, to see ... God truly worshipped and idolatry destroyed ... You are Supreme Head of the Church, elected of God, and only commanded by Him ...*' Cranmer then declared the Divine Right of Kings as being 'God's anointed ... in consideration of their power, which is ordained ... of their persons, which are elected of God, and endued with the gift of His Spirit, for the better raising and guiding of His people'.

After citing precedents from the Old Testament, Cranmer reached the climax of his adjuration.

'I openly declare, before the living God, and before the nobles of this land, *that I have no commission to declare Your Majesty deprived, if Your Majesty misses in part or in whole of these performances, much less to draw up indentures between God and Your Majesty, or to say you forfeit your crown with a clause for the Bishop of Rome, as has been done by Your Majesty's predecessors*. You are to reward virtue, to revenge sin, to justify the innocent, to relieve the poor, to procure peace, to repress violence, and to execute justice throughout your realms ... On those kings who fulfilled these things, the Lord poured out His blessings in abundance.'

The Archbishop concluded with his own blessing. The congregation joined him in a final prayer for His Sacred and Royal Majesty Edward VI, Defender of the Faith, King of England, Scotland, Ireland and France. [23]

Cranmer's declaration would have been impressive and memorable in the case of the stupidest and most heedless boy. To Edward, who had been trained to feel his duty and prerogative as deeply as any of his family, they became the inspiration of his heart and mind; every subsequent action, every speech relating to his position, carries their weight and imprint. At nine years old, his commitments as Supreme Head of the Church (no other monarch throughout the history of England had been crowned with this title or given this supremacy) became the mainspring of his life.

Some twenty minutes must have passed between the end of Cranmer's address and Edward's departure from the Abbey to Westminster Hall, where the coronation banquet was to be held. Walking back under the canopy held by the Wardens of the Cinque Ports, he noticed that three swords were now being carried in front of him, and asked why. He was told that they symbolized his three kingdoms. 'One is wanting — the Bible, the sword of the spirit', he said, and commanded that it should be taken from the lectern and borne before the emblems of earthly power. [24]

The rapidity of this reaction caused no tenderness, no surprise in the potentates who were using Edward as a figurehead. In the 1540s, as for the next three hundred years, the idealization of innocence and immaturity had no place; and the spectacle of an orphaned child, isolated in a concourse of men, most of them middle-aged, had no element of pathos, and no dramatic appeal. Certainly Edward himself would have rejected any such response to his public appearances, on this as on any other occasion. He stood alone. He saw the stated and official extent of his duty, and his power. Of its actual limitations he was told nothing. The discrepancy between Cranmer's pronouncements and Somerset's actions did not become apparent to him until some weeks after his coronation.

The banquet, at which Edward sat between Somerset and Cranmer, lasted some four hours; each course was brought in to the sound of trumpets and preceded by two noblemen on horseback. After the second course, Dymoke, 'upon a courser richly trapped with gold', holding a mace and followed by a page carrying his spear and shield, rode up to the high table and saluted the King. Then he turned to the rest of the company and three times repeated the medieval challenge — 'If there be any manner of man, of whatsoever estate, condition or degree, that will say and maintain that our Sovereign Lord Edward VI, this day here present, is not the rightful and undoubtful heir to the imperial crown of this realm of England, and that of right he ought not to be crowned king, I say he lieth like a false traitor, and that I am ready the same to maintain with him whilst breath is in my body, either now at this time, or any other time whensoever it shall please the King's Highness to appoint. And here upon the same I cast him my gage!' 'And then,' says the chronicler, 'he cast his gauntlet from him, the which no man would take up.' Garter-King-of-Arms then proclaimed Edward's titles and estate in Latin, French and English.[25]

Wafers and hippocras were now brought in on trays and there was a second ceremonial washing of hands. Then Edward, still wearing his crown and robes, left the table and came down the hall to receive the Ministers of State and the foreign ambassadors. It is from the reports of the Spanish and French envoys — Van der Delft and Odet de Selve — that the most unbiased impression of his social manner can be obtained, for these personages were not only expert in criticism, but politically hostile to everything that Edward represented. Somerset was standing by his nephew when Van der Delft approached and greeted him in French. Edward hesitated, and Somerset told the envoy to speak Latin, which he did, adding in his report: 'But truth to tell, he seemed to me to understand the one as little as the other.'[26] This is an excellent illustration of the contemporary attitude towards the child who is also a public figure: no allowances were to be made on the grounds that Edward might be feeling the strain of the last two days.

By the time de Selve, with his second in command, de la Garde, came up, Edward had regained his poise. De Selve, aware that he was not yet fluent in French, began at once in Latin, with condolences and messages of friendship from Francis I, and Edward thanked him, 'very heartily', in that tongue, 'avec la plus honnête façon et le meilleur visage qu'il était possible', says de Selve, noting that he then turned to greet the Scottish Ambassador with the same ease and readiness.[27]

Throughout the reception Edward's grace of bearing and charm of manner were sustained; he showed no sign of fatigue or awkwardness during the private audience of the Knights of the Garter that immediately followed it, nor at the feasting and the *Masque of Orpheus* performed that evening, nor at the jousts held the next day, when he again received the foreign ambassadors. He was in great spirits, and much taken with the skill and boldness of Thomas Seymour, who especially distinguished himself in all the tournaments.[28] The Protector's high position and new responsibilities barred him from joining in this or any future display of the kind; Seymour's, lightly carried, allowed him plenty of time for his own amusements and schemes.

During the week of the coronation the clergy followed Cranmer's lead in sermons that emphasized and reiterated Edward's autocracy and his fitness to exercise it. Day after day, he was compared to a series of Old Testament heroes: David, Samuel, Josias, the young Solomon. The speakers dwelt on his qualities — of which they had no personal knowledge — and poured out fulsome descriptions of the piety and learning that they themselves had not troubled to acquire; nor did they forget, the Spanish Ambassador says acidly, to 'vie with one another in abusing the old religion', whenever they preached before the King.[29] They discoursed ceaselessly and at enormous length on Edward's 'representing his father's majesty and virtues', and on his own 'great excellency and singular towardliness'.[30] His grave demeanour was especially admired. 'It should seem,' one courtier remarked, 'he were already a father, yet passeth he not the age of ten years. Your heart would melt to hear him named — the beautifullest creature that liveth under the sun; the wittiest, the most amiable and gentlest thing of all the world.'[31] Only Francis Godwin, Bishop of Hereford, seems to have allowed himself a momentary doubt as to the result of placing a child, 'of an age infirm, and opportune to treacheries', in such a position. Among His Majesty's so-called servants there were few or none, Godwin perceived, on whose loyalty he could rely.[32]

For Edward, who had found the City's tribute too heavy to carry, the issue was simple, and his duty clear. Long before he absorbed Cranmer's sonorous and dramatic definition of his calling, the motto over the chimney-piece in the Presence-Chamber of the Palace of Enfield Chase had summed it up for him in nine words, one for each year of his life: 'Service alone is virtue: the rest is a cheat.'

NOTES TO CHAPTER V

[1] Tytler, *Edward and Mary*, vol. I, pp. 15-16.
[2] Ibid., p. 17.
[3] Hayward, p. 9.
[4] Tytler, vol. I, p. 17.
[5] Ibid., p. 19.
[6] Muller, *Stephen Gardiner*, p. 89.
[7] Lloyd, *State Worthies*, vol. I, p. 189.
[8] Pollard, *Tudor Tracts*, p. 68.
[9] Hayward, p. 8.
[10] *Lit. Rem.*, vol. II, p. 211.
[11] Ibid.
[12] Ibid.
[13] Ibid., p. 212.
[14] Strickland, *Queens of England*, vol. III, p. 443 (from Sloane MSS).
[15] Hayward, p. 195.
[16] Ibid.
[17] Strickland, *Queens of England*, vol. III, p. 415.
[18] Tytler, vol. I, pp. 19-22.
[19] *Lit. Rem.*, vol. I, p. 51.
[20] Ibid., pp. cclxx-ccv.
[21] Hume, p. 153.
[22] *Lit. Rem.*, vol. I, p. cclxxi.
[23] Strype, *Life of Cranmer*, vol. II, pp. 205-7.
[24] Strype, *Ecclesiastical Memorials*, vol. I, part 2, p. 32.
[25] *Lit. Rem.*, vol. I, p. cclxxx.
[26] *Cal. Span. P.*, vol. IX, p. 46.
[27] De Selve, *Correspondence Politique*, p. 104.
[28] *Cal. Span. P.*, vol. IX, p. 46.
[29] Ibid., p. 493.
[30] *Tudor Tracts*, p. 68.
[31] Thomas, p. 56.
[32] Godwin, p. 203.

CHAPTER SIX

THE TWO BROTHERS

DURING the first month of Edward's reign the Council was dominated by a triumvirate: Cranmer, Somerset and Lisle, Earl of Warwick; they were seconded by Paget, who had now received his barony. The noblemen were apparently loyal to one another, and in agreement on matters of foreign and religious policy. In fact, Warwick was looking for a weak spot in Somerset's defences, but so unobtrusively that not even Paget realized what he was doing. Within a few weeks they combined in ousting Wriothesley, who was forced to hand over the Great Seal to Somerset; the Protector added to his other titles those of High Steward and Treasurer of England. The chagrin of Thomas Seymour could no longer be hidden when he realized that, by becoming Lord High Admiral instead of Warwick, he had committed himself to leaving the country for long stretches of time at his brother's command, while Warwick remained on the spot and in touch with the King, the Archbishop and the Protector.

Meanwhile, Somerset's attitude and behaviour became increasingly dictatorial and dominating. He began to relegate Edward, treating him rather as the adjunct to than the fount of power, thus tacitly contradicting all that the King had been told about his own prerogative. This volte-face, at first bewildering and then antagonizing Edward, was expressed in comparatively trivial changes of tone that would have conveyed more to a child than to a grown person. First, the Protector began to use the regal 'we' in letters and proclamations that were sometimes issued without any preliminary reference to Edward at all; and there were, of course, plenty of people to comment on these assumptions of power to the King, while deprecating the arrogance from which they sprang. In the official statement of his duty to God and the realm, Somerset's opening phrase struck the possessive note — 'Thou, Lord, hast caused me to rule. I am, by Thy appointment, minister for Thy

King, shepherd for Thy people'[1] — and in a letter to the King of France he addressed that monarch as 'brother', with the result that the resident English Ambassador was desired by Francis I to remind His Grace of Somerset who and what he was.[2] Somerset rose above this snub; he had greater affairs on his mind: he knew and declared himself to be, the chosen of God, and the sword-bearer of His justice.[3] The King's distress at this denial of his own status as God's Vicar and Vice-Regent was observed by de Vieilleville, the envoy who came to announce the death of Francis I and the succession of Henry II.

The resident French Ambassador, de Selve, had now become openly critical of Somerset's pretensions. Paget assured him that the Protector was signing the dispatches without reference to Edward simply because the King was still learning to make his signature in a different form from that used before his accession. 'Now', he went on, 'he knows how to do it, and in future he will sign all official papers.' De Selve had to accept the excuse, although he did not believe it.[4]

De Vieilleville and his gentlemen were received by Somerset and Edward together. Before Edward could reply to the announcement of Francis's death, Somerset struck in with expressions of sorrow in fluent French. 'His Majesty hath lost both a father and a brother', he went on, adding that his nephew did not as yet speak that language well enough to declare his friendship for the new King. De Vieilleville might have continued the interview in Latin, but he preferred to conduct the complicated arrangements for a new alliance and the Anglo-French defences of Calais and Boulogne in his own tongue; as neither he nor any of his suite understood English they had to guess what was being said when Edward's ministers spoke to him, or to one another.[5]

On the day following de Vieilleville's reception he and Somerset got down to business at a Council meeting presided over by Edward that the Protector opened in the high-handed manner which annoyed so many foreign ministers. He had, in fact, already decided partly to rescind the terms formerly agreed on for the defences of Calais and Boulogne. He therefore began by expressing his pleasure that the Sire de Vieilleville had not come to break his contract by insisting on the restoration to France of certain fortresses. De Vieilleville reiterated his royal master's good faith in

99

his English allies, and prepared to read out the new articles. Somerset said: 'There is no need to do so if the articles concerning Boulogne are altered.' 'In a solemn oath sworn between two great Kings', de Vieilleville replied, 'naught already agreed upon may be altered, save to forget past quarrels, above all those between the French and English officers who command the said fortresses.'

'That is true,' said Somerset, 'but the article of Boulogne is in that treaty, word for word, as I shall show your lordship. If the King of France destroyeth any of the Boulogne fortresses, whether it be secretly or in open warfare, that giveth him no right over Calais, or any place else held by His Majesty of England in the Comté d'Oye. This is the rightful heritage of the English kings, as it hath been for three hundred years past.' De Vieilleville remained contemptuously silent; Somerset went on angrily: 'In our business with France this article hath, in the reign of the King that dead is, been somewhat neglected — for reason of my absence in Scotland. But your lordship's people are more accustomed to cunning than we; yet, when we must hold what is ours, we know well how to show Frenchmen what Englishmen be.'

De Vieilleville kept command of his temper, and replied in an ironic strain. 'I think, my lord,' he said, 'that your lordship understands very well that no people may hide their true nature. Indeed, as with a man, the nature of a people is shown, not only by deed and word, but by that which he saith when he forgetteth his estate — and, as to courage, the French have ever shown the English what theirs was worth.' 'I will say no more of that', Somerset replied, adding as if in afterthought: 'Have your people ever held parts of England? And were the Kings of France crowned in London, as were our Kings in Paris?' At this de Vieilleville burst out — was his hand on his sword-hilt? — 'Ha! my lord — enough! It lieth not in the power of six Kings of England to make such conquests — unless, forsooth, they have the Dukes of Burgundy and Brittany for their confederates.' 'And in Boulogne?' Somerset blandly pursued. 'Since those kingdoms no longer remain, how does your lordship think we tarry?' 'Your lordship should not call that a conquest', retorted de Vieilleville. 'It is, rather, a rape, for we hold as prisoners in the Bastille the traitors who sold it to you.'

Carloix, de Vieilleville's secretary, who was making notes of the conversation, saw the Protector's angry flush — 'for he was one concerned in that deal'. He also perceived that the King was looking very much distressed; so, perhaps, did de Vieilleville, for he proceeded to the next point in the agreement, to which Somerset and the rest of the Council agreed; then he begged the Protector to continue the conference, and to take the lead. Somerset assented with a similar display of courtesy, and his nephew's face cleared. De Vieilleville wound up the interview by the reiteration of his master's loyalty and faith; he was ready to say a great deal more in this strain, as custom required; but Somerset broke up the meeting. [6]

The effect on Edward of his uncle's behaviour was apparent only to Carloix; that he brooded over it in resentful silence is proved by his comments later on, during the Protector's absence. The jealous rage of Somerset's fellow-Councillors was not so concealed. Lord Cobham, whose duty it was to escort de Vieilleville and his gentlemen to the river palace of Durham Place — referred to by the Frenchmen as Darompier — hastened to assure the envoy of Somerset's and his brother's unpopularity; he said much about ill-gained power and riches that Carloix recalled rather cynically when he observed the magnificence with which his master was entertained during the six days of their stay in London. The whole city revelled in wealth: goldsmiths' shops abounded; far too much was eaten and drunk at every meal; everybody was overdressed. And at Court this ostentation contrasted oddly, in the Frenchman's eyes, with the exaggerated subservience used towards Edward, Somerset and their guests. At one banquet de Vieilleville sat between Edward and Somerset, with the Lord Admiral opposite them, at a table raised above the rest. They were served by the Knights of the Garter, who carried in the dishes after the Master of the Household, bareheaded; when they reached the table they knelt; then the Master took the dishes from them and, himself kneeling, presented them to the King. To see gentlemen of high birth doing the office of pages and valets seemed to the French 'fort étrange' — in fact, ridiculous. The French custom of remaining bareheaded, and making a single bow when going in and coming out of the King's presence, was in better taste. When they returned to Durham Place, Carloix and his comrades discussed the absurdities of their hosts at some length, forgetting, presumably, that some of those who had escorted them to the Palace might understand what they were saying.

Suddenly they were interrupted by a tall, dark Englishman, whose name they had not heard; he said in excellent French: 'That your lordships should find gentlemen of experience and breeding practising these fooleries is because they have been ordered so to impress strangers with the power and greatness of our King. If they did not, they might fall to lose their places at Court — nay, even their lives. So much for tyranny!' They seem to have stared at him in silence, for he went on: 'As for the bared heads and bent knees in His Majesty's honour, those gestures are for God only; but your King beseemeth himself like a Christian; nor doth he use such Turkish rigour. Here, it is another gear; for out of twelve who kneel, seven would willingly cut the throats of both the King and the Duke of Somerset.' Their informant then went on to explain how unfairly the Catholics had been treated, speaking with horror and disgust of the late King's religious policy.

At last one of de Vieilleville's gentlemen asked why no one rebelled against the Duke's dictatorship. Another recalled Henry IV's dethronement and murder of Richard II; 'That was a great *coup d'état*', he added. 'The Duke and the Lord Admiral have made themselves impregnable', said the Englishman. 'We must needs wait for a *coup de main*, from God. But within these three years we shall see an end of their greatness ... ' and abruptly departed.

Some time afterwards Carloix and his friends found out that this indiscreet and passionate rebel was the Earl of Warwick, whom they never, during the rest of their stay, saw again, though they looked out for him wherever they were entertained, '*parceque nous le tenions pour fort habile homme*'. Recalling that strange scene four years later, the secretary adds that Warwick, in addition to his other gifts, must have had the spirit of prophecy, for all that he said came to pass.[7]

Warwick's seemingly uncharacteristic outburst was calculated, like every other action that forwarded his career. His policy of making allies among all parties could not always be subtly effected; in the case of de Vieilleville's entourage — Carloix gives the impression that the envoy himself was not present — a display of patriotic indignation against Somerset and his brother was more destructive, although risky, than hints of disloyalty: and Warwick was sometimes ready to gamble on his own judgment of a risk. In any case, he covered up his tracks by keeping his identity a secret and himself out of the way till de Vieilleville's mission was at an end; if any of the French had been so clumsy as to repeat what he had said of the Protector, Warwick would have bluffed his way out of the situation as he did on later occasions, trusting to Somerset's self-sufficiency and his own powers of persuasion. As it was, he succeeded in undermining the French belief in the stability of the regime; thereafter, his censure coloured their criticisms of the festivities that occupied the rest of their stay, when they watched jousts, tournaments, running at the ring, bull- and bear-baiting and naval manœuvres, and joined a hunt in Windsor Great Park.

The childish excitement of the English noblemen about sport, and their disregard of the formalities used in most hunting circles, amused the cool-headed French visitors. All sense of propriety was lost when the islanders sighted the deer or went in for the kill. Edward's courtiers, Carloix noted, 'could not have shouted more than if they had been in battle, using expressions common only in war'. Also they boasted about their prowess and showed off their riding in the most ludicrous manner. Although the guests were not much impressed by this part of the entertainment, the bear- and bull-baiting was new to them ('*passe-temps assez agréable*') and they later introduced it into France with great success. Among the King's parting presents to de Vieilleville, to whom he seemed to take a fancy, were three mastiffs and a young bull.[8]

De Vieilleville thought the naval review very remarkable indeed; he said to Carloix that it was a pity their king did not copy the English custom of employing his younger nobles as officers, instead of encouraging them to idle about at the Louvre; he added: 'Only through naval and military strength can peace be assured all over the world', and the secretary, much struck with the profundity and vision of this remark, made it the conclusion of his record of a visit that Edward seems to have enjoyed as much as anyone.[9]

Edward continued to enjoy his lessons; that was largely due to Cheke, whose integrity, devotion and outspokenness were in marked contrast to the sycophancy of the courtiers still trying to climb into the King's favour by distracting him from the strenuous but varied routine devised by his tutors. Cheke was firm; whatever his official duties, His Majesty must keep to his set times of study and relaxation. Both Cranmer and the Protector supported Cheke — the one because he realized the value of such training, and the other because it kept his nephew in the background during certain hours. In Cheke's correspondence with Ascham, who came several times a week for the writing-lessons that Edward still found rather irksome, there were references to the King's beginning Plutarch's *Apophthegms*, *Morals* and *Lives*, to his starting geometry and Italian, and to his geography and history lessons in Latin; his English reading was still mainly that of the Bible; in the first year of his reign he made a special study of Proverbs, Ecclesiastes and the four Gospels. In all subjects Cheke 'sugared the more austere parts of learning with the pleasures of poetry', while insinuating Elyot's maxim that 'the name of a sovereign without [self-] governance is but a shadow', and recalling to Edward his father's affability of manner.[10] At the same time Cheke created an informal, easy atmosphere, highly necessary for a boy treated with the elaborate deference that foreigners found so absurd.

In fact, Cheke seems to have been the only responsible person in Edward's entourage who perceived that there must be some antidote to the formality that is best illustrated by the Princesses' attitude when they talked or dined with him. Although Elizabeth was now nearly fifteen and Mary in her thirty-second year, neither their seniority nor their presumptive heirship counted against the sacrosanctity of their brother's person. They sat at some distance from him during meals, and never in armchairs when conversing; benches and cushions were placed for them in Edward's private apartments. 'I have seen the Lady Elizabeth kneel before her brother five times', says an Italian visitor, 'before she sat down; and then so far from the head of the table and the King, that the canopy did not hang over her ... It is the same whenever anyone speaks to him.'[11] Even Ascham, genuinely devoted though he was, could not help approaching his pupil with the humility of a subject and the hints of one who has his way to make in the world. He would first remind Edward that all England prayed daily that 'he, passing his tutor in learning and knowledge, following his father in wisdom and felicity ... may so set out and maintain

God's word to the abolishment of all papistry ... that thereby he, feared of his enemies, loved of all his subjects, may bring to his own glory immortal fame ... to his realm wealth, honour and felicity'. Then he would revert to his own position, to which Edward generally answered: 'I promise you one day to do you good.' 'Nay,' Ascham said, on one of these occasions, 'Your Majesty will soon forget me when I shall be absent from you.' 'I will never do that', Edward assured him. 'I do not mistrust these words,' Ascham went on, when he had repeated them to William Cecil, 'because they were spoken of a child, but rather I have laid up my sure hope because they were uttered by a King'[12] — thus making it clear to the Protector's increasingly influential secretary that his progress was on a sound basis. Edward's 'one day' indicates that he was already beginning to doubt the omnipotence conveyed by Cranmer's coronation address and the supple knees and bent heads of his courtiers.

Cheke's direct approach was reinforced by that of Edward's school-fellows, who in all their competitive games treated him as an equal; as he was the youngest, he often had to accept defeat. When they were not out of doors wrestling, shooting at a mark or running at the ring, they amused themselves in the great halls and galleries of Westminster, Whitehall or Hampton Court; and here also Cheke's tall gowned figure and freckled, bearded face were always somewhere in the background, although he was sensible enough not to supervise too closely. Yet, whatever he was doing, Edward seems to have felt the presence of this much-loved tutor, just as he was never able to throw off the whole weight of his own position. So it was that when they were all vainly reaching up for some lost possession — a ball, most likely — during one of these indoor playtimes, and one of his companions threw down a large Bible for Edward to stand on, he angrily refused.[13] If he glanced towards Cheke before he withdrew from the game altogether, it was not only because he relied on the tutor's approval, but because his sense of the difference between himself and other children was endemic and instinctive.

From such stories as this the modern reader recoils; yet no intelligent and sensitive boy trained as Edward had been trained could have behaved in any other way. And this incident has in any case an aspect that the Protestant hagiographers who so rejoiced in it have chosen to ignore. In the 1540s an English Bible (this was probably the Great Bible of 1539) was, in an entirely material sense, a rare and valuable possession, much more difficult to replace than, say, a piece of jewellery; the volume in question had no doubt belonged to Henry VIII, and was therefore doubly precious in Edward's eyes, quite apart from what it represented.

That Edward was, at this time, quite ready to indulge in other kinds of naughtiness was shown, a few weeks after his accession, by his newly acquired trick of swearing. Accustomed to hearing many of those about him invoke Christ's Passion or God's Blood on the most trivial occasions, it must have seemed to him a very natural thing to do so too. When questioned, he replied that one of his comrades — he would not say which — had told him that kings always swore, it was expected of them. Further inquiries were made, and the boy who had given Edward this information confessed. Both children were to be punished; as it was not possible to lay hands on the anointed of God, Edward was made to stand by while his friend was whipped. When it was over, Cheke told the King that the fault was really his, and that if he were heard swearing again his status would be ignored, and he himself would be beaten.[14] The other child's name is not recorded; but it is significant that with this incident the legend that Barnaby Fitzpatrick became Edward's whipping-boy has been intertwined. In fact, by the 1540s, such an employment had been long discontinued, and was thought as old-fashioned and barbarous as it would be today. Edward's bastard half-brother, the Duke of Richmond, had had a whipping-boy; but the place was honorary and the practice had been abandoned some years before Henry VIII's accession.[15] The tradition that Barnaby became Edward's 'breeching-boy', if connected with the swearing incident and the King's enduring affection for him, might conceivably point to the young Irish noble having led Edward into mischief, perhaps just for the fun of seeing what would happen.

At the beginning of his reign, Edward was very far from being the bigot that such historians as Foxe have delighted to describe; nor was he as fanatical or as prejudiced as some of his contemporaries would have had him be. He disliked intolerance; and his practical side, so characteristic of the Tudors, instinctively censured the waste that intolerance causes. Riding out into the

EDWARD AT 6 YEARS

country soon after his accession, he passed the ruins of a great monastery and asked what buildings had stood there. He was told: 'Religious houses, dissolved and demolished by order of the King Your Grace's father, for abuses.' According to a Catholic historian, Edward asked: 'Could not the King my father punish the offenders and suffer so goodly buildings to stand? And put in better men, that might have inhabited and governed them?' The answer to this matter-of-fact suggestion, exactly what might have been expected from the pupil of Ascham and Cheke, has not survived.[16]

Edward's dislike of neglect and waste sprang from a kindness of heart that throughout his life was made use of by the majority of those who had access to him. One of the surest ways of gaining his confidence was through his generosity. It is noticeable that Somerset, acute and intuitive as he was, never perceived that he might have done well to appeal to this side of his nephew's temperament; he had too many great schemes on hand to trouble himself with the feelings of a small boy. But Thomas Seymour, who was more cunning than he appeared, and by no means so well placed as his brother, saw at once how to endear himself to Edward, and from the moment of his accession set himself to work on the child's affections. The Lord Admiral was sharp enough not to do this, at first, for himself; he was well aware how observant Edward was.

The first step that Thomas Seymour contemplated was an advantageous marriage; he was indeed a very good match: but not quite so good as he believed. Within a week or so of Henry's death he proposed to the Princess Elizabeth, from whom he received a polite but uncompromising refusal. He then approached the Princess Mary, with the same result.[17]

These set-backs made it clear to Seymour that he could not proceed unaided, and he decided to make Edward his advocate; but in such a manner that the Protector should not guess what he was planning. He began by installing in the King's Privy Chamber a creature of his own, Thomas Fowler, who almost at once managed to insinuate himself into Edward's confidence and, somehow, to have conversations with him when no one else could hear what they were saying.

The ritual of the King's getting up and going to bed was so

elaborate and involved so many attendants that Fowler's in-
genuity must have been of a very high order for him to achieve
this privacy; that he was a man of remarkable ability is proved by
the verbatim reports of his talks with Edward after he turned
king's evidence, and by the manner in which he drew out this
naturally reserved child, to whom isolation with a single person
was in itself an odd experience. Fowler's practical management
appears particularly skilful when set against the background of the
state bedchambers in the great palaces where these interviews took
place, and where the ceremonial was unalterable and prolonged.

The huge painted and gilded bed, hung with cloth of silver and
gold filigree and trimmed with purple velvet embroidered with
crowns, roses and fleur-de-lis, stood on a dais. It was stripped every
day. Each evening, some hours before the King's bed-time, a
procession consisting of four Yeomen of the Bedchamber, four
Yeomen of the Wardrobe, a Groom of the Privy Chamber and a
Gentleman-Usher, passed through the ante-rooms leading into it
— these were guarded by halberdiers — and took up their respective positions round the bed. The eight Yeomen then brought the
bed-clothes to the Gentleman-Usher, and they were examined by
him and the Groom of the Privy Chamber; the Yeomen took them
back and ranged themselves on either side of the bed, holding the
blankets and sheets above it. The Groom called for his flambeau
and stood holding it at the foot. The curtains were drawn back by
the pages in waiting, and the senior Yeoman of the Bedchamber
searched the underlying straw mattress with his dagger. The
feather mattress was produced, placed on top and searched by
another official. The blankets and sheets were then severally laid
down by the eight yeomen together, each at the word of command
from the Gentleman-Usher, so that the bed was covered at all
points at the same moment, thus ensuring perfect evenness of
surface. In the same manner the bed-clothes were tucked in and
the pillows placed, each Yeoman making the sign of the cross and
kissing the spot his hands had touched.

The King was escorted to bed by a concourse of nobles, each of
whom had hereditary charge of some accessory (the towel, the
ewer, the posset-cup) while those who awaited him there had
each some duty connected with his undressing, one removing his
shoes, another his hose, a third his shirt, and so on; another section

stood ready with the shirt and cap he wore in bed. One or two attendants slept on pallets or benches in the ante-chambers, which all had double doors that were locked by the Gentlemen-Ushers on duty. Edward's little dog was usually put to bed in a basket between the main doors of his bedroom.

In the morning, the Gentlemen of the Privy Chamber were called at six, and, having dressed themselves, entered the bed-chamber to sweep away the ashes and light the fire; they warmed the King's clothes while he washed and said prayers with his chaplains; then they dressed him in 'a reverent, discreet and sober manner'. Anyone whispering or edging in to listen to what His Majesty said to those nearest him was punished, as were those who took this opportunity to gossip or to disturb, in any way, the solemn rhythm of the procedure.[18]

Such were the rules, as officially laid down, and — more or less — observed. Yet the bedchamber was very large, the minor attendants bribable and Edward himself perfectly willing to dispense, every now and then, with some of the formalities, especially when he came in from a day's hunting or a particularly strenuous game of tennis. Even so, he would not have lent himself to Fowler's machinations if Fowler had not been his uncle Seymour's mouth-piece. Edward was becoming fonder every day of the lively Lord High Admiral, who seemed to have so much more time for him than the Protector, and whose go-between knew exactly how to attract his nephew's attention and amuse him when the bed-chamber ceremonies became fatiguing or monotonous.

The situation was easier for Fowler than for the Lord Admiral who, like many people playing for high stakes, became impatient and nervy at the outset; he did not trust Fowler — rightly, as it happened — to do his business expeditiously; and Fowler was apt to answer his employer's cross-questioning in a brief and some-times insolent manner. The Admiral would begin, with uneasy heartiness: 'Now, Mr Fowler, how does the King's Majesty?' 'Well, thanks be to God.' 'Does he lack anything?' 'No.' 'Doth not His Majesty ask for me, or move any question of me?' 'Sometimes,' Fowler answered coolly on one of these occasions, 'But what question should His Majesty ask of [about] you?' 'Nay, nothing,' said Seymour hastily, 'unless sometimes His Highness would ask why I married not.' 'I never heard him ask any such question', said Fowler, and silence fell. Then Seymour resumed: 'Mr Fowler, I pray you, if you have any communication with the King's Majesty soon — or tomorrow — ask His Highness if he would be content I should marry or not. And if he says he will be content, I pray you ask His Grace whom he would have to be my wife.' Fowler agreed to approach Edward; their first recorded conversation took place some time between the end of February and the beginning of March 1547.

Fowler's report shows that the King's confidence had been already won. It was evening, and they were alone in one of the ante-rooms. Edward asked how his uncle Seymour was, as he did most evenings, and Fowler replied with an affectionate message from the Admiral. There was a pause. Then Fowler said casually: 'An't please Your Grace, I marvel my Lord Admiral marrieth not.' His uncle's matrimonial schemes had not till then come into Edward's mind, and he said nothing. A moment later Fowler pursued: 'Could Your Grace be contented he should marry?' 'Yea, very well', said Edward, apparently not much interested. 'Whom would Your Grace he should marry?' Fowler asked. Edward replied: 'My Lady Anne of Cleves' — still, it seems, in the same off-hand manner. In the pause that followed he deliberated; then he said eagerly: 'Nay, nay, wot you what? I would he married my sister Mary, to change her opinions.' 'His Highness,' Fowler goes on, 'went his ways' — into the bedchamber, presumably — 'and said no more at that time.'[19]

The turn of phrase, rather than its content, shows the terms on which Fowler now stood with the King. Only with a near-equal would the heiress-presumptive have been spoken of as 'my sister Mary', instead of 'the Lady Mary's Grace'. Fowler, of course, kept scrupulously to the accepted formula: his familiarity of approach was masked by a subservient correctness, combined with an inviting manner; no doubt he had a certain superficial charm and gaiety; in any case, he now had the whip-hand of the Lord Admiral. Seymour was aiming higher than Anne of Cleves; he had begun to consider the Queen-Dowager, to whom he had been betrothed before her marriage to Henry, and who was still in love with him; she coloured up when he spoke to her, and looked very pleased when one of her attendants described him as 'the prettiest man in the Court'.[20] Her subjugation should be an easy matter;

Seymour set about it immediately, first warning Fowler to prepare Edward's mind for a step that would, he knew, antagonize the Protector and shock the rather serious circle of the newly widowed Queen.[21]

At this point the Court moved to St James's Palace. On the morning after Fowler's conversation with Edward about Seymour's marriage, the Admiral walked up and down the great gallery till he saw Fowler alone; even then, he had to call him, and, after that, Fowler kept him waiting before he spoke. At last Seymour said sharply: 'Have you done as I bade you or not?' Fowler repeated what Edward had said about the Princess Mary and Anne of Cleves. Seymour laughed, no doubt rather forcedly; then he said: 'I pray you, Mr Fowler, if you may soon, ask His Grace if he could be contented I should marry the Queen — and, in case I be a suitor to His Highness for a letter to the Queen, whether His Majesty would write for me [to her] or not.' Fowler agreed to do this that same night.

Seymour then obtained a private interview with his nephew, of which he said nothing to Fowler; but the Gentleman-Usher kept his eyes open, and found that Edward, bound to secrecy by Seymour, had written to Katherine on his uncle's behalf.[22]

During the next few weeks the Admiral hurried on his courtship, visiting Katherine after dark or early in the morning at her country palace in Chelsea. She longed to marry him; but, fearful of the Protector's wrath and clinging to the proprieties, begged for delay. Her heart was his; 'for', she wrote, 'as truly as God is God, my mind was fully bent, the other time I was at liberty, to marry you before any man I know'.[23] Seymour soon bore down her last faint scruples, and some time in March they exchanged rings; a little later they were secretly married, by Cranmer. Edward remained under the impression that the wedding did not take place until May, a month before it was made public; the exact date was never revealed.[24]

Seymour had now to consolidate his position by making sure of Edward's support. With regard to his marriage, this was easy, for the King was much more dependent on Katherine than he had been when his father required all her attention. She kept her apartments in his palaces, and he was in the habit of walking unaccompanied through galleries and ante-chambers to see her privately. Now, whenever he did so, the Lord Admiral was always somewhere about[25] and, although no records of their conversation survive, it is clear that the three spent much time alone together, discussing how best to break the news of Seymour's marriage to his formidable brother; that it should have taken place without his knowledge, or that of the Council, was a breach of custom, and extremely detrimental to the solidarity of the regime.

Having so far prospered, the Admiral behaved with circumspection — for a time. When at last he told Somerset of the marriage, he appealed to his family feeling, and the Protector eventually responded to the point of speaking to the Council on his brother's behalf. The thing was done: he accepted it; but he was at first very angry, and his violence alarmed Edward, who, increasingly aware of his elder uncle's stern yet passionate temperament, recalled Somerset's outbursts in his journal three years later.[26]

The furious spite of the Duchess of Somerset — 'a woman for many imperfections intolerable, and for pride monstrous, subtle and violent', who ruled her husband 'by persuasions cunningly intermixed with tears'[27] — was raised to fever pitch as soon as she heard what had happened. From the moment of Edward's accession she had been struggling to deprive Katherine of her privileges and status, refusing to carry her train at one ceremony, upbraiding Somerset for his neglect of her personal precedence after another, and warning him of the Admiral's intended treachery. 'What between the train of the Queen and the long gown of the Duchess,' according to one observer, 'they raised so much dust as at last to put out the eyes of their husbands.'[28] Now Seymour irritated the Duchess by constantly drawing attention to his wife's superior rank. He made a point of remaining uncovered in Katherine's presence and continued, on all public occasions, to pay her royal honours; even his letters to her were suffused with the most respectful humility, interlaced with the compliments that, in this time of soaring power and influence, he could so well afford.[29]

Edward, temporarily subjugated by the vitality and warmth of this exuberant *faux bonhomme*, and perhaps rather proud of having been privy to his great secret, lost much of his reserve in the Admiral's company, and, encouraged by the assiduous Fowler, found himself complaining to Seymour about his own troubles. The eagerness with which Seymour fell upon the King's very natural resentment of the Protector's domination can be imagined. Now he held all the cards, and had only to play them skilfully. His conceit, his insatiable greed, his limited understanding and his total disregard of the potentialities of others, made this impossible. Thomas Seymour was aware of one person alone — himself. That dazzling vision lured him to his doom.

The Admiral's energy was only equalled by the range of his activities — all nefarious — and the speed with which he set about doing everything at once, except, naturally, his official duties; for these he had neither time nor inclination. The Protector, who now worked some fourteen or fifteen hours a day, and was engaged in forcing Edward's marriage with Mary Stuart on the Scots, did not notice his brother's negligence at first. When he had to prepare for a war with Scotland by land and sea, the other members of the Admiralty Board told him that Seymour's behaviour was causing complaints of such laziness and cupidity as amounted to corruption.[30]

Even then, Somerset was lenient; instead of dismissing Seymour, he reprimanded him. Lectures from elder brothers are seldom palatable, especially when, as in this case, they are founded on facts. The Admiral, enraged by what he considered insufferable interference with his prerogative, rushed to Edward's private apartments at St James's to complain of Somerset and put his own case. He met Fowler in the outer gallery and, ignoring him, went into the inner gallery, where he found Thomas Wroth, another Gentleman of the Bedchamber, who told him that His Majesty was in the one place where no interruption, even from the most privileged, could be allowed.[31]

The Admiral chafed and stamped about for a little while; his nephew, no doubt aware of what he had come for, remained in the privy. Finally, Seymour returned to his own apartments, telling Fowler to come with him; he sent his own attendants away, and asked if the Protector had been with the King that morning, to which Fowler replied in the negative. 'My lord hath fallen out with me concerning the Admiralty — he takes their part before mine', Seymour burst out. Fowler, who knew what had been going on, replied: 'I pray you, pacify yourself, and bear with my lord's Grace. Considering he is the Protector of the realm, and your elder brother, for God's love let there be no unkindness between you.' 'Nay,' said Seymour, 'my lord will have my head under his girdle', speaking with bitter passion. Fowler repeated: 'Yet pacify yourself, for the love of God, and bear with my lord's Grace.' There was a pause, while Seymour struggled with his rage; then he said more calmly: 'I trust we shall do well enough, for all this. Yet I pray you, tell the King's Majesty of it, lest my lord should tell him, and that His Highness should be ignorant of the matter.' As if suddenly remembering who had the greatest influence over Edward, he went on: 'Tell Mr Cheke of it. I will tell Mr Cheke myself. Tell the King — ' Here Fowler broke in: 'Why, what would your lordship that the King should say, if my lord's Grace told him?' (i.e. about the complaints made by the Board of Admiralty). 'Nothing', Seymour replied, 'but that His Grace would be indifferent between [fair to] us, and to consider we be both brethren, and that we must agree as brethren.' 'God forbid else!' remarked Fowler piously. 'I promise your lordship I will break [raise the point] with the King in it.' 'Pray Mr Cheke to break with the King also,' Seymour urged, 'and Mr Wroth too.' Once more, Fowler agreed to approach Edward on these lines.[32]

Edward, who did not at this time attend the meetings of the Admiralty Board, seems to have taken neither side in the matter, and Seymour, perceiving that he was not likely to get support from a boy who was as conscientious and hard-working as was compatible with his age, started to work on one of the complaints that the King had made of the Protector.

Coming to power when the national exchequer was at its lowest, Somerset had begun an economy campaign which he wished Edward to share and understand. Although his intentions were good, he did not, as far as his nephew was concerned, present them very convincingly. He allowed the King little or no pocket-money; Edward would probably have been ready to co-operate — although he loved to give presents — if he had not known that Somerset himself was daily acquiring more and richer grants of land, and had pulled down two churches in the Strand in order to build his great palace of Somerset House. (It may well have been that the Duchess instigated this particular piece of folly and greed;

in any case, Somerset was blamed for it.) Edward, therefore, did not take at all kindly to the Protector's strict measures with regard to his private expenditure; and to discontinue helping those he was fond of embarrassed and distressed him. Seymour at once seized the opportunity to enhance the King's dependence on himself, telling him, through Fowler, that he would supply him with any sum, large or small, that he needed, at the same time complaining, in his turn, of Somerset's refusal to let him keep the crown jewels that his wife had been given on her marriage to Henry VIII. If he had those, his messages seemed to imply, there need be no limit to his or Edward's generosity. He so pressed Edward on this point, emphasizing the meanness with which the Queen-Dowager was being treated, that the King wrote to her, promising he would do what he could. This letter is the first extant of those written without supervision; it contrasts oddly with the platitudinous correctness of the King's earlier correspondence; the phrases are those of a schoolboy writing in a hurry, as thought dictates. It is dated June 25th, 1547. The writer begins with thanks for the expression of the Queen-Dowager's affection, assures her of his own, and goes on: 'Wherefore, ye shall not need to fear any grief to come, or to suspect lack of aid in need; seeing that, being mine uncle [Somerset] is of so good a nature that he will not be troublesome any means unto you ... But even as without cause [anyway] you merely require help against [for] him whom you have put in trust with the carriage of these letters ... so that he may live with you without grief [anxiety] ... I will so provide for you both that hereafter, if any grief shall befall, I shall be a sufficient succour ... '[33]

Meanwhile the Admiral, more impatient than ever, pressed his own cause through the ubiquitous Fowler, whose response was now that of the high-principled and patronizing adviser. Fowler had taken a note from Seymour to Cheke, to which Cheke did not reply; then Fowler obtained from Edward what might be described as a compromising, letter in that it would be a proof, if Seymour got into trouble, that Edward had called for his help and support; it ran: 'My lord, because you are busied in your affairs that you cannot come to see me, I recommend me to you by this bearer. E.R.' Cheke saw this message, and let it go; he was not then aware of the extent of Seymour's machinations.[34] At this point Edward moved from St James's to Greenwich and thence to Hampton Court, while Somerset took up his residence at the Palace of Sheen, a few miles away; all this time Seymour continued to send the King reminders that he could count on him for ready cash. 'If His Highness lacks any money, send to me for it — and nobody else', he said to Fowler, adding: 'If you lack anything, you shall have it.'[35]

A little later Edward returned to the Palace of Westminster, where private access to him was more difficult. Immediately Seymour sent for Fowler, and began in his usual manner: 'How does the King's Majesty?' 'Very well, thanks be to God.' 'I must go to supper to the Queen,' Seymour went on hurriedly, 'or else I would tarry and speak with His Highness myself.' He added: 'Forasmuch as I would do nothing but that I would His Majesty should be privy of it, I pray you tell His Grace I would be a suitor to my lord my brother for certain jewels which the King that dead is gave the Queen, thinking the law would she should have them — whereof one is her wedding ring.' 'Alas! my lord,' was the rather trying rejoinder, 'that ever jewels, or muck of this world, should make you begin a new matter between my lord's Grace and you.' 'Nay,' Seymour assured him, 'there will be no business for this matter, for I trust my lord my brother will be content' — and then, calling to his servants for his riding-boots, he left the Palace. Fowler decided to say nothing of this conversation to Edward.

A few days later Seymour returned to London. It seems that he was beginning to feel Fowler's disapproval, for he now had to prime himself by drinking in the privy buttery before beginning: 'Hath the King's Majesty said anything of me?' 'Nay, in good faith,' Fowler said primly. Seymour muttered: 'I would the King were five or six years older ... when doth His Majesty rise?' 'I will bring your lordship word,' Fowler promised.[36]

The Protector was far too busy to attend Edward's getting up and going to bed; in any case, such an action would have reduced his status, outwardly at least, to that of a courtier. His interviews with his nephew generally took place after Council meetings and at state banquets; this gave the Admiral more opportunity for his private talks with the King. Yet here again Seymour was over-eager in poisoning Edward's mind against Somerset, although his warnings had effect. For some time now Edward's liking for and trust in the Protector had been shadowed by fear and suspicion, as if he were wondering whether he himself were king in name only; and among the many whose business it was to intrigue against the Protector, there must have been some who took care to remind Edward of the fate of the last boy king and his brother when their uncle, Gloucester, proclaimed himself Protector, and, later, Richard III by the Grace of God — for already Somerset headed his letters with the last five words. The Admiral never grasped that, when he frightened Edward about Somerset, this might lead to his identifying himself, too, with that other, long-dead wicked uncle, although, in the first months after his marriage, Seymour's easy open-handedness and spurious jollity were extremely persuasive. 'My uncle of Somerset', Edward told Dorset, one of Seymour's allies, 'dealeth very hardly with me, and keepeth me so straight that I cannot have money at my will. But my Lord Admiral both sends me money, and gives me money.'[37]

In the summer of 1547, when the Admiral was in the country, Edward told Fowler to tell Seymour how grateful he was, adding: 'I should like some money now.' 'What sum?' Fowler asked. 'As it pleaseth his lordship', Edward answered. In his report to Seymour, Fowler said: 'His Majesty desireth it for presents, but I cannot tell for whom — I pray your lordship to burn this letter.' Like many other such documents, it survives.[38]

In the early autumn, when Edward's loyalty was wavering between the two brothers, the Protector led the expeditionary force into Scotland, having told Paget to keep an eye on the Lord Admiral who, not surprisingly, had decided to administer the naval arm from London; his refusal of an active command made a bad impression on many of Edward's circle, especially on Cheke, who now began to see what Seymour was planning. Within a few days of Somerset's departure, Edward told his tutor that Seymour had said to him: 'My Lord Protector hath gone into Scotland, but he shall never pass the Pease without loss of a great number of men — or of himself. He spends a great sum of money in vain', thus further weakening Edward's belief in Somerset's administrative ability.[39]

In November the Protector returned to attend Edward's first Parliament, and it then became obvious that the Admiral's last criticism was in one sense justified. The expedition had been victorious; but the marriage was farther off than ever, for in July 1548 the little Queen of Scots was smuggled out of the kingdom into France. Edward, who realized as well as any of his elders how important this alliance was, took a still darker view of the Protector's policy.

At this point Seymour, in a private interview of which Edward himself gives a full account, struck the first blow in the campaign that was designed to destroy his brother and put himself in his place. He said to Edward, more peremptorily, it seems, than he had yet spoken: 'I desire you to write a thing to the Lords of the Council for me.' 'What?' Edward asked. Seymour's reply indicates the King's uneasiness. 'It is none ill thing,' he said hastily; 'it is for the Queen's Majesty.' The reference to Katherine failed to reassure her stepson, as it would have a few months earlier. 'If it is good,' he said, 'the Lords will allow it. If it is ill, I will not write it.' 'The Lords will take it in better part if you will write it', Seymour urged. His tone must have been threatening, but he did not observe the effect it had. Edward said: 'Let me alone ... ', and although Seymour obeyed, his shifting mind began on another means of undermining Somerset's authority over the King, who took the problem to Cheke — what had he better do? 'Ye were best not to write', was the tutor's advice.

The Admiral, still feeling himself in the ascendant with his nephew, came to him at Westminster a few days later and gave him a friendly lecture: 'You must take upon yourself to rule,' he said, 'for ye shall be able enough, as well as other kings; and then ye may give your men somewhat.' This opening struck Edward on his tenderest points — his prerogative, and his generosity. He did not answer at once; and Seymour, perhaps seeing his resentment, went on: 'Your uncle is old, and I trust he will not live long.' Edward's reply shows that Somerset's violent temper and Seymour's insinuations had combined to break his nerve. He said: 'It were better he should die.' Seymour pursued: 'Ye are but even a very beggarly king now. Ye have not to play [dice], or to give your servants.' The commiserating tone seems to have stirred Edward's pride, and with it his caution; he said: 'Mr Stanhope [the Duchess of Somerset's half-brother and one of his cofferers] hath for me.' 'I will give Fowler money for you', Seymour assured him; then he returned to the previous theme. 'You are too bashful in your own matters — why do you not speak to bear rule, as other kings do?' 'I am well enough,' was the answer, 'I need not.' Seymour tried another tack — for whom did Edward want money? The offer was irresistible, the list a long one: Cheke, Belmaine, a book-binder, Latimer, a musician, Barnaby Fitz-patrick, a trumpet-player, a tumbler, and several more; naturally Edward felt humiliated and annoyed at not being able to keep up the royal tradition of giving these people the money he knew they needed and at having to receive them with empty pockets: a beggarly king, indeed.

When the money matters had been settled, Seymour could not leave well alone. 'If anything is said against me,' he went on, 'do not believe it until I speak to you myself' — and departed, leaving his interests in Fowler's hands. When Fowler had conveyed the money to the King, he told him: 'Your Grace should thank the Lord Admiral for his gentleness that he showed you, and for his money' — and went on to speak of Seymour in fulsome terms, adding: 'It would much please his lordship if Your Grace could write some little recommendation with your own hand — for it will comfort the Queen much.' By this time the presents had been given, and Edward was again penniless; he therefore scribbled on a torn and dirty piece of paper: 'My lord, I recommend me unto you and the Queen, praying you to send me such money as ye think good, to give away to them as Fowler doth write in his letter.'

When he sent the list of beneficiaries, Fowler urged Seymour to continue on these lines, and a few days later, finding Edward alone, he began: 'Would Your Grace write anything to the Lord Admiral?' 'Nothing', was the rather daunting answer. Fowler persisted: 'If it were Your Grace's pleasure to write some recom-mendations, with thanks for his gentleness, it were well done' — his tone indicating, presumably, that only by this means would the Admiral be induced to disgorge again. By this time, Edward knew that what he was doing was wrong: but the thought of the presents he would be able to give was too much for him. A few hours later he told Fowler to go into his private dining-room and look underneath the carpet by one of the windows; there, on another crumpled bit of paper, he had scrawled: 'My lord, I recommend me unto you and the Queen, thanking you always for your remembrance. Edward.'[40]

As soon as Edward's debt to Seymour had run into three figures he was faced with the Admiral's terms, which were that he should write the letter to the Lords that Cheke had advised him not to write; it was to contain a request that the King should transfer the Protectorate from Somerset to Seymour. Edward no longer felt free to refuse; his increasing fear of Somerset and mistrust of Seymour had made him their joint victim — but a victim of spirit and resource. Forced by Seymour into some sort of verbal promise, Edward managed to avoid signing anything, and referred the Admiral to Cheke. Seymour, at last perceiving that he had come up against Tudor obstinacy and acuteness, and hoping that Cheke might be bribed, brought the tutor a slip of paper on which he had written, as from Edward: 'My Lords, I pray you favour my Lord Admiral mine uncle's suit', and suggested that Cheke should persuade Edward to sign it and then take it to the Council: he would do the rest. Cheke refused, and Seymour left him in a rage. Cheke then spoke seriously to Edward, who promised him: 'The Lord Admiral shall have no bill signed nor written by me.'[41]

Seymour's position was now considerably weakened; he had nothing from Edward but the evidence of a trivial debt that might be repudiated — for the Admiral's income and estates came from the sovereign and could be withdrawn at his pleasure. Urged on by the infatuated Katherine, bursting with hatred and jealousy of Somerset, and supremely confident of his own ability to overcome all obstacles (unaware, too, that Edward had begun to see through him) Seymour began to canvass the Lords of the Council. His plan was to get them to alter Somerset's patent as Protector on the grounds that Edward's prerogative gave him the power to choose his own Governor — and whom should he choose but his uncle Seymour? Convinced that such a scheme was not only feasible but easy, Seymour instructed Fowler to point out to His Majesty how much pleasanter this change would be, while he himself continued to sympathize with his nephew about the way Somerset treated him; at the same time he told Katherine to complain of Somerset to Edward, and to make friends with Mrs Cheke. Finally, in order to show that self-interest had no part in these activities, he announced that he was going to make over his manor of Sudeley Castle to the King, and began, with some success, to rally the party he had formed against the Protector during his absence in Scotland.[42]

Seymour knew that the subornation of the Council would be an expensive business; so he set in hand a pact with the Master of the Mint, Sir Thomas Sherington, by which Sir Thomas was first to debase and then embezzle his trust, sharing the profits with Seymour and his allies, of whom the principal was the Marquis of Dorset, the father of Lady Jane Grey; she was exactly the same age as Edward, and Seymour now promised Dorset that he would arrange a marriage between her and the King.[43] Riding to the opening of Parliament between Dorset and Lord Clinton, Seymour, as if attacked by sudden doubt of his own hopes, began to grumble about the way he had been relegated — why should he not at least share the Protectorate with his brother? 'If I be thus used,' he burst out, 'they speak of a black Parliament — by God's precious soul! I will make this the blackest Parliament that ever was in England!' 'If you speak such words,' said Clinton, 'you shall lose my lord [i.e. the favour of the Protector] utterly, and undo yourself.' Shaking with rage, Seymour reined in his horse, and shouted: 'I would you should know, by God's precious soul! I may better live without him than he without me! And whosoever shall go about to speak evil of the Queen, I will take my fist — from the first ears to the last!' Dorset intervened with: 'My lord, these words need not, for I think there is no nobleman that would speak evil of her, for he should then speak evil of the King that dead is. You have no cause to doubt therein,' he went on soothingly, 'and I trust all shall be well, and you [and the Protector] friends again.' The Admiral subsided, muttering; when he was in a temper he spoke so fast and confusedly that it was impossible to hear all he said. It was well for him that on this occasion the rest of his speech was inaudible.[44]

When reports reached Somerset of Seymour's behaviour, he ignored the Duchess's prophetic outburst — 'I tell you that if your brother does not die, he will be your death'[45] — and merely ordered him to appear before the Council. Seymour confronted them in his most belligerent mood. He denied that he had said to Fowler when they met outside St James's Palace, 'A man might steal away the King now, for there came more with me than is in all the house besides.' He denied neglect of his duties, threatened, blustered and dared them to send him to the Tower.[46]

For once his self-confidence was justified. He had already persuaded Somerset that his intentions were honourable, and his words distorted by traitors and tale-bearers; he swore to amend his ways. The Council could do nothing. A few weeks later Seymour received a further grant of land valued at £800 a year; during the first months of 1548 he gave no more trouble, and seemed to be keeping his promise. No one made inquiries of, or kept a watch on, Dorset and Sir Thomas Sherington.

Edward said nothing to anyone. None of those nearest him — neither Cheke, nor any of his schoolfellows — knew what he was thinking.

NOTES TO CHAPTER VI

[1] Strype, *Ecclesiastical Memorials*, vol. IV, part 1, p. 3111.
[2] Ibid.
[3] Ibid.
[4] De Selve, p. 111.
[5] Carloix, pp. 48-52.
[6] Ibid.
[7] Ibid.
[8] Ibid.
[9] Ibid.
[10] Strype, *Life of Sir John Cheke*, p. 19; Elyot, *The Governor*, p. 207; Baldwin, *Shakespeare's Small Latin and Less Greek*, pp. 200-56.
[11] Von Raumer, vol. II, p. 71.
[12] H.M.C. Lansdowne MSS, vol. III, part. 2.
[13] Burnet, *History of the Reformation*, vol. II, part 1, p. 2.
[14] *Lit. Rem.*, vol. I, p. lxxiv.
[15] Ibid.
[16] Clifford, p. 59.
[17] Haynes, *Burghley MSS*, pp. 61-153.
[18] Law, vol. I, p. 69.
[19] *Lit. Rem.*, vol. I, p. cxv; Haynes, pp. 61-153.
[20] Hume, p. 158.
[21] *Lit. Rem.*, vol. I, p. cxv.
[22] Ibid., p. cclv.
[23] Ibid., vol. II, pp. 41-4.
[24] Ibid.
[25] Rapin de Thoyras, *History of England*, vol. VII, p. 28.
[26] *Lit. Rem.*, vol. II, p. 215.
[27] Hayward, p. 198.
[28] Lloyd, vol. I, p. 189.
[29] Hume, p. 159.
[30] *Lit. Rem.*, vol. I, pp. 56-7.
[31] Ibid., p. cxv.
[32] Ibid., p. 55.
[33] Ibid., p. 46.
[34] Ibid., pp. 58-60.
[35] Ibid.
[36] Ibid., p. cxv.
[37] Ibid., p. cxiii.
[38] Ibid., p. 59.
[39] Ibid., p. 58.
[40] Ibid., p. 59.
[41] Ibid., p. 57.
[42] Ibid.
[43] Tytler, vol. I, p. 131; *Lit. Rem.*, vol. I, p. cxc.
[44] Ibid., vol. I, p. 55.
[45] Hume, p. 164.
[46] Haynes, pp. 61-153.

❈

CHAPTER SEVEN

THE FALL OF THE LORD HIGH ADMIRAL

WITHIN two years of Edward's accession the forcing process that sprang from his calling and had nothing to do with his school-room education had begun and was having effect. To all appearances, he was developing naturally: the reports of the foreign ambassadors, however critical of what he stood for, show him as a lively and agreeable boy, slightly in advance of his age as far as aplomb was concerned, but not startlingly so; he was immensely popular, an admirable figurehead and rose to all occasions as if he enjoyed both his position and its duties. In February 1548 the French Ambassador, with other foreign envoys, was his guest at a mock siege at Greenwich, where he received them '*fort gracieusement*', according to Odet de Selve, speaking Latin so that the conversation could remain general. Edward seems to have found the French and Venetian Ambassadors easier to get on with than the Spanish. On this occasion, although absorbed in the contest of which he was the referee, he talked mostly to de Selve, who thought the siege admirably carried out, while criticizing the over-excitement of the teams which was then, as now, an English characteristic. After the cannon assaults had brought down the bastions, the hand-to-hand fighting became so fierce that Edward had to intervene; even then, he was not immediately obeyed. When both sides had been halted, the King received the leaders and told them they had all done equally well, being careful, de Selve observed, not to differentiate between them. Only then did they consent to join in the march past that concluded the display.[1]

A month later de Selve was present when Edward said goodbye to the Marquis of Huntly on his departure to Scotland, and noted the eagerness with which the King asked after Mary Stuart, begging Huntly to bring her back as his bride. In April de Selve accompanied Edward to Deptford to inspect *The Great Harry*, now rechristened *The Great Edward,* and reported his interest in her enlargement and modernization. A few months later, when the plague was again prevalent in London, many rumours, some of them from his own country, reached de Selve of the King's illness and approaching death; in fact, he had never been in better health: it was strange, the envoy thought, that so many people could not get it out of their heads that His Majesty was sickly, when the very opposite was true. At Oatlands, where the Court stayed during October, he saw Edward every day, when the Council, under Somerset's direction, was in session; the King did not attend these meetings. [2]

It is unlikely that de Selve, seeing Edward often but never alone, would have agreed with Lord Russell, a courtier of some forty years' standing, who thought him 'very suspicious' in temperament, just as his father and grandfather had been.[3] The ease and forthrightness that so charmed the Ambassador contrasted oddly with the unchildlike reserve that informed the King's attitude towards Seymour and Somerset, his rapidly developing powers of deception and the rather marked manner in which he referred to Lord Parr, Katherine's brother, as 'mine *honest* uncle'.[4] Now, if he did send any messages to Seymour, it was not for money or in writing; Fowler was instructed to tell the Admiral that His Majesty was 'not half a quarter of an hour alone'.[5] Yet Seymour shut his eyes to his nephew's withdrawal, for his plans for seizing the Protectorate were coming to a head, and his campaign for a popular demand for his services had spread beyond the nobility to the gentlemen and squires of the countryside. He and Sir Thomas Sherington between them had amassed £4000, and were spending it freely.[6] Seymour was enclosing land and distraining his tenants at a great rate; he had private agreements with a number of pirates by which he overlooked their activities while they shared their takings with him; for these reasons he seldom, if ever, attended the meetings of the Admiralty Board, where inconvenient questions might have been put to him. He had now bought from the Dorsets the guardianship of Lady Jane Grey; and through another bribe he had made a stamp of Edward's signature and sets of keys to many of his private apartments.[7]

How much Edward knew of the Admiral's preparations is not clear, but, although he did not show it at once, his attitude towards Seymour was one of fear and mistrust. He mistrusted Somerset also; whether he still believed it were better the Protector should die is doubtful; it is certain that by the autumn of 1548, when Katherine Parr (whom Seymour had treated with great brutality and neglect) died in child-bed, Edward felt himself exposed to the mercies of a powerful and dangerous intriguer, whose access to him was now established. He could have asked Cranmer or some of the Lords for help against his younger uncle; it is possible that he was too proud to do so, besides being unsure of the extent to which Somerset was prepared to shield his brother.

The only persons with whom Seymour shared any of his booty were Fowler (to whom Somerset had granted some land in Sussex), Sherington, Dorset and the tenants likely to supply him with men and arms. Although discretion was beyond him, he kept this part of his scheme from all but Dorset, who remained his ally, until he perceived that the Admiral was making no progress with the marriage between his daughter and the King, and was in fact talking of marrying her himself when she was older, if his renewed attentions to the Princess Elizabeth had no success. Elizabeth, who had left the Admiral's household before her stepmother's death, was too cautious to compromise herself further; although she had enjoyed Seymour's boisterous advances, she now assumed an indifference she did not feel. The Admiral fascinated her, as he did most young women; but he was not worth the risk of the imprisonment and disgrace that would have been the result of her marrying him without Edward's permission.

In all this turmoil of intrigue Seymour continued to demand the late Queen's jewels, and a share in the charge of the King's person, apparently forgetting that, if his rebellion was successful, both prizes would fall into his hands. He went from one Councillor to another, grumbling, cringing, blustering about his influence one moment, complaining that he had none the next, and bursting into threats that he contradicted almost in the same breath. He would not hurt a hair of his brother's head — fair shares were all he wanted — in any case, why could not His Majesty choose for himself who should govern him? 'I would the King should have the honour of his own things,' he said to Dorset, 'for of his years he is wise and well learned. Let me alone, and I shall bring it to pass within these three years.'[8] Feeling himself on dangerous ground, Dorset changed the subject. He said: 'I hear say that there shall be a subsidy granted to the King', and advised Seymour to grant what was required of him. The Admiral flared up. 'Well, do as you will, I will not', he said, and after some further conversation about the Lady Jane, he tried to reassure Dorset by saying: 'I will not meddle with the doings either of the Protector nor the Council till I have seen the King's Majesty a year older, who then, I trust, should be able to rule his own.'[9] Dorset remained suspicious, and Seymour made the mistake of sending one of his servants to treat with him, who began: 'Be contented that the Lady Jane be with the Admiral — he shall place her in marriage to your comfort — I doubt not but that you shall see him marry her to the King. And fear you not that he will bring it to pass, and then shall you be able to help all the friends you have.' Dorset could not make up his mind. He removed his daughter: finally, accepting a further bribe, he sent her back to the Admiral, who promised him: 'If I might once get the King at liberty, I dare warrant you His Majesty shall marry her.' Seymour then advised Dorset to flatter and bribe the yeomen and small-holders, thus inducing them to join his party. 'Trust not too much to the gentlemen,' Seymour added, 'for they have somewhat to lose — but I will rather advise you to make much of the head yeomen. Go to their houses, now to one, now to another, carrying with you a flagon or two of wine, and a pasty of venison — and use a familiarity with them, for so shall you cause them to love you.' Dorset did not take to these democratic methods; they were indeed Seymour's speciality.[10]

Seymour then made advances to the Earl of Rutland, with whom he visited the Marquis of Dorset towards the end of 1548. He had grown careless by this time: the strain was beginning to tell. When, in the same sentence, he asked Rutland for his vote in the Lords and made inquiries about his income, he was rebuffed. 'I fear your lordship's power is much diminished by the Queen's death', Rutland said. This snub threw the Admiral into a frenzy. 'Judge, judge,' he exclaimed, 'the Council never feared me as much as they do now! My Lord of Rutland, how say ye, if I, a year or two hence — or sooner, as I see occasion — shall say unto the Council, "The King's Majesty, for whom I pray very much, is now of some discretion, therefore I would that he should have the honour and rule of his own doings, and not as that is now; for that which is now done, the King's Highness beareth the charges, and my brother receiveth the honour thereof". ' He went on hastily: 'I would not desire my brother's hurt — marry! I would wish he should rule — but as a chief Councillor. But I trust him not.'[11]

At last Lord Russell, one of the few wise and disinterested Lords of the Council, tried warning Seymour; he may have hoped to make peace between him and Somerset, for the Protector, although so far he had merely remonstrated with Seymour about his harshness to his tenants, was now in a mood to disgrace him, and soon. Russell and the Admiral were riding to the Parliament of January 1549, when the older man intervened: 'My Lord Admiral,' he began, 'there are certain rumours bruited of you that I am very sorry to hear. I am informed you make means to marry either with my Lady Mary or my Lady Elizabeth. And touching that, if ye go about any such thing, ye seek the means to undo yourself, and all those that shall come of you.' Seymour demanded where Russell had got his information. Russell said: 'Your near friends, and such as bear you much good will, as I do myself.' Seymour denied the charge, and Russell went on, 'My Lord, I am glad to hear you say so — do not attempt the matter.' Seymour waited a moment; then he said: 'Father Russell, you are very suspicious of me. I pray you, who showed you of the marriage that I should attempt?' Russell refused to answer this; he told Seymour that the King suspected his design of marrying one of the Princesses, and went on: 'In that case, you, being of alliance to His Highness, he may take occasion to have you in great suspect, and as often as he shall see you, to think that you gape and wish for his death — which thought, if it be once rooted in his head, much displeasure may ensue unto you thereupon. And what money, my lord,' he wound up, 'shall you have with either of them?' Seymour fell into the trap. '£3000 a year,' he replied. 'My Lord, it is not so,' said Russell earnestly. 'Ye may be well assured that ye shall have no more than £10,000 in money, plate and goods — and no land. What shall that be, to maintain your charges and estate?' 'They must have the £3000 a year also,' Seymour insisted. Russell lost his temper. 'By God! But they may not!' he exclaimed. 'By God! none of you all dare say nay to it!' blustered the Admiral.

128

facing: ADMIRAL SEYMOUR & THE PRINCESS MARY

'By God! but I will say nay to it,' repeated the old Earl, 'for it is clean against the [late] King's will.'[12]

Despairing of Russell, Seymour rushed to Sir George Blagge, from whom he received even less encouragement than from Russell. 'The Commons', he told Blagge, 'have asked that His Majesty shall be better ordered, and not kept close, that no man may see him. He is liker to grow a fool that way, than otherwise.' 'Who shall put this to the House [of Lords]?' Blagge inquired. 'Myself', was the answer. 'Why then,' said Blagge mockingly, 'you make no longer reckoning of your brother's friendship, if you purpose to go this way to work.' 'Well, for that I care not,' Seymour declared; 'I will do nothing but that I may abide by.' 'What an' my Lord Protector, understanding your mind, commit you to ward?' 'No, by God's precious soul!' Seymour exploded. 'He will not commit me to ward — no, no, I warrant you.' 'But if he do, how will you come out?' Blagge persisted. Seymour would not answer; as if to enrage him further, Blagge repeated the question. 'As for that, I care not,' said Seymour at last, 'but who shall have me to prison?' 'Your brother.' 'Which way?' the goaded Admiral asked. 'Marry,' Blagge replied, 'well enough, even send for you, and commit you — and I pray you, who shall let [hinder] him?' Seymour attempted to regain his dignity by saying: 'If the Council send for me, I will go — he will not be so hasty as to send me to prison.' 'No? But when you are there, how will you come out?' Blagge inquired. 'Why was he made Protector? There is no need of a Protector', was all Seymour would say; then, as Blagge went on asking him how he expected to get out of prison once he was arrested, he flung away in a rage, muttering: 'Care not for that', and avoided Blagge thereafter.[13]

At last Wightman, one of the Admiral's gentlemen, bolder than the rest, tried to prevent him rushing on his fate. When Seymour again began inveighing against Somerset's unfairness ('My brother is wondrous hot in helping every man to his right, saving me') and again said he was going to Edward about the Queen's jewels, Wightman replied: 'Sir, there is nothing shall discommend you more than your evil waiting and slackness in service in this time of the King's Majesty's tender years, when one day's service is worth a whole year's' — adding that, since Seymour no longer had the Queen's support, he should make up his mind to be 'a good waiter at Court, and more humble in heart and stomach to the Protector'. 'It maketh no matter,' said Seymour, 'it will come in again when the King cometh to his years, as he beginneth to grow lustily. By God's precious soul! I would not be in some of their coats for five marks, when he shall hear of these matters.'[14]

Yet somehow, try as he might, it was impossible, now, to see Edward alone. Frustration and impatience having combined to destroy such judgment as he had left, Seymour rode out to Hampton Court, where he found the King walking in the gallery with Somerset. He joined them, and at once began: 'Since I saw you last, you are grown to be a goodly gentleman' — they had been separated for less than two months — 'and I trust that within three or four years, you shall be ruler of your own things.' 'Nay', was the only answer. Somerset made no comment, and the Admiral went on: 'Within these three or four years, Your Grace shall be sixteen years old. I trust by that time Your Grace will help your men yourself, with such things as fall in Your Grace's gift.' Edward remained silent. For some minutes Seymour continued to talk on these lines, with the same result.[15]

The withdrawal of the confidence that had been the basis of his designs drove the Admiral to the last fatal step. If Edward was not to be approached except in company, then there was nothing for it but to come to him after he had gone to bed. On the night of January 16th, 1549, Seymour, taking two of his servants and — final, incredible folly — armed with a pistol, let himself into the Privy Garden and so reached the King's bedchamber without passing through the ante-chambers and passages. It had not occurred to him that Edward might have taken his own precautions. When everyone was asleep, the King had got out of bed and bolted the inner door on his own side, having put his little dog beyond the outer door. As soon as the Admiral and his men started fumbling with the lock, the dog — afterwards described by the virtuous Fowler as 'the most faithful guardian of the King's Majesty' — sprang up, barking furiously. Maddened, desperate, Seymour shot him.

As the report reverberated through the ante-chambers and galleries, yeomen, halberdiers and Gentlemen of the Privy Chamber came running. There stood the Admiral, the smoking pistol in his hand. To the torrent of questions he could only mumble:

'I wished to know whether His Majesty was safely guarded.' Within a few minutes he was under arrest, and next day in the Tower.[16]

It was, inevitably, Fowler who supplied the epilogue. 'Unless the King's Majesty had *accidentally* left his dog outside and bolted the inner door of his chamber — which is done very seldom — ' he observed, 'it would certainly have been all over with him.'[17]

Neither then nor later did Edward explain this coincidence. He was safe. His little dog was dead.

Proceedings for Seymour's attainder were set in hand, and a charge of thirty-five counts was laid against him. When Somerset heard all the evidence, he remarked gloomily that it looked as if his brother had planned to murder him as soon as he had kidnapped the King; urged on by the Duchess, he seemed to accept the fact that he must send the Admiral to the block. It was not until the Bill of Attainder had been passed in the Lords that he gave Edward a full account of Seymour's activities. The Protector seems to have been under the impression that his nephew was still attached to Seymour, and that the news of his treachery would come as a shock. If he had troubled to look at the Admiral's behaviour from Edward's point of view, he would have realized that no child is likely to forget or forgive the killing of a pet dog.[18]

It was for such a moment as this that the Earl of Warwick had been waiting. He joined in the Lords' condemnation of Seymour as a traitor. Edward did not live to realize that much of the ill-feeling between the Protector and the Admiral had been fomented by Warwick's subtle and judicious tale-bearing. A few weeks later Somerset seems to have considered the question of Seymour being granted an open trial and the chance of clearing himself publicly, instead of being examined privately by the Lords.[19] It is doubtful whether the Admiral's life would have been saved by this break with custom; in any case, Warwick, now on the point of stepping into his place, at once blocked that avenue, on the plea that Somerset's family affection might lead him into a dangerous leniency. Between Warwick and the Duchess, the Protector was overborne. Seymour, faced with the articles of a guilt that was reinforced by the evidence of Sherington (now also under arrest), Fowler, Wightman, Blagge, Dorset, Cheke, Rutland, Russell and Edward himself, denied everything. The Princess Elizabeth —

then not quite sixteen — cleared herself completely; she convinced Somerset and the Council that her relations with Seymour had been innocent.[20]

The Admiral's first denials were defiant and contemptuous. He feared no one; His Majesty would stand for him; he had nothing in his heart but the welfare of the King and the realm. Meanwhile, Warwick persuaded the Lords to prevent Seymour seeing the Protector; in his statement to the Council he implied that the Admiral had planned to murder Somerset, who, given the impression that his brother's mood was as impenitent as his intentions were sinister, could only let the law take its course.

At this point the Admiral began to break down. He had no one to advise him; he obtained no answer to his messages to Edward and the Protector — who, of course, never received them. Finally, he refused to answer all but two of the articles of the charge; then he refused to sign the answers that he had made; he believed that by confronting his accusers in a cataclysm of rage and defiance he would over-awe them. 'I am sure I can have no hurt,' he said to one of his guards, just before the Council meeting, 'if they do me right. They cannot kill me, except they do me wrong. And if they do, I shall die but once. And if they take my life from me, I have a master that will at once revenge it.' After the examination, he still boasted of his influence and power, reiterating that the Protector was frightened of what he might say. A few days later he burst out to the Keeper of the Tower: 'My friends are false. If there be any man in all England to accuse me that I should be a false knave to the King, or to his succession, or to the realm, I will wish no life. For if I had, I think the stones would rise against me.' He added that he had never had a key to Edward's private apartments, and had never thought of marriage with the Lady Mary or the Lady Elizabeth.[21]

The Council collated the evidence, and requested an interview with the King and the Protector. Early in the afternoon of February 24th, they were received at Westminster. Seymour's guilt was set forth, and proved on all counts. Somerset rose and said: 'This is a sorrowful case to me — yet I rather regard my bounden duty to the King's Majesty and the Crown of England than my own son or brother, and do more weigh my allegiance than my blood. And therefore, I will not be against the Lords' request [for indictment], but, as His Majesty would, I would most obediently be content. And if I myself should commit such offence against His Highness, I would not think myself worthy of life — and so much the more, as I am of all men the most bound to His Majesty. Therefore, I cannot refuse justice.'

The Council waited for Edward to speak. He did so in the formal terms required by the occasion; he had probably memorized them before the meeting: but there is a certain hesitation in the run of the phrases. He said: 'We do perceive that there is great things objected and laid to my Lord Admiral mine uncle — and they tend to treason — and we perceive that you require but justice to be done. We think it reasonable — and we will well that you proceed according to your request.'[22]

Several weeks passed between Seymour's attainder and the signing of the warrant for his execution. It was then usual, in cases of high treason, for the Council to present this document to the sovereign. The interval must have been an anxious time for Warwick; he succeeded in preventing all contact between Seymour and the Protector, who had been excused attendance at the Council meetings. On March 10th the Council asked Edward to receive them in order to wind up the case against the condemned man. When they entered the Presence-Chamber the King was seated under his canopy of state. Somerset stood beside him. The request for the signing of the death warrant was read out by the Marquis of Northampton. All the Lords then knelt to hear Edward's reply. This time it came as if long prepared. He said: 'I have well perceived your proceedings therein, and give you my hearty thanks for your pains and travail, and the great care you have for my surety. I will and command you that you proceed as you request — without further molestation of myself, or of the Lord Protector. I pray you, my Lords, do so.' A few hours later Somerset signed the warrant; his signature was almost illegible.[23]

When the news reached the public that the Lord Admiral was to die, popular feeling rose for him, and against the Protector — exactly as Warwick had calculated that it would. Somerset was spoken of as 'a blood-sucker and a ravenous wolf'. The bold and open-handed Lord High Admiral had become a hero and a martyr.[24]

On the scaffold Seymour, while showing the dauntless front

that was expected of him, made one last attempt to bring down his brother and revenge himself, not on those who had born witness against him, but on the Princesses. Before he knelt down he removed his shoe in which he had concealed two notes, pricked out with the point of an aglet. He told his servant to give one to the Lady Mary, and one to the Lady Elizabeth. As soon as his head fell they were seized and taken to the Protector, who showed them to the Council. They contained instructions as to how best to continue the revolution against himself that Seymour had not been able to pursue.[25] Two years later, Edward, giving a brief account of the events of this year wrote: 'Also the Lord Sudeley, Admiral of England, was condemned to death, and died the March ensuing. Sir Thomas Sherington was also condemned for making false coin, which he himself confessed; divers [others] also were put in the Tower.'[26]

A few days after Seymour's execution, Latimer, preaching before the King and the Protector, wound up his sermon with a diatribe against the Admiral, whom he described as 'a man furthest from the fear of God than any in England. He was a covetous man' — he went on — 'I would there were no more in England. He was a seditious man, a contemner of common prayer — I would there were no more in England. Well! He is gone! *I would he had left none behind him.*'[27]

To Edward, that last phrase, uttered by the only man in the kingdom who had the courage to beard the Protector in public, must have sounded a note of fear and warning. Seymour was no more: but his brother — the brother who had sent him to his death, whose power was absolute, whose ambition had no limits — remained. And behind the figure of the Protector another was rising, whose manners were reassuring, whose loyalty had been proved in peace and war: that high-minded, hard-working, selfless public servant, the Earl of Warwick.

NOTES TO CHAPTER VII

[1] De Selve, p. 284.
[2] Ibid.
[3] Tytler, vol. I, p. 147.
[4] Lloyd, p. 204.
[5] *Lit. Rem.*, vol. I, p. 59.
[6] Haynes, pp. 61-153.
[7] *Lit Rem.*, vol. I, p. 55.
[8] Haynes, pp. 61-153.
[9] Ibid.
[10] Ibid.
[11] Tytler, vol. I, pp. 138-45.
[12] Ibid., p. 147.
[13] Ibid.
[14] Ibid.
[15] Haynes, pp. 61-153.
[16] *Original Letters*, Parker Society, 2nd ser., p. 648; *Cal. Span. P.*, vol. IX, p. 333.
[17] Ibid.; Haynes, pp. 61-153.
[18] Rapin de Thoyras, vol. VII, p. 47; *Lit. Rem.*, vol. I, p. 371.
[19] Tytler, vol. I, p. 151.
[20] Haynes, pp. 61-153.
[21] Tytler, vol. I, pp. 168-70; Haynes, pp. 61-153.
[22] *Lit. Rem.*, vol. I, p. cxv.
[23] Ibid., p. cxxiii.
[24] Tytler, vol. I, p. 136.
[25] Haynes, pp. 61-153.
[26] *Lit. Rem.*, vol. II, p. 224.
[27] *Sermons*, p. 91.

CHAPTER EIGHT

THE PROTECTOR

THE people who ran to cheer Edward when he rode in and out of his palaces with his train of nobles and yeomen of the guard, the magnificent and stately figure of the Protector at his side, continued to idolize him, although, after eighteen months, their golden age had not yet begun, and their faith in Somerset was temporarily shaken by the remembrance of his brother's execution. The public memory was short and horror of bloodshed, as such, non-existent; but certain conventions prevailed. Somerset, looking beyond personal conflict to his great schemes of reform, never grasped that, while Henry VIII could send two defenceless wives to the block, his own condemnation of the brother who would not have hesitated to murder him had affronted the popular notion of a great man. Disapproval of adultery and reverence for royalty – puritanism and snobbery combined – had sufficed to excuse Henry; the son of a country knight who appeared to place the letter of the law above family feeling was not so forgiven. And the fact that the Admiral's actions had put Somerset in an impossible position was unknown to all but a few; only those in government circles realized that as long as Seymour remained alive, whether captive, free, or in exile, it was within his power to rally a party and disrupt the regime.

How much remorse Somerset really felt has been disputed for four hundred years. He was in fact neither a self-dramatizing hypocrite nor a merciless autocrat; he had been very fond of the brother whom he had spared – for far too long – the consequences of his mad ambitions; when at last he let the axe fall, Somerset was probably sure that he was right, immensely relieved, deeply unhappy and quite unaware how far Warwick was responsible for the split between himself and Seymour. As so often, it was a newcomer, a foreigner, who perceived the whole pattern. De Noailles, joining de Selve's embassy, reported to Henry II that as soon as Seymour had irrevocably compromised himself,

Warwick first urged Somerset to arrest him (it seems as if the Protector had thought of letting him leave the country) and then demanded his death as the price of England's deliverance from civil war. '*Il poussa l'affaire*', was the Frenchman's summing up; and it is the only one that is historically acceptable.[1]

Somerset's attitude towards Edward is less easily defined, perhaps because his actions show an increasing disregard of his nephew's development and the inevitable effect on the ten-year-old boy of the ceaseless public references to the King's personal supremacy. Latimer, the most outspoken and unconventional of popular preachers, tried again and again to curb Somerset's fellow-Councillors in his sermons at Westminster. Inveighing against the corruption in high places, of which Sherington and Seymour were the most recent examples, he declared that it was partly the result of a lust for power, to which all succumbed, adding: 'There be some wicked people that will say, "Tush, this gear will not tarry; it is but my Lord Protector's and my Lord of Canterbury's doing; the King is but a child, and he knoweth not of it." Jesu, mercy! What people are they that say, "The King is but a child?" Have we not a noble King? So godly — brought up with so noble councillors, so excellent and well learned schoolmasters? I will tell you this, and I will speak it even as I think — His Majesty hath more godly wit and understanding, more learning and knowledge at this age, than twenty of his progenitors — that I could name — had, at any time of their life.' Then, directly addressing Edward, Latimer went on to warn him against pride and begged him to drive away 'flatterers and claw-backs'. 'Hear men's suits yourself,' he urged, 'I require you in God's behalf; and put it not to the hearing of these velvet coats, these upskips ... I beseech Your Grace that ye will look to these matters — hear them yourself.'[2] Edward, who was accustomed to make notes of all the sermons he heard (often using Greek characters) followed this advice throughout his reign.[3]

Although Latimer was one of Somerset's most valuable supporters, his peculiar brand of spirituality and common sense had little contact with the Protector's high-flown idealism and capricious benevolence that every now and then were submerged by the fashionable taste for theological disputation and dogmatizing shared by Edward. Somerset encouraged his nephew to concentrate on these shadows and symbols of power, while he himself tried to rush through the reforms that were neither understood nor appreciated by the majority. Cheke's temporary withdrawal from the Court to Cambridge (the result of his acceptance of £15 from the Lord Admiral) [4] intensified the isolation of the King during the summer of 1549, and may have turned him towards the uncle whose aims, in ecclesiastical matters, he approved of and followed. Without Cheke to show him his limitations, Edward was left to gulp down the heady mixture of religious iconoclasm for political ends that Somerset dispensed and that his hangers-on used to further their own ambitions.

In the summer of 1548 Gardiner's recalcitrance had so irked the Extreme Protestants of the Council that they decided the moment had come for him to put his cards on the table in a sermon preached before the King and the Protector. Gardiner was ready to go some of the way with this section, and would perhaps have gone farther than he eventually did, if Somerset had not first sent William Cecil to direct him as to what he should say. Naturally, the Bishop of Winchester much resented the intrusion of this clever and pushing young man into questions that did not concern him and in which he showed neither learning, reverence, nor respect for his elders and betters. Cecil, a 'new man', of the most suspect type from Gardiner's point of view, was no doubt aware that he offended: as the Protector's confidential secretary, he could afford to do so. He began by suggesting that Gardiner should emphasize the fact that Edward had as much power now as if he had attained his majority; he then gave the Bishop a paper in Edward's hand, outlining points for his St Peter's Day sermon (June 29th), pointing out how quick His Grace was to seize on what was said about his prerogative, and adding: 'If you speak of a King, you must give council withal.' Gardiner received this piece of impertinence without comment, and a few days later Cecil reappeared with a message from the Lord Protector. My Lord of Winchester was desired not to speak 'of the sacrament of the Mass'. Gardiner 'looked askance', and Cecil explained: 'I mean, doubtful matter.' 'What matter?' the Bishop asked. 'Transubstantiation,' was the answer. Gardiner could control himself no longer. 'You know nothing of transubstantiation', he said. 'I mean to preach of the Very Presence of Christ's Body and Blood in the Sacrament —

which is no doubtful matter.' He added that Mr Cecil would do well not to meddle in religious affairs; he should leave them to those whose business it was to declare them to the laity.[5] Eventually Somerset himself interviewed Gardiner, but 'wily Winchester', as his enemies called him, refused to outline the heads of his sermon in which, while advocating the Sacrament in both kinds for the laity and acknowledging the Royal Supremacy, he accused the Extreme Protestants of blasphemy by their denial of the Real Presence; he then spoke against the marriage of the clergy. These divagations might have been forgiven him, if he had not added: 'I mislike subjects that rule like kings, to the diminishing of the King's authority, and their own estate' — concluding as he pointed at Edward: 'I would have but one King, and he only to be obeyed!' with the result that he was sent to the Tower.[6]

After the removal of this adversary, Somerset had been able to pursue his reforms with more precipitation than tact. His Injunctions for the destruction of images and the reading of the greater part of the Mass — still so called — in English, had been followed by orders for the administration of the Sacrament in both kinds and the appointment of bishops by the sovereign: these commands were not enforced, as they would have been in Henry's reign, by punishments, or even threats; in this way Somerset lost the respect of a people used to sterner methods. When one of the workmen employed in the removal of statues from St Paul's was killed by the fall of the great cross, the Protector's leniency was thought to have been shown up by the revenge of an angry God:[7] and the point of view, some three hundred years in advance of his age, that made him repeal the laws against heresy, eliminate the Six Articles and allow the reading of the English Bible by all classes, not only disgusted both the Henricians and the Catholics, but confused those who had suffered under, but submitted to, Henry's prohibitions. Naturally, Somerset's extremely mild penalties for disobedience to his commands were despised — what sort of a ruler could he be who neither burnt nor hanged for the faith? He ignored all criticism. 'I know very well', he said to the horrified Spanish Ambassador, 'that whatever is done ill will be laid on my shoulders', adding that he contemplated no further religious innovations.[8] This perfectly sincere statement of his aims was disbelieved by the Catholic powers, while at home those who clung to the old ways were given the impression that the Lord Protector did not know his own mind.

Somerset had crowned this unsuitable tolerance by his attitude towards the Augsburg Interim of Charles V, an arrangement designed to lure back into the fold of Papal jurisdiction those who were attracted to, but had not yet been subjugated by, the varying tenets of Continental Protestantism. The Interim was, as its name implies, a temporary compromise, by which the marriage of the clergy and Communion in both kinds were allowed; in all other essentials the ancient dogmas were to be retained until such time as a general Council could be held. Some Protestant states agreed to the Interim: others withstood it. In England the Extreme Protestant party regarded it with horror, as a cunning and insidious infiltration of Popery, far more dangerous to the Reformation than open hostility. The very word was anathema, discussion of it abhorred. So it was that when Somerset allowed a pro-Interim bishop to speak in a disputation on the First Prayer Book in the House of Lords, at which he himself took the chair as Moderator, he was again censured for his scrupulously neutral attitude, perhaps because the Prayer Book of 1549, for which Cranmer was mainly responsible, was considered too moderate and ambiguous by the Extreme Protestants, although it eliminated reservation of the Sacrament, adoration of the Host, belief in purgatory and the veneration of images; in fact, it more closely resembled the one now used in the Church of England than that of 1552, and combined in a single volume a Breviary, a Missal and a Ritual. Its two chief sources were the English medieval service book known as the *Use of Sarum* and the fourteenth- and fifteenth-century books of devotion called Hours or Primers; it contained a few prayers translated from the Greek, and some newly composed; a small portion of the Liturgy was borrowed from the suggestions of the Continental Reformers. Its full title — *The Book of Common Prayer and Administration of the Sacraments and other Rites and Ceremonies of the Church after the Use of the Church of England* — shows the spirit of compromise in which it was evolved, more explicitly stated in part of Cranmer's reply to its less sophisticated detractors. 'It seemeth to you', he wrote, 'a new service, and indeed it is none other but the old: the self-same words in English which were in Latin, *saving a few things taken out*' — a bland and masterly meiosis. [9]

The intellectual taste of the 1540s fed rather on theological disputation than on the arts that were then regarded as part of the background to everyday life. A man like Somerset, a boy of Edward's type and training, found the pleasure and excitement in a three-day debate on the Sacrament in relation to the First Prayer Book that they would now look for in a musical or dramatic festival. All that was said on these occasions was taken down in shorthand and privately printed so that listeners and speakers could refer back to it during other debates. There is thus a full record of a discussion that was then sensational, partly because both setting and participants were rather of national than scholastic importance.

The teams consisted of Cranmer, Ridley and Heath on the Extreme Protestant side, and, for the Henricians, Tunstall, Bonner and Thirlby. Bishop Thirlby had just returned from an embassy to Charles V and was, of course, known to be in favour of the Interim that, throughout the debate, was not referred to, but seems to have been at the back of every disputant's mind; in fact, this is one of the few points that can be assimilated today, for the discussion as a whole appears so highly technical and so enclosed as to show each side apparently repeating, instead of confuting, the arguments of the other. What appear to be the original pros and cons gradually disintegrate through a process of metaphysical hair-splitting that now confounds the reason and numbs the understanding.

Some personal characteristics emerge from the clouds. Edward, passionately absorbed, reserved his comments until he could make them informally. Somerset's calm detachment only once gave way. Warwick took this opportunity to show his hand, or that part of it that he considered most acceptable. On the opening day Thirlby came out boldly against the First Prayer Book — the head and front of Somerset's reformation. 'No agreement hath been reached upon it,' he said — presumably unaware that the Protector's leniency was partly responsible for this — 'and for my part, I will never allow its doctrine.' Warwick exclaimed: 'That is a perilous word. He is worthy of displeasure that in such a time, when concord is sought for, casts such occasion for discord', thus making it clear that as an Extreme Protestant his point of view was unexceptionable.

Next day Somerset opened the debate with an appeal for unity

— in other words, acceptance of the Prayer Book. Thirlby said that he approved of some portions of it; but he desired the elevation and adoration of the Host to be reinserted, as in the reign of the late King. This amounted to an attack on one of Somerset's pet projects. He said angrily: 'These vehement sayings show wilfulness and obstinacy — how doth your lordship not consent to prove your doctrine by the Early Fathers?' Thirlby, overawed, as so many people were when the Protector lost his temper, remained silent, and Bonner took his side in the hectoring manner that made him almost as alarming as Somerset, whom he called heretical. Somerset overrode Bonner with quotations from the Apostles, and an immensely long and intricate discussion on the Real Presence followed, with one or two rather personal and discourteous interruptions from Warwick, now set on nailing his colours to the mast. Next day the Henricians struck the first blow.

In their arguments about the Eucharist, both sides admitted two constituent elements in the bread and wine — the Accidents and the Substance of each. By Accidents they meant the shape, colour and weight, as perceived by the senses: by Substance, the deepest underlying reality, not taken in by any of the senses, but assumed by the reason to exist. The Henrician dogma on this point was that of the orthodox Catholics. Both parties believed that at the moment of consecration the Accidents of the bread and wine remained unaltered, while the Substance of the bread changed into the substance of the true living Body of Christ, and the substance of the wine into the substance of His Blood. Thus, Christ's words, 'This is my Body', were not a figure of speech, as Zwingli maintained: nor did His Presence depend on the faith of the recipient; it was there, truly and substantially.

The Extreme Protestant reply was summed up by Cranmer, who said: 'Spiritually, He is in them that *worthily* eat and drink of the same — but really, corporeally and carnally, He is only in Heaven.'

Part of Gardiner's answer, in his *Detection of the Devil's Sophistry*, published in 1546, had been that the devil tempted people away from belief by this very appeal to reason and the senses, which — wrongly — tell them that the bread and wine remain bread and wine after consecration; this cannot be, he goes on, for God remains incorruptible, while the bread and wine may become mouldy, or be eaten by a mouse. Of course, he argues, the Accidents are corruptible, but the Substance is imperishable — 'a mouse cannot devour God'. Thus the humble man of faith does not attempt to explain such a miracle, but accepts it.

After Tunstall had developed this theme, a long duet ensued between Cranmer and Heath about the true meaning of 'spiritual' and 'corporal', interrupted by comments from Thomas Smith, the new Secretary of State; these now read as comic asides. 'It cannot be the true Body, or else He must want His head or His legs' is one example; upon which Heath very properly put Smith in his place by remarking that 'reason will not serve in matters of faith'.

At the time of the debate on the First Prayer Book, Cranmer had not made his final view — that the Communion Service was commemorative and symbolic, while essential to salvation owing to the soul's reception of the Sacrament — public and official, as he did in the Second Prayer Book, issued in 1552. (In this one, the words 'Take and eat this, *in remembrance of Me*' were inserted in the Rubric.) He now concluded by saying: 'I believe that Christ is eaten with the heart. The eating with our mouth cannot give us life, for then should a sinner have life. Only good men can eat Christ's Body. When the evil man eateth the Sacrament, bread and wine, he neither hath Christ's Body, nor eateth it. The good man hath the Word within him, and the Godhead, by reason of an indissoluble connection with the Manhood [of Christ]. Eating with his mouth giveth nothing to man, nor the Body being in the Bread. Christ gave to His disciples bread and wine, creatures amongst us, and called it His Body, saying, "*Hoc est corpus meum*".' Ridley added that the Substance of the bread was transformed into a divine influence, its Accidents remaining the same,[10] and the discussion closed. Thirteen Bishops declared in favour of the new Liturgy, and ten against it.

The super-subtleties — sometimes amounting, as it now seems, to fantasy — produced by such disputations as this were common knowledge and part of everyday talk among educated boys in Edward's day. When he was late for his lessons because he had been absorbed in some game, he would say: 'We forget ourselves that would not choose *Substantia pro Accidente*'[11] — not perhaps, as reverently as later Protestant historians would have had their readers believe, but much as a modern schoolboy might use the current jargon of sport or war: for although there were those, and not a few, who were ready to die in terrible agony for Bishop Gardiner's mouse, the thrilling pursuit of theological argument was apt to obscure the loathsome cruelties and hideous suffering that too close discussion might cause. So, when Somerset, irked by his failure to win over Bishop Thirlby, said to his nephew: 'How much the Bishop of Westminster has deceived my expectations!' Edward's reply was that of the boy who wants his side to win without a struggle and feels that someone is to blame for the delay in the issue. 'Your expectations he might deceive,' he said, 'but not mine.' Somerset, a man of great sincerity and no humour, could not accept the failure of his own powers of persuasion. 'How so?' he asked. 'I expected nothing else,' Edward answered, 'but that he, who has been so long a time with the Emperor, should smell of the Interim' — a pert, but natural riposte.[12]

In fact, Edward was temperamentally far more tolerant than most of his contemporaries, as was shown when a little later there arose the question of Joan Bocher's heresy. This poor creature persisted in believing — worse still, in preaching — that 'Christ did not take flesh from the Virgin Mary; He only passed through her body, as water through the pipe of a conduit, without participating anything of that body'. For some years Joan Bocher had been under restraint and attempts were continually made to persuade her of the sinfulness of this view; the more arguments were presented to her, the firmer she became. Before he was eleven Edward had become convinced, partly through Cheke's influence, that heretics should not be burnt but reasoned with, and, if necessary, punished; every chance of conversion should be provided; and this was also Somerset's view. At last, after Somerset had fallen from power, the moment came when the Bishops agreed that Joan Bocher must die, and the warrant for handing her over to the civil arm was made out. Edward did not refuse to sign this, as was later reported, because, at that time, he signed no warrants; but he pleaded with Cranmer for her life, begging the Archbishop to allow her another week of persuasion. She was certainly wicked; but she might be mad, and thus not responsible for her errors. These methods were tried in vain; and Cranmer told his godson that Joan Bocher must go to the fire. Edward exclaimed: 'What, my lord? Will ye have me send her quick to the devil, in all her error?' Cranmer pointed out that there was nothing else to be done: Edward burst into tears: the Archbishop persisted; at last the King dismissed him, saying: 'I lay the charge thereof upon you, before God' — and Joan Bocher went to the stake. Two years later Edward noted in his Chronicle how she had 'withstood' the Bishops sent to convert her, 'and reviled the preacher that preached at her death'.[18] She and a Dutchman, Parris, were the only persons burnt for heresy in Edward's reign; another example of the enlightenment for which the Protector was despised.

Edward and Somerset were therefore in sympathy over persecution and theology. Although the Protector's deepest affections were centred on his own family, he was loyal to his nephew, in spite of the fact that he made use of him. Edward had begun by admiring his distinguished and powerful uncle, first because his father did, and later because Somerset had been both helpful and considerate when he succeeded. In the formal phrases of his congratulatory letter about the Protector's victory over the Scots at Pinkie Cleugh there is genuine feeling, and some unconscious irony. 'Pray thank, in my name, the Earl of Warwick, and all the other noblemen and gentlemen ... God granting me life, I will show myself not unmindful of their service.'[14] Edward rated success in battle as highly as most boys, but during the first two years of his reign he became aware, as much through his own observation as through Seymour's malice, of the results of Pyrrhic victories; when it became clear that his marriage with Mary Stuart was farther off than in his father's day, he must have wondered whether the Protector's famous breach-of-promise invasion had been worth while, and felt some sympathy with the Earl of Huntly's summing up: 'I haud weel wi' the marriage but I like not this wooing.'[15]

While convincing Edward that his alliance with Mary Stuart was still of paramount importance, Somerset did not trouble to explain to him the whole extent of his plan; if he had, there might have been some mention of it in Edward's Chronicle for that year, in which he briefly describes his uncle's successful assaults and sieges, but nothing else. Somerset wished to unite Scotland, Ireland, England and Wales, giving Edward the title of Emperor of Great Britain. The Protector disliked war; he desired 'peace, unity and quietness ... of both nations, that the Scottish men and we might hereafter live in one love and amity, knit into one nation by the most happy and godly marriage of the King's Majesty our Sovereign Lord and the young Scottish Queen'. It is characteristic of Somerset's grandiose earnestness that in his proclamation reminding the Scots of the marriage contract he pointed out that they 'could not in reason expect that their Queen' (then aged five) 'should perpetually lead a virgin life', while suggesting that she should remain in Scotland till she was of marriageable age.[16]

Unfortunately — tragically — Somerset's theories were never borne out by his practice, partly because he could not visualize any point of view other than his own: he instinctively discounted Scottish national feeling and fear of absorption by the more prosperous kingdom; he did not understand why the Scots disregarded his assurance that his object was 'not to conquer: not to spoil and kill, but to save and keep: not to dissever and divorce, but to join in marriage, from high to low both the realms, to make of one Isle, one Realm ... If we two,' he went on lyrically, 'being made one, ... be the most able to defend against all nations; and having the sea for wall, mutual love for garrison and God for defence, should make so noble and well agreeing a monarchy, that neither in peace we may be ashamed nor in war afraid of any worldly or foreign power — why should you not be as desirous of the same?'[17] The Scots, who were not prepared to forgive Somerset's burning of Edinburgh in the previous reign, made no answer to this Shakespearian oratory; and the result was an increase of common hatred and a cruel expenditure of lives and money.

By the beginning of 1549, then, Seymour's intrigues, his execution, Somerset's failure over the Scottish marriage, and his long absence at the beginning of Edward's reign, had combined to estrange the King from his uncle. Meanwhile, worry and overwork so accumulated as to heighten Somerset's attacks of bad temper: he had begun to live on his nerves, and Edward was one of the first to feel the effect of the strain. Vainly Paget, the only person besides Cranmer who dared to speak his mind to the Lord Protector, remonstrated and warned; finally, he appealed to him through a pathetic description of one of the Councillors, 'poor Sir Richard Lee', who 'this afternoon, after Your Grace had very sore — and much more than needed — rebuked him, came to my chamber *weeping*, and there complaining, as far as became him, of your handling of him, seemed almost out of his wits, and out of heart; Your Grace, to be sure, had put him clean out of countenance' ... 'A *King*,' Paget added sagely, 'who shall give men discouragement to say their opinions frankly, receiveth thereby great hurt and peril to his realm; but a *Subject* in great authority, as Your Grace is, using such fashion, is like to fall into great danger, and peril of his own person which for the very love I bear to Your Grace, I beseech you, and for God's sake, consider and weigh well.'[18]

Somerset, struggling with an enfeebled army and navy, a bankrupt exchequer, an agricultural revolution and a ministry of swindlers, was beyond listening to this excellent advice. At every Council meeting he stormed and threatened, dominating by sheer strength of conviction. He knew, no matter what others might say, that he was the dedicated administrator of Henry's will, the people's 'good Duke', their saviour. He gave away all his lands round Hampton Court to the farmers and small-holders; he set up a private Court of Appeal, so that anyone who had been wronged might approach him personally; he tried to regulate the further enclosure of common land; he instituted schools where there had been chantries and monasteries. Then, fatally, he began his great campaign against what he described as superstition and idolatry; but over the removal of images he was always changing his mind.[19]

The laws against witchcraft were repealed; death by boiling in oil — the punishment for poisoners — was forbidden; creeping to the Cross on Good Friday, covering the head with ashes on Ash Wednesday, carrying palms on Palm Sunday, were discouraged, preached against and at last eliminated; orders went out that all over the country the painted and sculptured symbols of the old faith were to be effaced.

But some of the English people — the simple and the untaught — who for countless generations had accepted wizardry and enchantment, death by slow torture for certain sins and the acting out of Christ's suffering and triumph on certain days, were bewildered and appalled by these deprivations. The spirits that dwelt in wood and water and field, the power of the necromancer, the conjurations of the seer, were as much a part of their daily lives as the pictures and carvings that every Sunday and holy day had given them heroes and villains, devils and angels, in their own image, reproducing in dear familiarity the storied richness of a Hell, a Heaven, a far country that was, somehow, their own ageless and, as it had seemed, indestructible possession.

Suddenly strange workmen from the towns with their hammers and ropes and pails of whitewash were there again, as in the iron age of the dead King: in the church, around the wayside shrine, on the village green. Within a few hours the remaining saints and martyrs, the partially restored Paradise, God in his glory, Satan's fiery kingdom, the Virgin's bower, Christ's Passion and Resurrection, were no more; instead were scarred pediments, glassless windows; and on the walls that had borne all their knowledge, all their hope and fear, three prancing lions and a motto in the language of their ancient foes. And when a single, cracked bell — 'the least of the peal' [20] — called to them for the remembered ritual, they heard, instead of the spell-binding incantations of a marvellous and magical belief, clear-cut pronouncements in a disagreeably familiar English — not theirs: the English of the lord and the squire, the great lady, the dreaded justice of the peace. Beauty, excitement, awe and splendour, the treasures of the past and the guardians of a living faith were wiped out, ground into the dust to which their spiritual world was now reduced. This was the beginning of the Lord Protector's golden age.

Yet this bitter holocaust was ordained by the only statesman who cared and planned for the common people. Somerset made the mistake of counting on his popularity to sweep the illiterate and the impoverished towards intellectual conceptions for which they were not prepared. For images and ceremonies he substituted sermons; and in these the peasants would have found as much excitement and pleasure as the townsfolk did, if there had been more preachers like Latimer, Ridley and Hooper, whose discourses were so enthralling that no church, however large, could hold their congregations, and who, therefore, often had to preach in the open air. The association of sermonizing with boredom would have amazed our sixteenth-century ancestors who crowded to weep and laugh and be amused and awestruck and delightfully horrified by the pathos, the humour, the daring anecdotes and epigrammatic colloquialisms that Latimer — comedian, philosopher, story-teller and mob orator — produced for them, Sunday after Sunday. But there were none such in the smaller parishes, where Cranmer's *Book of Homilies* was generally the only fare, and where, in fact, Latimer's homely, allusive, reminiscent vein would not have been appreciated as it was by the congregations of Paul's Cross or Whitehall. Even today his outbursts of invective, his drama and rhetoric make wonderful reading; delivered by a master of technique, they must have been unforgettable. It is not surprising that Edward commanded him to speak again and again at Whitehall, where he appeared as a great actor giving a solo performance in a pulpit set up in the privy garden, so that as many as a thousand persons could listen. The old people and the women and children sat on the grass, just below him, Edward and Somerset at a window in the gallery facing the pulpit, with Cheke standing behind them. The rest of the congregation stood, walked about, or wandered in and out as their fancy took them.[21]

The most thrilling moment came when Latimer spoke his mind or gave advice to the sacrosanct figures of the King and the Protector, who seem to have enjoyed his personalities as much as anyone; indeed, the relief of being publicly addressed as an ordinary human being must have been considerable, especially when the speaker's turn of phrase was amusing, unexpected and sometimes what would now be described as slangy. Latimer's anecdotes became so famous that one may be given in full. In support of Somerset's policy of a more enlightened attitude towards injustice and abuse, Latimer first inveighed against the stupidity of sentimentalizing about the 'good old days', and then broke off to say: 'And here, by the way, I will tell you a pleasant tale. Master More [Sir Thomas] was once sent in commission into Kent to find out, if it might be, what was the cause of Goodwin Sands, and the shelf that stopped up Sandwich Haven. Thither came Master More, and called the country before him, such as were thought to be men of experience, and men that could most likely best certify him concerning the stoppage of Sandwich Haven. Among others, came before him an old man with a white head, one that was thought to be a little less than a hundred years old. When Master More saw this aged man, he thought it expedient to hear him say his mind in this matter; for being so old a man, it was likely that he knew most of any man in that company. So Master More called this old aged man unto him, and said, "Father, tell me, if you can, what is the cause of this great rising of the shelves and sands here about this haven, which stop it up, so that no ships can arrive here? You are the oldest man that I can espy here in all this company, so that if any man can tell any cause of it, you, it is likely, can say most in it, or at least more than any other man here assembled." "Yes, forsooth, good master," quoth this old man, "for I am well nigh an hundred years old, and no man here in this company is anything near unto mine age." "Well, then," quoth Master More, "How say you in this matter? What think you are the causes of these shelves and flats that stop up Sandwich Haven?" "Forsooth, sir," quoth he, "I am an old man. I think that Tenterden Steeple is the cause of Goodwin sands. For I am an old man, sir," quoth he, "and I may remember the building of Tenterden Steeple, and I may remember when there was no steeple at all there. And before that Tenterden Steeple was building, there was no speaking of any flats or sands that stopped the haven. And therefore I think that Tenterden Steeple is the cause of the destroying and decay of Sandwich Haven." '

For the less sophisticated audiences of the city Latimer provided his celebrated Sermons of the Card, in which his texts were 'trump-cards for the winning of virtues'. 'Now you have heard what is meant by the first card,' he would begin, 'and how you ought to play with it, I purpose again to deal unto you another card, almost of the same suit; for they are of such near affinity, that one cannot well be played without the other.' His most famous discourse of all — the Sermon of the Plough — was given at Paul's Cross, where from 'a covered place' on the north side, the people crowded to listen to him when it was rainy or cold: in this, Latimer gave the Bishops a fine trouncing. 'For ever since the prelates were made lords and nobles, their plough standeth, there is no work done, the people starve. They hawk, they hunt, they card, they dice, they pastime in their prelacies with gallant gentlemen, with their dancing minions, and their fresh companions, so that ploughing is set aside ... And now I would ask a strange question — who is the most diligent bishop and prelate in all England, that passes all the rest in doing his office? I can tell, for I know who it is:

I know him well. But now I think I see you listening and hearkening that I should name him ... And will ye know who it is? I will tell you — it is the Devil. He is the most diligent preacher of all others: he is never out of his diocese ... Call for him when you will, he is ever at home ... '[22]

Naturally Latimer's style and effects were copied, spreading through other preachers beyond the cities. By the summer of 1549 his diatribes were everywhere repeated, and not only by the clergy. Those humbler orators, whom Somerset had already inflamed by his promises and unequally distributed gifts of land, began at last to revolt — some against the most grievous of all their oppressions, the enclosures, others against the First Prayer Book. By the end of June 1549, the Protector had two revolutions on his hands, one economic, the other religious.

NOTES TO CHAPTER VIII

[1] *Ambassades de M. de Noailles* (ed. Vertot), vol. I, p. 141.
[2] *Sermons*, p. 95.
[3] *Lit. Rem.*, vol. I, p. civ.
[4] Strype, *Life of Sir John Cheke*, p. 40.
[5] Conyers Read, *Mr Secretary Cecil and Queen Elizabeth*, p. 47.
[6] Muller, p. 181.
[7] Wriothesley, vol. II, p. 9.
[8] *Cal. Span. P.*, vol. IX, p. 205.
[9] Foxe, *Acts and Monuments*, vol. V, p. 732.
[10] Gasquet and Bishop, *Edward VI and the Book of Common Prayer*, pp. 157-81.
[11] *Lit. Rem.*, vol. I, p. clxxv.
[12] Gasquet and Bishop, p. 177.
[13] Heylyn, p. 89; Foxe, vol. V, p. 699; Hayward, p. 16.
[14] *Lit. Rem.*, vol. I, p. 49.
[15] *Tudor Tracts*, p. 77.
[16] Godwin, p. 214.
[17] Hayward, p. 48
[18] Tytler, vol. I, p. 174.
[19] Constant, vol. I, p. 370.
[20] Pocock, *Troubles Connected with the Prayer-Book of 1549*, pp. 40-56.
[21] *Lit. Rem.*, vol. I, p. civ.
[22] *Sermons*, pp. 90-200.

✖

CHAPTER NINE

THE EARL OF WARWICK

IT has been generally assumed that Edward was neither an affectionate nor a sensitive child; this conclusion has been drawn from the entries in his diary in which the burning of Joan Bocher and the execution of his uncle Seymour are baldly set down; as that part of it was written in retrospect and supervised by Cheke, Edward could not have made any statement of feeling. The records of those who knew him best show that he was fond of few people — which is not surprising — and that his love for them was, considering his age, unselfish. When his father died, his affections were centred on Barnaby Fitzpatrick, the Princess Mary, Cheke and Henry Sidney. His friendship with Barnaby was interrupted shortly after his accession by the Irish boy's departure to the French Court, in itself a sign of Edward's care for his protégé, for he could have insisted on Barnaby remaining with him; that he would have liked to do so is proved by his recalling him in May 1548 in a note in which he thanks his 'dearest and most loving friend' for his letters, adding that the Protector has given leave for his return.[1] Edward's concern for Cheke and Henry Sidney was shown in practical ways; with the Princess Mary his relationship was difficult, and sometimes painful.

The Protector and Cranmer could not approve of or encourage the King's attempts to make life easier for the heiress-presumptive, whose popularity and adherence to the old faith continued to threaten the second phase of the Reformation. It was natural that they should discount Edward's instinctive but ambivalent sympathy with the half-sister whose piety was so like his own. The fact that each thought the other's beliefs dangerous and wrong made it easier for Edward's ministers to drive a wedge between them; during the first two years of his reign the Protector's omnipotence and his nephew's fear of his anger drew the King and the Princess together, in spite of her twenty years' seniority. Mary was sometimes prevented from visiting Edward, but, as appearances had to be kept up, total estrangement was out of the question; whenever they did meet informally, Edward somehow managed to spend a little time alone with her. Their Catholic friend, Jane Dormer, says that he took 'special content in her company', asking her many questions and promising her that he would do what he could for the private practice of her faith. He treated her as if she were his mother, confiding his own difficulties; then, inevitably, their warring beliefs would intervene, and he would burst into tears when he saw that she was not to be shaken, saying: 'Have patience till I have more years, then I will remedy all' — presumably meaning that with greater knowledge and the reality of power he expected to achieve her conversion. He was always sad when the moment of parting came, kissing her and giving her some jewel — 'regretting he had no better'. As soon as the effect on his spirits of these interviews became apparent, they were further discouraged.[2]

Such was Edward's situation in the spring and early summer of 1549, when Cheke was still at Cambridge, and the Protector, beset on every side, kept both Mary and Elizabeth from coming to Court, in case they might be used to influence the King against him. As if to make up for these deprivations, he allowed his nephew to take a share in the administration; he put his training in the hands of one of the clerks of the Council, William Thomas, an advanced Protestant and a very clever man. When Edward was eleven and a half Thomas began his political education much as Cheke would have done; he worked out analyses of the national situation for him, and set him simple examinations, to which the answers no longer exist, except for brief references in the first part of Edward's Chronicle. Is it expedient, Thomas asked, for a ruler to 'vary with the times' — i.e. to adapt himself to circumstances at the cost of principle? And if he does, 'what prince's amity is best?' He then explained that if forced into war, England must be 'a prey to the enemy'; therefore the best policy was to play off France and Spain against one another, and concentrate on the alliance with Scotland. He also gave Edward an explanation of the debasement of the currency, with suggestions for its reform, a matter that, after religion, became the King's chief concern as he grew older.[3] Thomas never got over Edward's death; he could not speak of him without tears, and persisted in the political and religious activities that had been their common interest, with the result that he was executed in Mary's reign for an alleged attempt at her assassination, when he became involved in Wyatt's rebellion.

Edward rose with enthusiasm to these new and fascinating directives; just when he was beginning to feel himself an active participant in public affairs, the risings broke out that might have brought on the overthrow of the government, if the people's loyalty to his person had been diminished by their revolt against hardship on one side and innovation on the other. That these rebellions were entirely separate, geographically and morally, was another reason for their ultimate failure.

On June 1st, 1549, Somerset issued a proclamation against the system of enclosures, a process which then fell into three categories: the first was the substitution of large holdings for small ones through the eviction (not always enforced) of tenants and the destruction of their cottages; the second was the conversion of arable land for sheep-runs, the sheep being bred for wool and not for meat (England's dependence on the wool trade made this a necessity); the third was the seizure of the waste land that had been common to all for the purposes of cultivation and improvement of the soil and also for deer-parks. Somerset wished to stop what might be described as the robber-baron behaviour of the landowners, while he worked out a scheme that would benefit all parties and that included economically desirable enclosures. His authority, unsupported by such an administration as Henry's had been, failed completely, although he was merely trying to enforce the anti-enclosure laws that already existed. In the three weeks that followed his proclamation the gentry continued to enclose the land — some for deer-parks and some for sheep — and the peasants of Norfolk and Suffolk, led by a wealthy tanner, Robert Kett, took over the countryside, tearing down palings, killing the deer and the sheep and removing the landmarks, heedless of appeals for patience and promises of justice made by Somerset's commissioners. At first the Protector could not bring himself to take up the sword; at a Council meeting he announced that he liked 'well the doings of the people', and pointed out that it was the greed of the gentry that had caused the mischief; then he issued a pardon for those taking part in the rising on condition that they returned to their homes and gave up their arms. This was ignored; the landlords thereupon decided to protect themselves, and proceeded to capture and hang the invaders of their property.[4]

This was the situation in the eastern counties when the command went forth that the Mass was forbidden and the Liturgy of the First Prayer Book was to be used in all churches from Whit-Sunday, June 9th. On Whit-Monday the people of Sampford Courtenay in Devonshire stopped the priest as he was going into the vestry, crowded round him and asked what service he was going to use. 'I must go by the law', was the answer. 'We will have none of the new fashions — we will have the old religion of our fathers — ' someone shouted, and another added that Henry VIII had ordained the Mass in his Will. The priest then put on his vestments and said Mass in Latin, 'the common people from all the country round clapping their hands for joy'.[5]

In the same week, a few miles away, Sir Walter Raleigh (father of the great Elizabethan, not yet born) riding home through St Mary's Clyst, overtook an old woman telling her beads on her way to church. Sir Walter, a Protestant and a strict landlord, told her that such mummeries were now forbidden, and that she would be punished for persisting in their use. 'This woman', says an Elizabethan historian, who received the account from an eye-witness, 'nothing liking nor well digesting this matter, went forth to the parish church ... and being impatient and in an agony with the speeches passed between her and the gentleman, began to upbraid in the open church' (i.e. to all the congregation) 'very hard and unseemly speeches concerning her religion, saying she was threatened.' She added, untruthfully, as it afterwards turned out, that Sir Walter had sworn to burn down her house if she kept her rosary and holy water: that he was going to burn all their houses. 'It is all gone from us, or to go — ' she screamed. The villagers rushed out of the church, barricaded the bridge between Sampford Courtenay and Exeter, whence they expected the magistrates to arrive, and hauled up the cannon from the vessels at Topsham quay; here they found Sir Walter, whom they would have lynched if he had not been rescued by a party of sailors.[6]

So the general revolt began. The Norfolk rebels, who were trying to organize agrarian Communism, used the Liturgy which the western peasants described as being no better than a Christmas game,[7] while both continued to affirm their loyalty to the King.

During July and August, sieges, pitched battles and assaults went on; the disparate revolutions spread from Devonshire to Somerset and Cornwall, and from Norfolk and Suffolk to the Midlands. The troops, sent from London to east and west, had to be reinforced by German and Italian mercenaries; at every meeting Somerset tried to mitigate the strong measures urged by the Council and already employed by the local gentry. Edward, 'much grieved and in great perplexity', interviewed some of the landowners who came for help against their tenants; one, who appeared 'in a great dump or study' before him and his uncle, never forgot his distress — nor the fact that Somerset was seriously considering whether to reinvade Scotland now, or in a few months' time.[8] As the slaughter continued, the people began to give way; at last, out of the confusion, some successful leaders emerged; the most notable was the Earl of Warwick. On August 29th he defeated the eastern rebels, killing three thousand five hundred in a series of cavalry charges; he was therefore able to show mercy to those who were left, and was much admired for his refusal to organize a reign of terror. So, with the capture of Kett and the other ringleaders, the Norfolk rising ended, a fortnight after Lord Russell's victory in the west, where four thousand peasants fell in the last struggle for the Mass and the Six Articles. Warwick's reputation soared far higher than Russell's; only the French Ambassador saw through his much-vaunted skill and moderation, reporting him as '*avide de gloire*', and making friends with persons whom he discarded as his power and influence rose.[9]

Somerset had played into Warwick's hands. The landowners never forgave the Protector their losses: nor did the Henricians and the Catholics their failure to restore the Six Articles. With the Londoners, who had suffered little and were mainly Protestant, he was still popular; but the city fathers, with whom Warwick was now allied, had been disgusted by Somerset's vacillations and disapproved of his issue of a general pardon. On this point, even judged by the merciless standards of his own day, Somerset was right; nearly ten thousand Englishmen had been killed; Henry II, seizing the opportunity to capture the Boulogne fortresses, had attempted an invasion, with the result that war was declared on France, and between the summer and the autumn of 1549 rebels became patriots and defenders.

The effect on Edward of taking part in the administration at a time of social and economic disaster (he was present at the Council meeting when the charge for 'wars and fortifications' of one million, three hundred and fifty-six thousand pounds, eighteen shillings and threepence three farthings was declared) stimulated his practical side.[10] His account of the troubles, written a year later, shows that he grasped all the points of the military situation, both at home and abroad; in this respect, his version is clearer and more informative than that of any other contemporary historian, partly because it is neither detailed nor picturesque, but detached and succinct; he describes, very briefly, the ebb and flow of battle as if from a height, but without minimizing the possibility of a recurrence of the Wars of the Roses; when he turns from the western rising, with an abrupt 'Now to Norfolk ... ', the pace of the narrative heightens a very little, especially in the outline of Warwick's exploits. Edward's objectivity is so sustained that reading between the lines is almost fruitless; a shade of criticism of Somerset's policy (was this the result of Warwick's influence?) can be discerned in his nephew's reference to the Midland enclosure riots. 'By fair persuasions,' he says, 'partly of honest men among themselves and partly by gentlemen, they were often appeased; and because certain commissions were sent down to pluck down enclosures, they did rise again ... ' adding: 'In the mean season, because there was a rumour that I was dead, I passed through London.'[11] This rumour was promptly used — if it had not already been created — by Warwick, who was now preparing his first open assault on the Protector.

The 1549 section of Edward's Chronicle contains no reference to the religious aspect of the struggle; of the Devonshire peasants, he merely says: 'They went about sedition, but were quickly repressed.' And this is partly because all his life he was able to count on the devotion of his people, which may have helped to conceal from him the dislike of many for his Prayer Books. It was those nearest him he was made to fear; he never doubted his hold over persons who, even in their declaration of defiance, announced that they were his 'very humble and obedient subjects, whose desire is to be the dogs appointed to keep your house and your kingdom, and the oxen to cultivate your lands, the asses to carry your burdens'.[12] Nor could he any longer doubt his own supremacy;

for in his official answer to the rebels' demand, his prerogative and authority were emphasized in a highly dramatic and personal manner. Although Edward had no hand in the composition of this document (it was mainly the work of Cheke, who thus obtained his re-entry to Court), he had to associate himself with its odd combination of ferocity and fatherliness.

With the publication of the First Prayer Book Edward had been described as 'the most noble ruler of his ship, even our most comfortable Noah',[13] and it was on these lines that the Norfolk rebels were adjured by Cheke to 'learn, learn, to know this one point of religion ... disobedience to His Majesty is an abominable sin ... But what talk I of disobedience so quietly? ... Have not such mad rages run in your heads that, forsaking and bursting the quietness of the common peace, ye have heinously and traitorously encamped yourselves in the field, and there, like a bile in a body, have gathered together all the nasty vagabonds and idle loiterers to bear arms against His Majesty, whom all godly and good subjects will die for withal? ... Shall not strangers think that the King's Majesty — in whose mind God hath powered so much hope for a child, as we may look for gifts in a man — is despised, if they judge him by your behaviour? Thus all England is despised by other countries ... The shame of your mischief [will] blemish ye for ever.'[14]

The western rebels, whose demands, under fifteen heads, began with 'We will have the laws of our sovereign lord King Henry VIII concerning the Six Articles to be used again ... ' were scolded as if personally by his son — who were they, to give orders to the Lord's Anointed? — and each theological point in their petition was dealt with at length. The exordium that the less sophisticated received as from Edward himself, beginning in mild reproof, rises to a crescendo of wrath. 'Ye would have them [the Articles] stand in force till our full age ... If ye knew what ye spake, ye would never have uttered that notion, nor ever have given breath to such a thought. Be we of less authority for our age? Be we not your King now, as we shall be? ... Ye must first know that, as a King, we have no difference of years or time, but as a natural man and creature of God, we have youth, and, by His sufferance, shall have age. We are your rightful King, your liege lord, your King anointed, your King crowned, the sovereign King of England, not by our age, but by God's ordinance ... We possess our crown, not by years, but by the blood and descent from our father King Henry VIII ... and rule we will, because God hath willed it ... Thus far, ye see we have descended from our high majesty for love, to consider you in your base and simple ignorance, and have been content to send you instruction like a fatherly prince, who, of justice, might have sent you to your destruction ... We swear to you, by the living God, by Whom we reign, ye shall feel the power of the same God, in our sword, which how mighty it is, no subject knoweth; how puissant it is, no man can judge; how mortal it is, no English heart dare think. Repent yourselves, and take our mercy without delay.'[15]

For his contribution to the settlement Cheke was made Provost of King's College and given large grants of land. It is rather by Latimer, speaking for those whom his contemporaries called 'the country gruffs, Hob, Dick and Hick',[16] than from Cheke's accomplished pamphleteering that the relationship between King and people is most memorably defined. 'The noblemen ... in Christ are equal with you. Peers of the realm there must needs be. But the poorest ploughman is, in Christ, equal with the greatest prince that is ... It is thy bounden duty to pay His Majesty that which is granted ... upon peril of thy soul ... Yea, I will say more; if the King should require of thee an unjust request, yet art thou bound to pay it, and not to resist and rebel against the King ... God is the King's judge, and will grievously punish him if he do anything unrighteously. Therefore pray thou for thy King, and pay him his duty and disobey him not.'[17]

So outward rebellion was crushed; yet here and there, not only in hearts and minds, but in secret hiding places, fragmentary records of the ancient faith survived — 'for repairing and soldering Joseph, sixpence: for cleaning and anointing the Holy Ghost, sixpence: for repairing the Virgin Mary behind and before and making a new Child, four shillings and eightpence: for screwing the nose on the Devil's face, putting a new hair on his head and gluing a bit on his tail, five shillings and sixpence ... '[18]

Unaware, as it seems, of the resentments, divisions and bitter memories that were the aftermath of the struggle, Somerset went on stubbornly with the campaign against his two bugbears, superstition and idolatry. His sense of duty had now begun to obscure his judgment: his care for detail was becoming an obsession. When Robert Allen, 'wizard and bawd', was called before the Council for foretelling Edward's death, the Protector insisted on interviewing him personally, but in so mild a manner that the culprit was emboldened to defend one of his trades. 'Necromancy', he explained, 'is a lawful craft.' 'Thou foolish knave,' said the Protector, 'if thou and all that be of thy science tell me what I shall do tomorrow, I will give thee all that I have' — and sentenced him to a year's imprisonment in the Tower. Perhaps Somerset remembered that a few months earlier a group of 'prophesiers and conjurors' had been found operating in his own household with crystal balls, magic swords and holy water, and had been released after 'speaking with the fairies', calling up 'Oriental and Septentrial spirits' and finding some of his stolen plate by a conveniently secret method.[19] The terrifying rages that cowed and antagonized his equals were not caused by such offenders as these, any more than by a deputation of London butchers whom he received with the same tolerance, promising them redress when their spokesman accused certain members of the Council of fraud and tyranny.[20] Towards the Princess Mary he showed a similar kindness, partly because of her friendship with his wife, when the Council tried to prevent Mass being celebrated in her household.

On this occasion Edward was present throughout the interview, but the Protector did not appear — no doubt purposely — till the Princess had made her defence, and this further irritated his peers. 'Do you not know me?' she exclaimed. 'How is it you make so small account of me? I am the daughter of Henry VIII and the sister of Edward VI. It was great pity that my brother's kingdom should fall into your hands.' Turning to Edward, she went on: 'Your Grace doth not understand what I do' — presumably meaning that her Mass was still privately celebrated. Edward was prevented from answering by the entrance of Somerset, to whom he said: 'I would that the Lady Mary's Grace were always here.' Mary remarked: 'I pray to God that when Your Grace knows what is done in your name, you may find a remedy.'[21]

A few days later the French Ambassador reported that the Princess had managed to clear up the mischief made between Edward and herself, that he had increased her allowance and that the Protector had been most considerate. One of Warwick's

agents, whom he had placed in Edward's household, told his
employer of these proceedings: they were to become part of the
case against Somerset. The pattern of tale-bearing and intrigue
that had begun with Fowler and the Lord Admiral was being
worked out again, this time by a subtler hand.[22]

Somerset, burdened by a mass of these and other trivialities,
was still blind to the gulf that was opening just ahead of him.
There was, for instance, the theological instruction of the newly
ordained clergy to be dealt with as soon as the rebellion ended;
the results were not always happy. The Reverend John Card-
maker of St Bride's informed his congregation that if God were a
man He would be six or seven feet high; therefore how could He
be contained in a piece of bread 'in a round cake on the altar?
What an erroneous opinion is this of the lay people!'[23] Somerset
turned from curbing this preacher to a lengthy and embittered
correspondence with the exiled Cardinal Pole; his return and
reinstallation having been required by the western rebels, Pole
now took it upon himself to advise about, and indeed dictate, the
Protector's future policy. In reply to Somerset's letter giving him
leave to come back on condition that he conformed, Pole, angrily
conscious of his Plantagenet lineage and his nearness to the
dynasty (he was Edward's second cousin), sent off a diatribe that
was at the same time unrealistic and factual. Almost everything he
said was true; this made his reasoning completely unacceptable.

'The King,' wrote Pole, 'if he wisheth for the pardon and grace
of God, hath much greater need to ask pardon of me, for the
injuries and losses suffered by me' — going on to suggest that
Edward should restore the property taken from his family by
Henry VIII. He then denied Edward's supremacy, and announced
that although he had no intention of obeying the new laws, he
was willing to return in order to put Somerset right on religious
matters; naturally, he was not going to waste his time with Edward
himself, as he had been corrupted by the Protector — an insolent
upstart, who had made a great mistake in flattering and deluding
his nephew. That Somerset had had to behead his own brother
was proof enough of the instability of the regime — 'why did you
not consult me when the late King died?' (The Cardinal took
particular exception to a letter from Cecil, in which it was hinted
that, after nearly twenty years' absence, he might be out of

touch with English affairs.) He went on to say that as Edward's title had not been acknowledged by the Pope, he was schismatic and excommunicate — 'although you do not choose to admit this to be a danger'. Pole wound up by telling Somerset that he had neither faith nor religious feeling, and was therefore not fit to be in charge of Edward, although no one else had dared to tell him so. The conclusion was obvious: Somerset must at once return to the true faith, send for Pole, give him the Protectorate and retire to repent of his misdeeds. At about the same time the Cardinal sent Edward the books he had written against Henry VIII. 'I send you these ... ' he wrote, 'to show you your father's faults, that you may wipe away his stains ... I cannot assist you better than in emphasizing your father's disgrace and treachery.' He added that Edward would do well to model himself on his grandfather, that admirable servant of Christ.[24]

It was characteristic of Somerset that he wasted time and energy on Pole, instead of leaving the correspondence to Cecil, or abandoning it altogether; yet it seems that he believed in the possibility of the Cardinal's conversion, much as he believed that he could heal the breach between his wife and Mrs Cheke, whose quarrelling added to the innumerable complications that helped to conceal from him Warwick's activities during September 1549. No details of these survive, except a justly censorious report of Somerset's administration that the Council drew up and sent to the Emperor Charles V, thus giving the impression that they were going over to the Henrician party. In the first week of October someone who had a foot in both camps gave Somerset the alarm.

The Protector, however obsessed and preoccupied, was neither timorous nor, in a crisis, ineffectual. He grasped the situation in all its essentials (save that of the range of Warwick's influence), and of these the possession and control of Edward came first. Unfortunately for Somerset, though he could and did seize his nephew's person, he no longer had command of his spirit.

By the morning of October 5th Somerset had had printed a handbill that was distributed during the next few days over the countryside; it called upon the people of England to defend the King and the Lord Protector 'against certain lords, gentlemen and chief-masters which would depose the Lord Protector and so endanger the King's royal person, because we, the poor Commons, being injured by the extortion of gentlemen, had our pardon this year, by the mercy of the King and the goodness of the Lord Protector ... '[25] The dramatic simplicity of this warning is typical of Somerset's gift for contact with illiterate and simple people, and goes far to explain their loyalty to him, quite apart from what he tried to do for them. A second leaflet, given out in the streets of London on the same date, contrasts sadly with the first; it shows the Protector's lack of method and his inability to choose the right men for the right jobs. He could not have read it until it was too late to withdraw a piece of propaganda that contradicted almost everything he had been working for; it seems extraordinary that, with such men as Thomas and Cecil in his employ, he should entrust the composition of this vital message to an anonymous writer whose attack was inept, diffuse and hopelessly amateurish. The preamble is vague and redundant: the content strikes one wrong note after another. 'Be not carried away with the painted eloquence of a sort of crafty traitors ... They now of mere malice have conspired the Lord Protector's death ... to plant again the doctrine of the Devil and Anti-Christ of Rome ... and here also note, how they be come up but late from the dung-hill ... more meet to keep swine than to occupy the offices they do occupy ... ' Set against the Protector's recent campaign, the last sentence is as pitiable as it is ludicrous. 'And as for London, called Troy Untrue, Merlin sayeth that twenty-three aldermen shall lose their heads on one day, which God grant to be shortly. Amen!' It says much for Somerset's hold over the city authorities that their loyalty to him remained unaffected by this absurd appeal.[26]

From Hampton Court, where he and his nephew were now guarded by five hundred armed men in the Seymour liveries, the Protector sent his son, Sir Edward Seymour, with a letter from the King dictated by himself, asking Lord Russell and Lord Herbert to raise all the forces they could to rescue them from the conspirators. All that day and the rest of the night he waited for the answer that never came.[27]

On the morning of the 6th the Council, headed by Warwick, held a meeting at his residence in Holborn. They decided to go out to Hampton Court, 'but in a friendly manner, with their own servants only' — as they afterwards declared. That this was not the case is shown by the fact that just as they were setting off they were approached by one of Somerset's gentlemen, Sir William Petre, who asked them 'for what they had gathered their powers together', and added that, if they wished to interview the Protector, they should come in peaceable array; if they tried to besiege Hampton Court, he went on, they would be arrested as traitors.

A short discussion ensued, of which no details are extant; one result was the subjugation, by Warwick, of Sir William Petre; he joined the Council, and did not return to Hampton Court. On the same day five more Lords, then resident in London, also declared for the Council and against Somerset, who now had with him no one of note but Cranmer, Paget, William Cecil, and Edward's Secretary of State, Sir Thomas Smith. [28]

By the night of the 6th it had become clear to Somerset that his allies in London were falling away, and that it was not possible to keep command of the situation from an unfortified position. He therefore woke the King and brought him down to the Base Court of the Palace, just within the main entrance. A great crowd had collected, and this was what he had hoped for; during the last twelve hours he had primed Edward with the story of the conspiracy and of the threat to his own person. In the flicker of torchlight Somerset, Cranmer, Paget and Cecil came out under the archway of the Clock Tower, preceded by trumpeters and yeomen of the guard. Edward was in the midst of them. [29]

The little group went on over the stone bridge and across the moat, which had just been filled up. There they stopped and, at a sign from the Protector, Edward stepped forward. In the sudden silence his voice rang out. 'Good people,' he said, 'I pray you be good to us — and to our uncle.' [30]

The answer was a burst of cheering. The Protector came to stand beside his nephew and took his hand. As soon as he could be heard, he said: 'I shall not fall alone. If I am destroyed, the King will be destroyed. Kingdom, commonwealth — all will be destroyed together.' Pointing at Edward and thrusting him forward, he went on: 'It is not I that they shoot at — this is the mark that they shoot at — ' and, turning, led the King back into the courtyard where the horses were waiting. They mounted; then, with a clatter and a rush, spurred through the gateway; here they had to slow down between the ranks of staring people.

Suddenly, if a contemporary chronicler is to be believed,

Edward decided to speak for himself. He also had been armed, no doubt at his own insistence. He drew the jewelled dagger that had been one of his father's presents and waved it, shouting: 'Will ye help me against those who would kill me?' The answer came in a full-throated roar: 'God save Your Grace! We will die for you!'[31]

But Somerset was hurrying him on; they galloped out into the darkness. Before it was daylight they had reached Windsor, into which Somerset moved as for a siege or a civil war. He and Edward had gone ahead of the others. When they were joined by Paget and Cranmer with three hundred armed men, Edward's terrors woke again. He said to Cranmer: 'What do you here at such an hour?' 'Sir,' said the Archbishop grimly, 'suffice it that we are here.'[32]

The effect of these scenes on a child so often warned and frightened is not difficult to imagine. It must have seemed to Edward that everything that other uncle had threatened him with was happening — flight, kidnapping, intimidation. The inter-rupted nightmare of the Admiral standing pistol in hand between his bed and the body of his little dog was now renewed, more horribly, with the glare, the shouting, Somerset's harangue, and the wild ride through the cold dark to the castle in the forest, where no one, save at his captor's pleasure, could break in, once the gates had shut behind them. That the Protector would not have laid a finger on him — that he would have guarded his nephew's life at the cost of his own — was neither then nor later realized by Edward, although at first he believed what Somerset told him of plots against them both and of the dangers from which they were escaping. For this helpless king of eleven there was danger, terror, everywhere, and no one to trust. Somerset, too desperate to consider anything but his own plans, had no notion of their effect on Edward, nor that they would be used, again and again, to re-create his nephew's fear of him. Nor would it have occurred to him that an intelligent boy who is constantly told that his person is sacred must have been appalled by the Protector's talk of shooting at marks and this sudden flight from a palace to a fortress.

On the morning of the 7th, Somerset was still sure of his power. During the whole of that day and the next messengers galloped between Windsor and London. The Council asseverated that, though criticisms had been made, no attack on his person was in question. Paget and Cranmer advised him to see the Lords and come to an agreement rather than risk civil war. On the 8th, Edward wrote a letter at Somerset's dictation, in which he assured the Council of his trust in his uncle. 'We and our Council here find him tractable', he wrote, going on to recall Somerset's past services. 'Each man hath his faults, he his and you yours; and if therefore we shall as rigorously weigh yours, as we hear that with cruelty you intend to purge his, which of you shall be able to stand before us? ... He meaneth us no hurt ... He is our uncle, whom you know we love ... Proceed not to extremities against him ... '[33] To this Somerset added the assurance of his good intentions. It was at this point that, finding himself alone with Paget, Edward said: 'Methinks I am in prison — here are no galleries nor no gardens to walk in — ' and it was then that Paget noticed he had caught cold,[34] upon which he consulted with Cranmer; between them they persuaded Somerset to allow them to act as mediators between himself and the Council in London.

The Council accepted Cranmer and Paget in a letter in which they begged the Protector not to frighten his nephew; this touch is characteristic of Warwick, whose eye for detail was unfailing, and who now assumed the role of the deliverer. At the same time the Council answered Somerset's propaganda with an appeal to the people against him. The heralds read it out at various points in the city, where it was received in silence. At a second reading near Paul's Cross, a citizen, George Stadlow, shouted: 'Let His Majesty hear the case of the Council against the Lord Protector!' — another example of Warwick's care for planning.[35] Sir Philip Hoby was then sent out to Windsor on a mission of compromise and reconciliation. Somerset was promised liberty and a fair deal, to which he replied that he meant his nephew no hurt and was anxious to come to a settlement. In a private letter to Warwick he appealed to his loyalty, their old friendship and long service to the Crown. Paget also wrote privately to Warwick, saying that he had persuaded Somerset to resign from the Protectorship, on condition that he was not put upon his trial for high treason; whether he showed Somerset this letter is not clear.[36]

On the morning of the 9th, Somerset received a written promise from the Lords. He would be deprived of neither honour nor property if he would submit to the formality of an arrest, after an agreement had been reached. By this time he knew that he was helpless. Through Sir Edward Seymour — who had been permitted to rejoin him — Herbert and Russell had protested against his actions and declared their loyalty to the Council. Sir Philip Hoby was therefore sent again to Windsor with an address that he read out to Edward, Somerset, Cranmer and Paget. Somerset's unconditional submission was asked from the King; the Council then declared their amazement that the Lord Protector should have written to them 'as though they sought nothing but blood and extremity'. On their faith and honour they promised him safety; reconstitution of the Protectorate was all they desired.

As soon as he finished reading, Hoby turned to the Duke and said: 'My Lord, be not you afraid. I will lose this' — he pointed to his neck — 'if you have any hurt. There is no such thing meant. And so they would have me tell you, and mark you well what I say.' He then read out a declaration of loyalty to the King. Another gentleman, seeing which way he must go, stepped forward and suggested that they should all 'thank God, and pray for the Lords'. Paget went farther. He knelt at Somerset's feet in floods of tears. 'Oh! my lord,' he exclaimed, 'you see now what my Lords be.'[37]

Somerset did not rise to these histrionics; he said that he would receive their Lordships, and next day, the 10th, they arrived at the Castle. They breakfasted first; then it was agreed that Somerset should be placed under guard in the Beauchamp Tower.

The Lords were then received by Edward. His cold had disappeared; he was 'in good health and merry, welcoming them all with a merry countenance and a loud voice'. 'How do your lordships?' he said, 'You shall be welcome whenever you come.' They lined up to kiss his hand. Next day they were joined by the rest of their fellow-Councillors, and a meeting was held, over which Edward presided. It was a long business; they had to tell him everything that had really happened, and how he had been misled. He behaved with great propriety, making no comment till they had finished, asking no inconvenient questions, and finally giving them his hand to kiss, with thanks for the care they had taken for himself and the realm. They rose from their knees masters of the situation.[38]

Three days later Somerset, with William Cecil and the Duchess, was escorted from Windsor to the Tower of London. But here the Lords made their first mistake, one that Warwick profited by in the weeks that followed, when he had to consolidate his position and work out his plans for the future. He had reckoned without Somerset's popularity. The Duke was received in state by the Mayor and followed all the way along by crowds of cheering people. A lesser man would have taken the opportunity to rally his side against those who had entrapped him; Somerset remained stately and aloof. At Mark Lane he reined in his horse and said — 'proudly', according to one hearer — 'I am as true a man to the King as any here.'³⁹

During the next few days a count of twelve charges was drawn up against the Duke. It seems that at this point his life hung in the balance. But Warwick, who had his finger on the pulse of the city, and who realized how high his great enemy still stood in the people's love, had decided to withdraw in order to fall upon him later: yet in such a manner that he himself would appear as the heroic patriot and faithful friend.

There was a story that the Duchess of Somerset had been granted an audience with Edward, who received her with Cranmer and Warwick.⁴⁰ She knelt and asked him to pardon her husband, to spare his life. Edward, as much taken aback as Warwick had guessed he would be, asked where Somerset was. 'A prisoner, in the Tower — and if Your Grace doth not pardon him, the Council will kill him,' the Duchess replied. 'Jesu!' Edward exclaimed. 'They told me the Duke was ill — why have they taken him prisoner?' There was no answer, and he turned to the Archbishop. 'Godfather, what hath become of my uncle the Duke?' 'He is a prisoner in the Tower,' Cranmer repeated. 'Why, what evil hath he done, that he should be arrested?' Edward demanded. 'May it please Your Majesty,' Cranmer replied, 'if God had not helped us, the country had been ruined, for the Lords were all up in arms, and we feared that he might kill you. If my lord had not been imprisoned, great harm had been done.' 'The Duke never did me any harm,' said Edward after a pause, adding: 'As he went to the Tower of his own will, it is a sign that he be not guilty.' He could not take in the sudden loss of his formidable uncle's power. Cranmer said oracularly: 'Your Majesty doth not know all. The

168

Lords know what they do.' Edward's instinct of authority rose at this. 'I would see my uncle,' he said. 'Your Majesty can do so,' was the reply — always from Cranmer: Warwick remained silent throughout the interview — 'His life is in your hands' — and the Duchess was dismissed with the promise of the King's mercy.[41]

At the next Council meeting Edward asked the Lords for Somerset's life. Warwick's moment had come. He rose and said: 'My lords, we must return good for evil. And as it is the King's will that the Duke should be pardoned, and it is the first matter he hath asked of us, we ought to accede to His Grace's wish.'[42] The conclusion was subtly but inescapably drawn. The Council was new; a better, brighter rule had now begun, in which Edward was to take, at last, his rightful place and the authority so wrongly usurped by his disgraced and unfortunate uncle.

NOTES TO CHAPTER IX

[1] *Lit. Rem.*, vol. II, p. 65.
[2] Clifford, pp. 60-2.
[3] William Thomas, *The Pilgrim*, p. 170.
[4] Holinshed, pp. 939-42.
[5] Ibid.
[6] Ibid.
[7] Strype, *Life of Cranmer*, App. xl.
[8] Holinshed, p. 944.
[9] *De Noailles*, p. 158.
[10] Rapin de Thoyras, vol. VII, p. 35.
[11] *Lit. Rem.*, vol. II, p. 228.
[12] Pocock, p. 20.
[13] Strype, *Ecclesiastical Memorials*, vol. I, part 2, p. 102.
[14] Holinshed, pp. 1000-11.
[15] Ibid.
[16] Froude, *Edward VI*, p. 128.
[17] *Sermons*, p. 99.
[18] Winchester Cathedral MS. (in the possession of the author).
[19] Strype, *Ecclesiastical Memorials*, vol. I, part 2, pp. 176-83.
[20] Hume, p. 170.
[21] Ibid.
[22] De Selve, p. 334.
[23] Greyfriars' *Chronicle*, p. 63.
[24] *Ven. S.P.*, vol. V, p. 258.
[25] Tytler, vol. I, p. 210.
[26] Ibid., p. 212.
[27] Pocock, p. 30.
[28] Ibid., p. 56.
[29] Ibid.
[30] *Lit. Rem.*, vol. I, p. cviii.
[31] Hume, p. 187.
[32] Ibid., p. 189.
[33] Halliwell-Philipps, *Letters*, vol. II, p. 35.
[34] Strype, *Life of Cranmer*, pp. 317-26.
[35] Holinshed, p. 1018.
[36] Tytler, vol. I, p. 212.
[37] Ibid., p. 239.
[38] Ibid.
[39] Ibid., p. 240
[40] Hume, pp. 190-1.
[41] Ibid., p. 192.
[42] Ibid.

✿

THE PROTESTANT KING

NINE years before Edward's birth a book was published that
Henry VIII said all kings should read. This was *The
Obedience of a Christian Man* by William Tyndale, who in
1536 was strangled and burnt as a heretic in Brussels. In Edward's
reign this work helped to form the political and hierarchic creed
of his government (it ran into eight editions before 1562) and was
chiefly remembered for its pronouncements on kingship, the
most famous being that 'the King is in this world without law, and
may, at his lust, do right and wrong, and shall give accounts to
God only ... God hath therefore ... in all lands put kings, governors and rulers in His own stead ... Whosoever therefore resisteth
them, resisteth God ... and they that resist shall receive their
damnation'.[1] In this book Tyndale developed his theme of the
vulnerability of kings, as apt to be lured into tyranny by bishops
and duped by that arch-enemy of true religion, the Pope, who
'giveth to one a rose, to another a cap of maintenance', thus
tempting them into lechery and pride, 'the common pestilence of
princes'.[2] Nevertheless, he continues, kings must be obeyed, because it is better to suffer one tyrant than many, and because their
office is ultimately derived from the people, who cannot, however, depose them.

That Edward subscribed not only to Tyndale's doctrines but to
his methods of reasoning is shown in his first literary work, a
treatise in French against the supremacy of the Pope, which he
wrote between December 1548 and March 1549 and dedicated to
Somerset. It is a remarkable production for a boy of ten, even
judged by contemporary standards; that it was entirely his own
and unsupervised is shown by the fact that he let his argument
carry him into irreverence — as when, in his eagerness to prove
that St Peter was not the chief Apostle, he criticizes him rather too
severely — and by a major error that both Cheke and Cox would
have corrected before letting their pupil's effort reach the Lord

Protector. After a brisk comparison of Jesus Christ with the Pope ('Jesus wore a crown of thorns and ... was set at naught ... the Pope has a triple crown ... Jesus paid tribute, but the Pope receives all and pays nothing'), Edward accuses his Holiness of 'stopping the mouths of Christians with his Six Articles, as with six fists' — forgetting, in his vehemence, that these were the creation of his own father. 'Seeing then,' he concludes, 'that the Pope is the minister of Lucifer, I entertain a strong hope that as Lucifer fell from Heaven into Hell, so the Pope, his Vicar, will fall from the glory of his papacy into utter contempt.'[3]

There is no record of Somerset having shown the least interest in the essay over which his nephew laboured for three months; but, whether he dismissed it as puerile or ignored it altogether, Warwick used Edward's crude theologizing and Tyndale's radical philosophy as slogans in his plan for the rule of the kingdom through the personal subjugation of the King, when Somerset fell from power. Warwick intended Edward to become the mask through which he spoke, the shield that protected him from his enemies and rivals; this could only be achieved by Edward's willing co-operation and unshakeable loyalty.

It was not until after Somerset's fall that Edward's twenty-four-page treatise was printed and bound in gilded quarto decorated with the Royal Arms. Although Warwick may not have had anything to do with this piece of flattery, it can be connected with his assumption that he and Edward were now launched on an anti-papal campaign — part of his reversal of Somerset's attitude towards his nephew. For some time since Edward's accession Warwick must have been learning and planning through Somerset's mistakes. His best weapon was his knowledge of human nature: as far as Edward was concerned, he did everything that Somerset should have done — and did not pause to think about — for and with the King; as in the political and religious divisions throughout the country, Somerset had played into his hands, and Warwick's course was obvious from the moment of his rival's first defeat.

To begin with, Edward must be reassured; this Warwick effected gradually, making it clear that he himself was merciful, disinterested, self-effacing and chiefly concerned with religious and economic reform. He was far too clever to vilify Somerset before Edward had had time to recover from the shock of his flight to Windsor; by deeds, rather than by pleasant speeches, Warwick set about creating an atmosphere of serenity and rehabilitation, soothing jealousies and making suggestions for equality in the Council, in which he appeared to be sharing the powers that Somerset had arrogated to himself. While temporarily crippling the Duke by imprisonment and heavy fines, Warwick unobtrusively set up an oligarchy in which he himself took fourth place. There was to be no Lord Protector — he agreed with the other members in rejecting the idea — and the royal prerogative must now become a reality instead of a pretence. Both these innovations pleased and encouraged Edward, especially when Warwick backed them with proofs of a Protestantism that at once transcended Somerset's comparatively tolerant and easy methods. The leaders of the Henrician party whom he had used in his campaign against the Protector — Wriothesley, Arundel and Gardiner — were already in a minority. Suddenly they found themselves relegated, while Paget was given a peerage and Cecil, after a short absence, became Warwick's secretary; various other noblemen attached to the Dudley interest were elected to the Council. So this remarkable man achieved the essence of power, without its outward show. The rapidity and smoothness of his reorganization were set off by the bewildered helplessness of his discarded allies. Gardiner, who had been told that with the Protector's fall his imprisonment would cease, made ready to rejoin the administration and, as the custom was, gave a little party for the Lieutenant of the Tower and a few friends, amusing them with 'merry tales' of his life under lock and key. When the moment came for his departure he was told that the Council had not issued the order of release; he wrote in protest and anger; the Lords took his diatribes 'very merrily, saying that he had a pleasant head', but the days went by, and then the weeks, and the order never came. He remained in the Tower until Mary's accession.[4] Arundel was accused of peculation, fined and disgraced; Wriothesley was quietly dropped from the Council board.

In these and other ways it was brought home to Edward that he was at last being treated according to Tyndale's theories and

Cranmer's coronation address, and that his hopes of religious reform were to be realized. Two days after Somerset entered the Tower, he celebrated his twelfth birthday, and three days later rode from Hampton Court through the city in state, wearing a coat and buskins of cloth of gold.[5] While continuing his education with Cheke and his other tutors, he now attended Council meetings as a matter of course, instead of being summoned to support decisions already made, as in his uncle's time. His self-confidence was further restored by Cheke, Barnaby Fitzpatrick and Henry Sidney being made Gentlemen of his Privy Chamber; Ascham, whom he had never been able to help as he had promised, was given a secretaryship in the embassy to the Emperor.

So, from the point of view of those in immediate contact with the brilliant and popular Earl of Warwick, bounties flowed — Edward knighted the Mayor and several sheriffs on his progress through the city[6] — and order was established. The Protestant party acclaimed their new patron as 'that intrepid soldier of Christ' and 'the thunderbolt and terror of the Papists',[7] and his praises echoed from the pulpit, the Treasury (where Sir Thomas Sherington was reinstalled) and the Council Chamber, sounding outwards to the manors of the countryside; for now the enclosure system was resumed, without much regard to the improvement of the soil, and under the *peine forte et dure* of Warwick's laws. In many districts, in all owned by the greedy and the unscrupulous, the peasant and his family faced three alternatives: death from starvation and exposure; hanging, for merely protesting against enclosure: semi-slavery under the pitiless hand of the newly enriched squire or merchant determined to buy himself into the aristocracy. The state of the yeoman-farmer and small-holder was almost as desperate, for the price of food had quadrupled in the last two years, while wages remained the same. Such persons — many of whom had seen their sons and brothers cut to pieces by Warwick's and Russell's German and Italian mercenaries — were no longer rebellious, or even articulate: fear and hunger had silenced them; and the fact that their standard of living (if it can be so called) had sunk lower than at any time since the Conquest, was ignored by all but a few. Only one — Latimer — dared to voice the miseries of the common people, in one of his last sermons before the King. Beginning with a tactful reference to the possibility of brighter prospects — 'Howbeit, there is now very good hope that the King's Majesty, being by the help of good governance ... trained and brought up in learning and knowledge of God's word, will shortly provide a remedy ... pray for him, good people. You have good cause and need to pray for him ... ' — he went on to speak of the peculation that had become habitual among the ruling class. ' "And so," said I, to a certain nobleman that is one of the King's Council, "if every man that has beguiled the King should make restitution ... it would cough up for the King £20,000, I think?" ... "Yea, that it would," quoth the other, "a whole £100,000." Alack, alack! make restitution, for God's sake ... Ye will cough in hell, else.' Then he turned to those who were climbing into wealth and power over the bodies of their tenants: 'Aldermen nowadays are become colliers — they are both wood-makers and makers of coals. I would wish they might eat coals for a while, till they had amended it.'

Edward, making his notes, with the imposing and benevolent figure of Cheke behind him, pondered these things, and looked in vain for a remedy. The brief entries in his Chronicle for this time show his awareness of the corruption of Somerset's ministers, and are the results of Warwick's propaganda. Obsessed with his uncle's perfidy and mismanagement, he seems to indicate that reform must come from the top, reaching downwards by degrees, but beginning with the Protector's faults — 'ambition, vain-glory, entering into rash wars in my youth, negligent looking on New-haven, enriching himself of my treasure, following of his own opinion, and doing all by his own authority, etc.'[8] Presumably the last word covers the writer's lapses of memory, as if his youth were too far off for detailed recollection; but in a long essay entitled *A Discourse about the Reformation of Many Abuses*, written a year later, the results of Latimer's protests emerge, and the thirteen-year-old father of his people sets down his conclusions and remedies. ' ... So must there be in a well-ordered commonwealth no person that shall have more than the proportion of the country will bear ... I think this country can bear no merchant to have more land than £100, no husbandman nor farmer above £100, or £200, no artifice [craftsman] above 200 marks; no labourer much more than he spendeth. I speak now generally ... but this is sure, this common-wealth may not bear one man to have more than two farms, than

175

one benefice, than 2000 sheep ... The gentleman ought to labour in service in his country. True gentlemen ... have little or nothing increased their rents ... yet their house-keeping is dearer, their meat is dearer ... their liveries [arms] dearer ... their wages greater; which thing at length, if speedy remedy be not had, will bring that state [estate] into utter ruin ... ' After a long passage about the avariciousness, snobbery and self-seeking of the ruling classes, Edward goes on: 'These sores must be cured with these medicines or plasters. 1. Good education. 2. Devising of good laws. 3. Executing the laws justly, without respect of persons. 4. Example of rulers. 5. Punishing of vagabonds and idle persons. 6. Encouraging the good. 7. Ordering well the customers. 8. Engendering friendship in all parts of the commonwealth.' He then develops each of his 'medicines' at length, concluding: 'Wherefore I would wish ... that those noblemen, except a few that should be with me, went to their countries, and there should see the statutes fully and duly executed; and that these men should be put [prevented] from being Justices of the Peace that be touched or blotted with those vices that be against these new laws to be established; for no man that is in fault himself can punish another for the same offence. And these Justices being put out, there is no doubt for execution of the laws.'⁹

It is not surprising that these naive notions were courteously ignored. By the time they had been put forward and disposed of, Latimer had retired, Somerset was executed and Warwick's ascendancy absolute.

With the disgrace and imprisonment of his uncle, Edward's spirits sank; later, some said that the 'lamentable tragedy' of the quarrel between Somerset and the Lord Admiral was the original cause of his fatal disease; a wrong, yet symbolical judgment.¹⁰ It became clear that he must be distracted with outdoor sports and pastimes; and he was allowed to enjoy the company of persons of whom his uncle had disapproved because they encouraged the wilful, high-spirited side of his character.

Among the gentlemen of Edward's household there were probably only two — Barnaby Fitzpatrick and Henry Sidney — who were disinterestedly fond of him; of those who combined the furtherance of their careers with genuine affection for the King, Sir Nicholas Throckmorton stands out, chiefly because, many years after Edward's death, he wrote a short rhyming chronicle of their friendship, in which the narrator's unabashed self-seeking is made palatable by the gaiety and warmth that amused and stimulated his master.

Throckmorton, the younger son of an impoverished country squire, had been attached to the Lord High Admiral's household; Seymour placed him in Edward's before his downfall. Throckmorton thought Somerset a 'beast' for allowing his brother to be executed and so 'defiling his nest', and remained loyal to Seymour's memory; 'Thus guiltless, he, through malice, went to pot', he says. When Seymour was arrested, Throckmorton retired from Court; after Somerset's disgrace he returned and rose to favour by treating Edward as a schoolboy rather than as a potentate, amusing him with his absurd stories and crude humour. Edward, he records, 'would jest with me most merrily ... Wearied much with Lords, and others more, Alone with me into some place would go' — in order to enjoy his jokes uninterrupted by ceremony. Coming back to the palace from one of his progresses through the city — where he had knighted a number of persons in whom he took no interest — Edward came upon Throckmorton, and drew out his sword of state; why should not his friend be similarly honoured? 'Kneel!' he said. Throckmorton hesitated, not because he did not wish to be knighted, but for fear of causing jealousy, and so losing what he had already gained. He tried to explain this to the King; but Edward, relaxing after the strain of his progress, was in wild spirits, and would not be denied. There was nothing for it but to withdraw; before Throckmorton was half way across the room Edward, bursting with laughter, was behind him, sword in hand. Throckmorton ran off, Edward in pursuit; when Throckmorton was out of sight in a dark lobby, he hid himself in a cupboard; but the King guessed what he had done, flung open the door, and 'there', says Throckmorton, 'against my will, he dubbed me knight, Which was an eyesore unto some men's sight,' — for naturally the spectacle of His Majesty chasing one of his gentlemen with a sword through corridors and ante-chambers had created an audience of shocked and disgusted courtiers for the final scene.

After this, Throckmorton prudently withdrew to his Oxfordshire home where his wife and father were living; when he told them what had happened, adding that he was now in a position to bring the new Lady Throckmorton to Court, her father-in-law fell into a passion; Nicholas was the younger; he should have seen to it that his brother was knighted first. 'He thumped me on the breast,' says Throckmorton, 'and thus began — "Sir knight, sir knave! a foolish boy art thou, And yet thou think'st thyself a goodly man. Why shouldst thou scorn thy father's daily fare, Or send me word when I should see thee here, As who should say, I should provide good cheer?"' Sir Nicholas prevented a quarrel by promising that he would do what he could, not only for his brother, but for the whole family, and returned to Court with his wife. As they were still too poor for him to buy her a Court dress, she appeared before Edward 'meanly clad', according to her husband, upon which the King reproached Throckmorton with selfishness and neglect. Lady Throckmorton, well primed, 'excused the fault with poverty, Which we enforced to keep her beggarly' — and Throckmorton struck in: 'For her it was no way, To bear the merchant's stock upon her back, Unless I knew some means it to repay, Or us to save from ruin or from wrack.' 'Dost thou want?' said Edward, 'I will give you what you need.' Throckmorton again demurred: he was afraid of going too far; when he consulted his friends, they advised him 'while the iron was hot, to strike the stroke', and 'while May doth last, make choice of May' — with the result that he acquired some church lands and retained his place at Court during the rest of the reign. 'The King', he goes on complacently, 'fancied me daily, more and more', and the new knight began to give himself airs. No tale-bearing or spite lessened Edward's affection for this friend; Throckmorton was 'the King's familiar ... and spat in Fortune's face' — until the Earl of Warwick became aware of the hold he had achieved.[11]

A more suspect but equally jovial climber was John Perrot, some years Throckmorton's senior. Tall, athletic, red-haired and boisterous, he was one of those high-living, reckless young men whom misfortune does not overtake until the provocation of it has become a fatal habit. Henry VIII's eye fell upon him when he was having a free fight with two Yeomen of the Guard — an offence for which he was liable to lose his right hand — and Perrot managed to make capital out of his physical prowess and so get a place at Court. On Edward's accession he was knighted (because, his biographer says, the King found him irresistible) and sent on a mission to France, where he hunted boars with Henry II and enjoyed himself immensely. Returning to England, he began a course of life that ran him into debts of some seven or eight thousand pounds; and how was he to pay? He had borrowed all he could, and was faced with bankruptcy. After some thought, he hit upon a simple yet effective plan: 'He walked into a place where commonly the King used to come about that hour; and there he began to complain, as it were, against himself, unto himself — how unfortunate and how unwise he was, so to consume his living ... ' Finally, he launched into a dramatic soliloquy, taking care not to speak too loud. 'Must I be the man that shall overthrow my house, which hath continued so long?' he began. 'It had been better I had never been born. What shall I do? ... Had I best leave the Court and follow the wars? Shall I retire into the country?' with a great deal more to the same effect. At last the King appeared. Perrot continued to walk and mutter to himself. Edward came up to him and said: 'How now, Perrot, what is the matter that you make this great moan?' Perrot started back. 'An it like Your Majesty,' he faltered, 'I did not think that Your Majesty had been there.' Edward said: 'Yes, we heard you well enough. And have you spent your living in our service?' Sir John acknowledged that it was so, but implied that nothing could be done. This hint at the uncertainty of the royal prerogative had the desired effect. 'Am I so young and under government, that I cannot give you anything in recompense of your service?' Edward demanded. 'Spy out somewhat, and you shall see whether I have not power to bestow it on you.' Perrot 'humbly thanked' his Majesty, and told him what he needed. It was a good deal more than Edward had imagined: he was not able to provide the whole sum; but most of Perrot's debts were paid. He remained in Edward's service till the end of his reign, and often amused the King with stories of his wild youth; how he was so hot-tempered that he 'could not brook any crosses' and made many enemies; how he swore, and was lecherous, and a spendthrift; how, when he was attached to the Marquis of Winchester's household, he and young Lord Abergavenny planned a drinking-party for some of their friends, but 'before their guests came, they came to some contention, and so to blows, that they took the glasses and brake them about one another's ears; when the guests came thither, they found, instead of claret wine, blood besprinkled about the chamber'.*

The charm of such stories for a sheltered and strictly brought up boy (apparently they improved with constant repetition) can be imagined; Perrot's anonymous biographer gives the impression that those in which the figure of 'the King my father' appeared pleased his son best.

Some allowance must be made for exaggeration and planned effect in the narratives of both Throckmorton and Perrot; yet they unwittingly bear one another out, and repeat the pattern of circumstantial evidence provided by Fowler and the rest of the Lord Admiral's circle. Through the trivial and self-glorifying reminiscences of these two courtiers that side of Edward emerges from which such historians as Strype and Hayward averted their eyes; yet their rhapsodical descriptions of the Protestant phenomenon's piety, earnestness and learning do not contradict, but complete, the picture of a temperament that delighted to express itself in a variety of interests and pursuits and that Edward's own writings make clearer still. Dignity of demeanour, intellectual grasp, a deeply serious attitude towards all religious and political questions alternated, as in the case of Henry VIII and Queen Elizabeth, with bursts of animal spirits, a passion for games and pleasure in very simple fun; the dual nature of the Tudors is here seen with one difference — that of immaturity, the hard, enclosed immaturity of a boy whose responsibilities have made a wall between him and the rest of the world. The child whom Foxe described as 'dearly and tenderly beloved of all his subjects: but especially of the good and learned sort: and ... also admirable, by reason of his ... virtue and learning, which in him appeared above the capacity of his years',[12] would rush away from books and Council meetings to wrestle, ride and shoot at rovers with the same absorption; his 'elegant' speaking and writing of Greek and Latin[13] went hand in hand with a love of finery partly shown by adherence to certain colours and materials — crimson damask, white velvet, and violet silk embroidered with gold, silver and pearls; he so often wore violet that it became part of his prerogative, none of his courtiers venturing to imitate him.[14] When a consignment of textiles, furs

* Sir John was thought to be a son of Henry VIII by 'a lady of great honour, of the King's familiarity', and he himself believed this. Naunton, *Fragmenta Regalia*, p. 43.

and jewels arrived from Italy at the Port of London, no merchant was allowed to look through it until His Majesty had made his choice.[15] His generosity was carried to recklessness; yet it related to an extreme sensitivity as to the value of money and the importance of a sound economy in public and private affairs. His innate stubbornness and the wary reserve that Lord Russell had observed in his father and grandfather were set off by an innocent credulity that Seymour, Somerset and Warwick all made use of — Warwick in such a manner that his phraseology can be discerned throughout Edward's correspondence. Cheke's influence is most apparent in the diary; Edward did not keep this regularly till after the Christmas of 1549.

When Cheke returned from Cambridge, he suggested that Edward should write down briefly, each day, 'debates in Council, dispatch of Ambassadors, honours conferred, and other remarks as he thought good', adding that 'a dark and imperfect reflection upon affairs floating in the memory is like words dispersed and insignificant: whereas a view of them in a book is like the same words digested and disposed in good order, and so made significant'.[16] Edward therefore prefaced his diary proper with a short résumé of the principal events of his reign; this is probably why he called the record that began in full in March 1550 and ended in November 1552, seven months before his death, his Chronicle. Its first editor, Bishop Burnet, who published it in his *History of the Reformation* (completed in 1714) describes it as a diary, thus giving the impression that it contains more personal matter than is the case; Edward's daily entries rather resemble the minutes taken by the secretary of some organization — which, in a sense, is what he was — and the 'other remarks as he thought good' are of a private but trivial nature, relating to games, parties, journeys and dress. Cheke, of course, saw the diary, but does not seem to have tampered with it. A rough analysis divides its contents under four headings, here listed in proportion to the amount of space accorded to each: foreign and military affairs come first; then religion; civil and economic matters tie with social events and court ceremonies; the smallest section is devoted to dress and games. There is only one mention of the First Prayer Book, and none at all of the schools and hospitals traditionally associated with Edward's name.

Many historians have judged Edward's character by the cold brevity of certain entries, deducing an extreme heartlessness from such phrases as 'the rebels were constrained, for lack of meat, to remove; whom the Earl of Warwick followed, with 1000 Almains, and his horsemen ... and overcame them in plain battle, killing 2000 of them, and taking Kett, their captain, who in January following was hanged at Norwich, and his head hanged out ... '[17]

From babyhood Edward had lived publicly; all that he said or wrote was liable to be repeated, distorted and used against him, as his notes to the Lord Admiral were; it is therefore not surprising that although he kept his diary, with other treasures, in a locked desk of black velvet, decorated with plates of gilded copper, it provides no self-revelation. The diary itself, now in the British Museum, is in folio. If Ascham ever looked through it, he would have censured the hand in which Edward scribbled his entries; for, although perfectly legible, it is inelegant and uneven; but there are not many corrections or insertions, and the standard of spelling and punctuation is remarkably high. This is the result of Cheke's passion for clarity, and his efforts to modernize the writing and pronunciation of English. He would never allow a mute E to be added to such words as 'excuse', 'give', or 'deceive'; he preferred a double E to Y, writing 'necessitee' and 'adversitee'; when A and I had a long sound he wrote 'maad' for 'mad' and 'desiir' for 'desire'. Y was one of his bugbears; he taught Edward to write 'mi', 'awai' and 'sai', and put a stroke above long-sounding U's — 'presūme' — while all words ending in 'le' were given their proper value by transposing 'brittle' to 'brittil', 'praisable' to 'praisabil', and so on; these innovations were carried through as his campaign in Greek at Cambridge had been — he told Gardiner that the old-fashioned pronunciation of that language was like 'the hissing of a snake or the peeping of a sparrow'[18] — and his influence on Edward's written work was excellent. The opening paragraph of the Chronicle, composed when Edward was twelve and a half and here transcribed exactly as he spelt it, reads like a passage from a memoirist of the early eighteenth century. 'The yere of our Lord 1537, was a prince born to king harry th'eight, by Jane Seymour, when quene, who w'in few days after the Birth of her soone died, and was buried at the castel of Windsore. This child was christened by the duke of Northfolke, the duke of Southfolke, and the archbishop of Caunterbury. Afterward was brought up till he came to six yeres old among the women. At the sixt yere of his age, he was brought up in learning by Mr. Doctour Cox who was after his amner, and Jhon Cheke, Mr. of Arts, tow wel learned men, who sought to bring him up in learning of toungues, of the scripture, of philosophie, and all liberal sciences. Also Jhon Belmaine frenchman did teach him the french language. The 10 yere not yet ended, it was apointed he should be created prince of Wales, Duke of Cornwal, and Conte Palatine of Chester. At wich time, being the year of our L. 1547 the said king died of a dropsie as it was thought. After whos death incontinent came Edward erle of Hartford, and S. Anthony Brown, Mr. of the horse, to convey this prince to Enfild, where the earle of Hertford declared to him, and his younger Sister Elizabeth, the death of their father.'[19]

Thereafter the narrative changes every now and then from the third to the first person, and becomes less condensed. Edward did not begin to use the diary form till some months after the imprisonment of Somerset, whose list of crimes against the state rose from twelve to twenty and then to twenty-nine separate charges, the principal being his acquisition of money and lands and the *coup d'état* that had made him Protector. One item in the list, whether true or false, is oddly symbolic. The Duke was found guilty of having taken for himself the City's gift of a thousand crowns that had been too heavy for Edward to hold.[20] As he had no grounds of defence against the main accusations, Somerset acknowledged them and appealed for mercy to the King and Council. At this point — January 14th, 1550 — a less acute observer than Warwick would have raised an outcry about letting off such an offender with a fine of £2000 and the loss of the Protectorate; but between this date and the preceding autumn, it had become plain that Somerset's popularity with the people had rather increased than diminished; and a charge of felony or high treason would have re-created in Edward the suspiciousness that, on a long-term policy, would lessen his utility as the instrument of Warwick's power. All that need be done was to hamstring Somerset by taking away his authority, and, temporarily, removing him from Edward.

On February 6th the Duke was released from the Tower on condition that he lived as a private gentleman and did not come within ten miles of the King's person. On April 1st most of his lands were restored, and he was allowed to return to Court; on the 8th he was admitted to the Privy Council and dined with His Majesty.

By this time, Edward's fears must have been soothed; if Somerset had ever been a danger to the realm, he was one no longer; the uncle and nephew embraced and seemed on excellent terms.[21]

The effect on the Duke of this rehabilitation was a renewal of his trust in, and friendship with, Warwick; it may not have occurred to him at once that their new alliance left him defenceless and Warwick in control. Now it only remained for Warwick to tighten the bond between himself and Somerset by a personal tie; on June 3rd his eldest son, Lord Lisle, was married to Somerset's daughter, Anne Seymour, at Sheen, after which, says Edward, 'a fair dinner was made, and, dancing finished, the King and the ladies went into two antechambers made of boughs'. From this woodland pavilion Edward and his companions watched two teams of six persons a side run at the ring; this was followed by a tournament, then a great supper; when the bride and bridegroom had been put to bed, Edward returned to Westminster, having given the bride a ring worth £40.[22]

Next day a much less important wedding was celebrated, that of Warwick's fourth son Robert, to Amy Robsart, the daughter of an obscure country knight; it was noted by William Cecil that the seventeen-year-old couple were deeply in love; many years later he recorded this observation in disapproving terms: '*Nuptiae carnales a laetitia incipiunt et in luctu terminatur.*'[23]

Edward enjoyed himself very much, although the Dudley-Robsart wedding was a mild affair compared to that of Warwick's heir, and the festivities were rather rustic than chivalric. 'There were certain gentlemen', he says, 'that did strive who should first take away a goose's head, which was hanged alive on two cross posts.'[24] A nineteenth-century biographer has been much pained by this mark of indifference to animal suffering.

Thereafter, says an Elizabethan historian, 'great love and friendship' prevailed, outwardly at least, between Warwick and Somerset.[25] Warwick, his reputation enhanced by his successful negotiation of peace with France, remained serenely indifferent to the chagrin of the Henrician and Catholic parties, who had counted on his taking up their cause. The Spanish Ambassador observed this change of front with sardonic disgust. It was what he had anticipated — a typical English trick; yet he could not help being sorry for the King, for whom he was beginning to feel something like affection. Edward, he told the Emperor, 'is beginning to debate the question of religion, and oppose ours, as he is being taught to do. It is a sad thing to see the righteous suffer and the kingdom be lost, with its young King, who is naturally of a gentle nature, but is being corrupted by false doctrines and practices'. It seemed to Van der Delft that Warwick and Somerset were firmly allied in this odious campaign — 'because the King, who is but too good by nature, changes his mind from day to day under their influences, and yields himself up to their vagaries; so that, in the Court, there is no man of learning or bishop so ready to argue in support of the new doctrine as the King — according to what his masters tell him — and he learns from his preachers, whose sermons he often writes with his own hand beforehand; and this is a source of pride to his courtiers. It may be feared', he went on, 'that the King's natural goodness may be perverted ... and he will never learn to aspire to things he has never learnt to know.'[12]

This report shows how completely yet unobtrusively Warwick had altered Edward's status. All of it is true, except the remark about the King changing his mind from day to day, according to the whims of his Protestant advisers.[27] Van der Delft, presumably remembering that Somerset had said there would be no further religious innovations, did not grasp that the Duke had now no power to stop those that Warwick was putting in hand; nor that this phase of the Reformation was being effected by dogmatic variations that to an orthodox Catholic appeared not only wicked but ridiculous: nor could he understand that Edward was at last in a position openly to discuss ideas that he had absorbed over a number of years: nor that he was being allowed — he needed no encouragement — to take, as it seemed, a leading part in a movement that Henry VIII would have condemned in its present form, but that he might have gradually adapted to the national use.

Of course, Warwick had no interest at all in this or any other religious question for itself; when he no longer had anything to lose in this world, he prepared for the next by reconciliation with

the old faith. Now he perceived that the quickest way of sub-
jugating Edward and gaining control of the government and of
episcopal property was to stand out for an advanced form of
Protestantism; in this he had not only Edward behind him, but
Cranmer and a posse of clever and pushing 'new' men, much more
suited to his subtly moulding hand than either the Henrician or
the Catholic nobles, who despised him as the upstart representative of a bourgeois and tainted stock.

Warwick's rise to power brought Edward the responsibilities
and duties of which Somerset had deprived him. He accepted them
with the same enthusiasm that informed his study of national and
foreign politics. The points now raised by William Thomas for his
private study reveal Warwick's system of general appeal — was it
'better for the commonwealth that the power be in the com-
monalty or in the nobility'? What was the best way of reforming
the currency? What was His Majesty's opinion of the realm 'within
itself'?[28] Before the Council meetings Thomas would discuss these
questions with the King, sometimes refuting, sometimes agreeing
with, the arguments that he put forward. At the meetings Edward
waited till everyone else had spoken, and then gave his own
opinion; he was sensible enough to defer to the Lords before putting his ideas into practice, 'by which means,' says the Venetian
Ambassador, 'he became so popular with his councillors and the
whole country, that there is perhaps no instance of any other King
of that time being so much beloved, or who gave greater promise'.[29]
With Dr Cox, who was still his almoner, Edward heard appeals
for his private charities 'at set times'; of these there is no record in
his diary, in which the entries for May 1550 relate chiefly to the
new alliance with France.

Under this agreement, some of Edward's schoolfellows went as
hostages to the Court of Henry II, while MM. de la Trémouille, de
Henaudie and the Vidame de Chartres replaced them in his
circle; gay and athletic young men, bent on enjoying themselves,
they were surprised at the number of duties their twelve-year-old
host took as a matter of course, and the amount of time he spent
over his books; the Vidame de Chartres was quite pained by this
passion for reading. 'What need has Your Majesty of so many
books?' he would say, and urge Edward out to play, without
much difficulty.[30] When the French envoy arrived to sign the

treaty a state dinner was given, and then Edward and his guests watched two teams, one dressed in yellow and the other in blue, running at the ring; this was followed by bull- and bear-baiting, a hunt, and supper at Hampton Court Palace. Before the embassy left, Edward and Somerset received them together at Sheen, where the Duke provided 'a fair supper', according to his nephew, 'and afterwards went into the Thames, and saw both the bear hunted in the river, and also wild-fire cast out of boats, and many pretty conceits.[31] A week later Chartres asked Edward and his uncle to supper at Durham Place, with 'masques and other conceits' to follow. Both the French and Spanish envoys noticed the King's high spirits; he enjoyed everything, pageants especially; and he seemed to get as much pleasure out of watching tournaments as of joining in them. When he took Chartres and Henaudie to supper at Deptford with Clinton, the Lord Admiral, he was fascinated by an exhibition of tilting over the water and a mock sea battle, of which he recorded every detail in his diary. The most exciting moment was when Clinton himself 'went forth to take the yellow ship, and at length clasped with her, took her, and assaulted her top, and won it, by compulsion'.[32] The Spanish Ambassador was much struck with Edward's health and vigour, and his natural aptitude for all outdoor games.[33]

From the point of view of the French Ambassador, Edward's physique was now of paramount importance; for Warwick had decided to abandon, temporarily, any hope of a Scottish alliance, and was considering a marriage between the King and Madame Elisabeth, Henry II's daughter. There was some feeling against this plan among those who still looked on France as the ancient enemy; it was thought that if Mary Stuart were brought into England she would be converted, which would be less likely in the case of a French princess; in non-political circles the aspect of the marriage that mattered most was defined by Latimer in a sermon preached before the King at Whitehall. 'And here I would say a thing to Your Majesty — marry in the Lord', he began, going on to warn Edward against looking on marriage as a bargain, which, he explained, 'causes much whoredom and divorcing'. After a resounding censure of the incontinence and greed that prevailed among Edward's courtiers, Latimer begged him not to fall into self-indulgence and frivolity, and then reverted to the marriage theme. 'Let Your Grace choose a wife that is of God,' he urged, 'of the household of faith ... such an one as Your Grace can find it in your heart to love and lead your life in pure and chaste espousage with ... Let Your Majesty not choose a proud wanton, and one full only of rich treasures, and worldly pomp.'[34]

These last items were in fact exactly what Warwick considered essential. Edward appeared to agree with him during the first year of the negotiations for the French marriage; privately, he seems to have thought that his father's scheme of the Scottish alliance was not only better, but still feasible. A year later, when Mary of Guise, the Queen-Dowager and Regent of Scotland, was storm-bound on the south coast and asked leave to pass through England on her journey from France to her own kingdom, he gave orders that she was to be received with special honours.[35]

Edward was at Westminster when Mary of Guise reached Portsmouth; from there, she and her train, numbering some fifty persons, journeyed slowly to Hampton Court, staying at various country houses on the way; from Hampton Court she proceeded to Southwark Palace, where she held a reception for the ladies of the English Court. Warwick and a party of gentlemen then called on her to convey Edward's welcome. 'If she lacked anything,' the King said, 'she should have it for her better furniture; and I would willingly see her the day following.'[36] So the still beautiful widow of thirty-five was received with the most elaborate cere-monial that the English Court could provide.

She was met at the gates of the Palace of Westminster by thirty gentlemen. Edward, standing under his canopy of state, waited for her at the end of the Great Hall. As soon as the Queen-Dowager reached the dais she knelt; Edward raised her, kissing her on the cheek; she then presented her ladies, each of whom he kissed as she told him their names and titles. At midday she was conducted by Edward to her apartment to rest. 'The Court, the hall and the stairs', he says, 'were full of serving-men; the presence-chamber, great-chamber, and her presence-chamber, of gentlemen. And so, having brought her to her chamber, I retired to mine. I went to her to dinner; she dined under the same cloth of state, at my left hand; at her rereward dined my cousin Francis [the Duke of Suffolk] and my cousin Margaret [Margaret Clifford, daughter of Lord Cumberland]; at mine sat the French Ambassador. We were served by two services, two sewers, cup-bearers, carvers, and gentlemen. Her master-hostel [major-domo] came before her service, and my officers before mine. There were two cupboards [displays of plate], one of gold, four stages high, another of massy silver, six stages. In her great-chamber, dined at three boards [tables] the ladies only. After dinner, when she had heard some music, I brought her to the hall.'[37]

During the meal the conversation was formal; after the concert, Edward took his guest round the gardens and galleries; as they walked, he tried to persuade her to reverse her decision of marrying Mary Stuart to the Dauphin. He reminded her of her contract with his father, begging her to renew it, as 'most meet for the unions of both the realms, staunching of blood, and for a perpetual quietness'. She seems to have demurred, for he went on, more earnestly: 'Otherwise, whoever marries her should not have her with half my kindness — but I shall be his enemy.' The Queen-Dowager explained that the contract had really been broken by Somerset, 'and others of his Council, against the realm of Scotland', adding that after the holocaust of Pinkie Cleugh, she had been forced to seek an alliance with France. Then she went on — and the phrase gives the impression that she was rather amused by Edward's persistence — 'Such a fashion of dealing is not the nearest way to conquer a lady.' Edward had never thought of marriage in that light; he had nothing to say. The Queen-Dowager added: 'Your Majesty should have approached me more gently. But I will speak to the King of France.' No more was said, then; afterwards, Mary told her chaplain, Bishop Lesley, who was present during their conversation, that she thought Edward had wisdom and judgment. Compliments were interchanged, farewells made, and this oddly assorted pair of potentates parted, never to meet again. The only blot on the proceedings had been the elopement of one of the Queen-Dowager's ladies — 'the fairest' — with a city merchant.[38]

It is doubtful whether Warwick would have approved of Edward's independent action; but thenceforth no more was heard of the Scottish marriage. Warwick had in fact a greater matter on hand; the introduction, followed by the enforcement, of a more extreme Protestantism into England; this he began with a series of attacks on the Princess Mary.

NOTES TO CHAPTER X

[1] Op. cit., p. 178.
[2] Op. cit., p. 186.
[3] *Lit. Rem.*, vol. II, pp. 181-205.
[4] Strype, *Ecclesiastical Memorials*, vol. I, part 2, p. 380.
[5] Wriothesley, vol. II, p. 28.
[6] Greyfriars, p. 65.
[7] *Original Letters*, 1st ser., p. 82.
[8] *Lit. Rem.*, vol. II, pp. 475-510.
[9] Ibid.
[10] Speed, *Chronicle*, p. 809.
[11] *The Legend of Sir Nicholas Throckmorton*, ed. J. G. Nichols.
[12] Foxe, vol. V, p. 699.
[13] Strype, *Life of Sir John Cheke*, p. 40.
[14] Von Raumer, vol. II, p. 71.
[15] *Calendar of Patent Rolls*, Nov. 1550.
[16] Strype, *Life of Sir John Cheke*, p. 20.
[17] *Lit. Rem.*, vol. II, p. 231.
[18] Strype, *Life of Sir John Cheke*, p. 88.
[19] B.M. Cotton MSS.
[20] *Cal. D.S.P.*, vol. XIX, p. 742.
[21] Hume, p. 193.
[22] *Cal. Span. P.*, vol. X, p. 97.
[23] Haynes, pp. 61-153.
[24] *Lit. Rem.*, vol. II, p. 273; Strickland's *Edward VI*.
[25] Holinshed, p. 1025.
[26] *Cal. Span. P.*, vol. X, p. 97.
[27] *Lit. Rem.*, vol. II, p. 387.
[28] Thomas, p. 170.
[29] *Ven. S.P.*, vol. V, p. 339.
[30] Ibid.
[31] *Lit. Rem.*, vol. II, p. 279.
[32] Ibid.
[33] *Cal. Span. P.*, vol. X, p. 98.
[34] *Sermons*, p. 94.
[35] *Lit. Rem.*, vol. II, p. 359.
[36] Ibid., p. 360.
[37] Ibid., p. 363.
[38] Lesley, *History of Scotland*, p. 240.

CHAPTER ELEVEN

THE PRINCESS MARY'S MASS

BETWEEN the autumn of 1549 and the summer of 1550 the full strength of Edward's personality was released. This sudden development was partly the result of his escape from Somerset's rule and partly created by Warwick, who now began a process of violent stimulation that combined incitement to fanaticism with appeals to Edward's sense of duty. In three and a half years this treatment defeated Warwick's object, bringing with it his own ruin and disgrace. Edward's fatal illness was to some extent hurried on by Warwick's merciless pressure and his savage lust for power; thus Warwick himself lost everything he had acquired, and was executed within a month of his victim's death. So it was that from his twelfth to his thirteenth year Edward's temperament shot out of the chrysalis created by Somerset into the fiery light of a scene designed by Warwick for the ultimate supremacy of the Dudleys. If Edward had lived, they might have become as famous and terrible a dynasty as the Borgias, or the Bonapartes; or Edward himself might have destroyed them, as Henry VIII had destroyed Wolsey and Cromwell, and Elizabeth was forced to destroy Mary Stuart and Essex.

This revolution in Edward's professional and inner life did not affect the pace of an education that Cheke continued to direct on lines originally mapped out by himself and Henry VIII, as if unaware of Warwick's impetus; indeed, Edward kept the same hours, played the same games and gave the same number of public receptions as he had when he succeeded. In his correspondence with Ascham, Cheke reported that His Majesty was studying the *Dialectic* and *Ethic* of Aristotle, and translating Cicero's *Philosophy* into Greek; Ascham recommended the *Cyropaedia* of Xenophon; Cheke replied that, though this might be more amusing, it was less instructive, and added that Edward was translating his tutor's favourite authors, Demosthenes and Isocrates, into Italian or French; he now spoke these languages fluently, and was beginning to learn Spanish. 'I would have a good student pass rejoicing through all authors,' Cheke went on, 'both Greek and Latin; but he that will dwell in these few books only, first in God's Holy Bible, and then join with it Tully, Plato, Aristotle, Xenophon, Isocrates and Demosthenes, must needs prove an excellent man.' In respect of enjoyment the tutor's success was sustained. Edward liked his classical reading as much as, perhaps more than, the ten chapters of the Bible that, with his schoolfellows, he was supposed to get through every day; like most children, he preferred to read alone, in a window-seat, unsupervised. When he showed temper or self-will, which was fairly often, Cheke would tell him that 'every fault is greater in a King than in a mean man', and that he must be 'slow to judge, glad to hear all men, mistrusting his own reason, taking truth to be hidden ... and persuading himself that which Socrates believed when he was old, that he knoweth only this thing, that he knew nothing'.[1]

Fortunately for Edward, the Socratic ideal, although it contradicted the Calvinist influences that Warwick was now bringing to bear, still prevailed in his private life which in June 1550 touched those of the common people through a short progress when he abandoned his daily routine. Starting from Greenwich, he passed through Westminster to Hampton Court, thence to Windsor and on to Guildford, coming back via Oatlands and Woking to Richmond, in so leisurely a manner that he did not return to London till October.[2] At Greenwich he crowned Gilbert Dethick Garter-King-of-Arms with all the splendour of the ancient ritual that reached its climax when he poured a cup of wine over Dethick's head before investing him with the robes and the order.[3] Meanwhile, Warwick continued to build up his own reputation as a reformer by giving posts to Bullinger, Bucer, Melancthon and a number of other foreign and ultra-Protestant divines, recommending Edward to read their books and urging them to influence him in the reorganization of church affairs. In this movement Warwick's most enthusiastic supporter was Hooper, recently imprisoned by Somerset for heretical disobedience, and now presented to the see of Gloucester. Hooper would only accept the bishopric on his own conditions, which were that he dispensed with the episcopal vestments and the 'popish ceremony' in the consecration. This shocked many of the Council, and Edward was advised by Cranmer and some of the other bishops to order Hooper to conform. Everyone was at loggerheads, with the result that a few months before his twelfth birthday Edward had to decide what was to be done.

He sent for Hooper and began by telling him that he need only wear his episcopal robes when he preached at Court, so as not to offend the more orthodox members of the congregation; in his diocese and elsewhere, he could do as he liked. After some demur, Hooper agreed to this compromise; then, together, he and Edward went through the service of consecration. The last sentence of the oath ran 'So help me God, all saints and the holy evangelists'. In a letter describing this interview, Hooper said that His Majesty grew 'much excited' when his eye fell on these words, and he exclaimed: 'What wickedness is here, Hooper? Are these offices ordained in the name of the saints, or of God?' Hooper apologized, and the phrase was altered, in the King's own hand, to 'So help me God, through Jesus Christ', and so incorporated in the Prayer Book of 1552.[4]

This rather alarming anecdote is a milestone in the progress of the child who less than three years before had commanded the Bible to be carried in front of him out of Westminster Abbey. The logical piety that had inspired that order was becoming obsessive. Although Warwick and his visiting protégés may not have been entirely responsible for a bigotry that would be absurd if it were not pathetic, the shadow of an arrogant and alien faith seems to have crept across Edward's spiritual development; Cheke's pupil was temporarily replaced by the harsh reformer who in July of this year wrote to Bishop Gardiner that he could no longer endure his 'disordered doings and insolent wilfulness', desiring him to subscribe without reservation to the new rubric, 'upon pain of incurring such punishments and penalties as, by our laws, may be put upon you for not doing the same'.[5] In his diary Edward noted that Warwick, with three other members of the Council, having twice examined Gardiner, required him to sign a paper confessing his guilt. The Bishop refused to be thus humiliated. 'I would rather tumble myself desperately into the Thames', he declared. A few months later he was again tried for contumacy, and again imprisoned. The fact that Somerset, who had tolerated and to some extent supported him, was now powerless, was emphasized by Warwick's insistence on his disgrace; this was followed by an outburst of theological dispute that even Calvinists and Zwinglians found trivial and degraded.

One of Gardiner's chaplains, having appeared before him in highly coloured lay attire, was asked: 'Is this fit apparel for a Deacon?' and pertly answered: 'My vesture doth not so much vary from a Deacon's as doth your lordship's from that of an Apostle' and was supported by one of the Prebends of St Paul's announcing that 'If the Bishop require me to wear a cap and tippet, then it should be decreed that all popish priests, for a distinction between us and them, should be forced to wear upon their sleeves a chalice with a host upon it'. [6] Bonner, on the other hand, supported Gardiner and, denounced by Latimer and Hooper for 'demeaning' the King's authority, described his adversaries as 'daws, woodcocks and fools', to which Hooper replied that he was 'more ignorant than a boy of ten'. 'Put up your pipes,' Bonner retorted, 'I will meddle no more with you' and in 'a pelting chafe', according to an eye-witness, was sent to the Marshalsea. [7]

The foreign clergy stood aloof from these wranglings and, through Warwick, made Edward their protector. In the summer of 1550 Bullinger, who seems to have been highest in Warwick's favour, sent the King one of his books, refusing the present of money that Edward offered in return; when they did meet, Bullinger found Edward amazingly erudite (His Majesty discussed with him a new book on anabaptism) but thought that his minority would check the Protestant cause, adding that there were comparatively few true Protestants in England. [8] Hooper, who saw a good deal of Edward during the autumn of 1550, said to Bullinger: 'If he lives, he will be the wonder and terror of the world', and Dean Traheron, the King's librarian, saw a great future ahead of him, but both seemed to think that he was not very robust; others considered that too much pressure was being put upon him by a new preacher, Lever, who begged him to avoid the company of those young noblemen with whom he hunted and played games; this may have been the result of Edward losing a tilting wager — ten yards of black velvet — to Sir Thomas Wroth. [9] This pressure took different forms; another English bishop, Heath, said proudly that, when he and the King disagreed on some point, 'His Majesty used me more like a son than a subject'.[10] In advanced Protestant circles Warwick and Cheke were now compared with Somerset to the Duke's disadvantage, and the rumour went round that he might regain his hold over his nephew. Then Warwick contrived to lower Somerset's status by a gesture that combined social discourtesy with theological propaganda.

Somerset's widowed mother, who had lived quietly in Wiltshire since the year of Edward's birth, died on October 18th, two days after he returned from his progress. A state funeral and Court mourning should have marked the death of the King's grandmother; neither tribute was allowed by the Council, on the grounds that such demonstrations were papistical, extravagant and depressing for His Majesty. These excuses could not possibly have deceived Somerset, who, when he received the news of Lady Seymour's death, consulted the Lords and was thus personally slighted. The fact that he did consult them shows his awareness of his altered position, and of its dangers. If he had ordered, or asked Edward's leave to order, an official display of grief, such an assumption of privilege might have been used against him by Warwick's faction. In Edward's diary, which for this month is confined to nine brief entries relating to finance, trade and a dispute with the French Ambassador, his grandmother is not mentioned; it is unlikely that he ever saw her; and he was not present when the Council, having considered Somerset's appeal, announced that '*private* men should reserve their private sorrows to their own houses, and not diminish the presence of their prince with doleful token' adding that His Majesty 'did specially dispense with the said Duke for the wearing of doole, either upon himself, or upon his family ... as serving rather to pomp than to any edifying'.[11]

Having thus drawn attention to Somerset's loss of influence and position, Warwick began his long-planned attack on the heiress-presumptive, as if to make it clear that the Duke's support and his wife's friendship availed her nothing. Charles V had already provided the opportunity by a series of demands — hitherto courteously received but not acted upon — that his cousin should be allowed to celebrate Mass in her household. Warwick now inaugurated a systematized persecution of the Princess, using pressure on Edward to enforce her obedience and defy the

Emperor; he would not have done so if he had not been sure of his own predominance.

Although they met less regularly since his accession, Edward and Mary were still devoted to each other; but there was now a deeper gulf between the frail and melancholy woman of thirty-five and the boy of thirteen. The King's younger sister was described by an Elizabethan memoirist as his darling. 'There was between these two princes a concurrency and sympathy in their natures and affections,' he says, 'together with the celestial conformity in religion which made them one, and friends; for the King ever called her his sweetest and dearest sister, and was scarce his own man, she being absent, which was not so between him and the Lady Mary.'¹² It pleased the Protestant section to see Edward and Elizabeth in this happy light; from the comments of others who knew them equally well, a more complicated relationship may be perceived, in which Elizabeth's subtler intelligence and temperate Protestantism put her in the right, from her brother's point of view, while Mary's single-minded piety, caricaturing his own, created grief and disagreement, poisoning the last years of his life and deepening the shadow over hers. A fatal similarity of attitude towards their respective faiths made their disputes agonizing and pointless; meanwhile, their sufferings, although deplored, were accepted as inevitable by the partisans of either side, one section urging the brother to command, the other the sister to disobey; no one seems to have noticed that the resultant deadlock was being made permanent by this feverish persistence, creating scenes that began with reproaches and ended in recrimination.

Soon after he succeeded, Edward had told Mary that he would try to protect her from persecution. 'If you are troubled or molested,' he said, 'it is against my will, and I will see you contented.'¹³ Mary, realizing how powerless he then was, had made no complaints; she withdrew, preferring estrangement to dissension; when Warwick rose to command, she was forced into the open, and the fact that de Scheyfve, who had joined Van der Delft at the Spanish Embassy, made himself her champion on her imperial cousin's behalf, thrust upon her a more explicit and an infinitely more painful self-defence.

Edward began by an appeal to Elizabeth — surely she would

help him convert the sister of whom they were both so fond? Elizabeth appeared sympathetic; her Protestantism was irreproachable: but she would take no action, although she adapted herself to the prevailing trend by an outward simplicity that was dramatically effective on all public occasions; her plain dress and lack of jewels were much commented on, and her 'godly zeal' greatly admired.[14] Edward, whose acuteness was sometimes satirically expressed, referred to the Lady Elizabeth as 'my sweet sister Temperance', when she thus contrasted her unadorned youth and beauty with the splendours that emphasized Mary's fading looks.[15] At about this time, Elizabeth sent the King her portrait at his request, as 'not worthy the desiring for itself', adding, 'for the face I grant, I might well blush to offer, but the mind I shall never be ashamed to present', and ending her letter with a quotation from Horace.[16]

Such was the situation in the spring of 1550, when Mary had obtained leave from Edward to live quietly in the country so as to continue in the faith in which she had been brought up without offending him or drawing attention to herself. The celebration of Mass in her household had hitherto been winked at, and in return she had excused herself from spending the Christmas of 1549 with her brother. In April the Spanish Ambassador played into Warwick's hands by making a protest to some of the Council about the way she was being treated. One of the Lords replied: 'You talk much of the Lady Mary's conscience. You should consider that the King's conscience will receive a stain if he allow her to live in error ... ' and a heated argument ensued that ended by de Scheyfve threatening to complain to Edward. To Charles V he wrote: 'But as for speaking to the King, it is quite certain that he will only say what he is told to say. There is none about him, or among the gentlemen of the Bed-Chamber except those well known as partisans of the new doctrines. The King takes increasing pleasure in disputing and upholding the said doctrines, and there is no hope therefore that I may obtain anything from him. He would more likely pride himself on overthrowing my arguments.'[17] The envoy, who had just arrived in England, could not take in that this courteous and intelligent boy was as dedicated to his faith as the Lady Mary to hers; to the Catholic, these new doctrines were a fashionable craze that would not endure. The

Emperor seems to have shared this view; two months later he advised Edward to let his sister have her Mass until he was old enough to judge such matters for himself. It was all that was needed to spur Edward on to the enforcement of his authority. He made no comment when de Scheyfve and Van der Delft read him this message, merely referring them to the Council, and the envoys began to look for signs of dissension in the Court, with the result that they were able to report that a few persons still considered His Majesty 'the schismatic son of a schismatic father', born of a woman who had not been married according to the rites of Holy Church: another, casting his horoscope, had prophesied his death within the year.[18] Meanwhile, the Emperor was urging Mary to leave England and take refuge with him. When these plans for carrying off the heiress-presumptive were revealed to Edward, he began to consider the sterner measures recommended by the Council.

In September Mary was summoned to Windsor; she refused, on the grounds of health. Edward wrote to her suggesting that a change of air might do her good; she managed to postpone their meeting till the middle of December, when she visited him privately. Edward began by saying that he had heard 'strange rumours' about her Mass.

Agitation made Mary tactless. Instead of answering directly, she turned to Paulet, who with some of the Lords was in attendance, and asked him to take note of her reply. He approached, and with him Edward's step-uncle, William Parr (now Lord Northampton), Lord Rich, the Marquis of Dorset and two other noblemen. 'I declare', Mary then said, 'that the message I received from the Council through the Emperor's Ambassador [that the private celebration of Mass was permitted her] is true.' There was no answer, and in the pause that followed she began to cry. Edward tried to speak; then he also burst into tears. 'I think no harm of you ... ' he sobbed out. The courtiers, strangely moved, attempted to end the interview with a few soothing words; to Mary they said: 'His Majesty hath no other thought but to inquire and know all things.' 'His Majesty hath been hardened against me', exclaimed the Princess. When she was alone with the Lords, she went on: 'I hope His Grace will not be wroth with me, his poor suppliant, till he is of an age to judge for himself.' This quotation from the Emperor was disastrous; it resulted in an official and dictated letter from Edward of the kind he had sent to Gardiner, commanding her obedience. In his own hand, he added a postscript pointing out that exceptions had been made for far too long. 'I do but my duty,' it went on; 'my laws must be carried out. I could not suffer it to be otherwise as a true minister of God ... Truly, sister, I will not say more and worse things, because my duty would compel me to use harsher and angrier words ... but ... I will see my laws strictly obeyed.'[19] Mary replied humbly. She said that Edward's letter had made her very miserable, and reminded him of the promise made by the Council on his behalf; she rather foolishly implied that Edward had gone back on his word, and added: 'Your Majesty, praise the Lord, is gifted indeed with understanding far beyond that by others possessed at your age ... but both sides of the question are not brought before you ... Rather than go against my conscience I will lose my life. Yet I will live and die Your Majesty's most humble sister and loyal subject.'[20]

By the time this letter reached Edward, two of Mary's chaplains had been arrested and sent to the Tower for publicly celebrating Mass; and herein lay the quibble that was the basis of the Anglo-Spanish dispute. The Council understood private celebration to mean Mass heard by Mary alone; if all her household — some fifty persons — attended, the ritual became public, and punishable by law. It was now pointed out that divine punishment for this offence had already been visited on the nation through the new and terrible plague of the sweating sickness that by the end of January 1551 had killed nine hundred and fifty persons in London alone.[21] This disease — for which the slang terms were New Acquaintance and Know-Thy-Master[22] — first paralysed the limbs and caused agonizing pains all over the body; sweating then began from the head, making the hair stink and fall out; if, when the head was shaved, clippings fell into the eyes, blindness and death followed within three or four days.[23]

The death-rate shot up with the spring weather, intensifying the acrimony of religious and other dissensions; this may have had something to do with the formal summons of the Lady Mary to appear before the King and Council on March 16th. She rode into London in state, at the head of a great retinue of peers, knights and gentlemen-at-arms, whose loyalty to her and to the old faith was shown by the large rosaries they wore over their doublets. An answering demonstration came from the Catholic citizens who rushed out to cheer the procession from Fleet Street and along the Strand to the gates of the Palace of Whitehall. Supernatural support was observed by several Catholics in the form of armoured horsemen in the clouds, three suns appearing 'so that we could not tell which was the true sun', and a shaking of the earth throughout the city.[24]

It was characteristic of Mary to lend herself to an unnecessary and tactless demonstration, bound to irritate the Lords and upset her brother. Here bravery and defiance were out of place and extremely harmful to her cause; she could not have hoped for tolerance and kindness after thus drawing attention to Catholic feeling in the capital. Those who look for martyrdom are generally ready to inflict it; and Mary's rejection of a sensible and diplomatic approach, her apparent eagerness to suffer, may now be seen as a premonition of the attitude that was to make her reign so horrible and so disastrous to her faith.

The effect on Edward of her entry into London was cruelly distressing; she now appeared dangerously mistaken, a menace to his government and his religion. By the time he received her in the outer courtyard of the Palace it must have been borne in upon him that they were enemies, and that compromise and leniency were no longer possible, apart from the fact that since their last meeting the Emperor's pressure on him to allow her her Mass held hints and threats of a rupture that might end in attempted invasion or incitement to civil war.

When he had kissed and raised her from her knees, Edward led Mary into one of the galleries. She apologized for the delay caused by her illness. 'I am sorry God hath given me health and you sickness', he replied. Mary then dismissed her ladies and, turning to face Edward and the Council, waited for him to speak. He said: 'I wish to remind you of the letters sent you by my Lords.' 'I have received them', Mary answered, and there was silence for a moment or two.

Then the struggle began. Mary's conscious rectitude and Edward's uncompromising rejoinders reveal a common and perhaps unknowing self-identification with the father who had placed them on either side of an unbridgeable chasm. Surely the spirit of Henry VIII was evoked at that meeting, not only by reiterated appeals to his name and his laws, but by the tone of voice, the carriage and manner of his son and daughter. Both stood and moved as he had: in the faces of both — narrow-eyed, tight-lipped, formidable — his power was clearly marked, fine-drawn and fragile though they were.

One of the Lords opened the discussion by pointing out that no promise had been made to Her Grace about the public celebration of her Mass. She denied this, going over the disagreement of the year before, and recalling that everything had then been arranged to her brother's satisfaction, through the Spanish Ambassador. According to her own account — the only full one that survives — Edward admitted that this was true. She then complained of the Council's hectoring letters. 'I knew not of them ... ' Edward put in. 'In that case,' Mary rejoined, 'Your Majesty did not draw up the ordinances on the new religion.' Before Edward could reply another Councillor intervened. 'Your Grace will cause trouble by this obstinacy,' he said, 'although you had exemption from the said ordinances, it was not for always.' 'I had not understood so,' said the Princess; 'I pray your Lordships to wait until you should hear from the Emperor.' (She was referring to the Council's promise to de Scheyfve, who had now joined Charles V.) No reply was made to this, and she went on: 'I have always prayed for the King's prosperity and peace. As your Lordships have already praised His Majesty's great knowledge and understanding, then I will pray God that his virtues may increase.' Turning to Edward, she added: 'Riper age and experience will teach Your Majesty much more yet.' The patronizing tone was too much for Edward's self-control, and he replied sharply: 'You also may have somewhat to learn. None are too old for that.' 'It would be very hard for me to change my religion,' Mary answered, 'that in which the King my father bred me, and left me at his death.' One of the Council objected that the late King had altered many points in the faith before he died, and that if he had survived he would have done what was being done now. 'I will not speak of that,' said Mary, 'but I would that all had remained as it was.' She was told that she had been disobedient to her father's Will, and she retorted angrily: 'I have carefully read the Will, and am bound but on the point of my marriage. Your Lordships have said no Masses for the King my father's soul, as he commanded', she went on. 'That would be harmful to the King's Majesty and the state', was the answer. 'I know the King my father never ordered aught harmful to his present Majesty, because of his love for him. He cared more for the good of his kingdom than all his Council put together', said the Princess.

At this point Warwick said loudly: 'How now, my lady? It seemeth that Your Grace is trying to show us in a hateful light to the King our master without any cause whatsoever.' 'I have not come hither to do so,' said Mary, 'but you press me so hard I cannot dissemble.'

She then reverted to her Mass, using a more conciliatory tone. 'I have enough faith in the foresight and discretion of the King's Majesty and of his Council to hope that they will remember the ancient and close alliance between yourselves and the Emperor, and will await his reply.' Again she turned to Edward. 'I would have hoped', she went on, 'that because of the great and boundless goodness with which God hath endowed Your Majesty, and also because I am Your Majesty's near kindred and unworthy sister, that Your Majesty would have allowed me to continue in the old religion. There are but two things — soul and body. My soul I offer to God, and my body to Your Majesty's service. I would rather it pleased Your Majesty to take away my life than the old religion, in which I desire to live and die.' To this highly emotional appeal Edward replied as his father would have. 'I desire no such sacrifice', he said.

Some further and equally fruitless discussion ensued. At last the Princess said: 'I beg Your Majesty's leave to go — and that you give no credit to any who wish you to believe evil of me' — did she look towards Warwick as she said this? — 'I will always remain Your Majesty's humble, obedient and unworthy sister.' 'I do not doubt of that', said the King and there was another silence. Then he burst out: 'I have long suffered your Mass, in hope of your reconciliation. There now being no hope, unless we see some short amendment, I cannot bear it.' 'My soul is God's — my faith I will not change,' Mary repeated, 'nor dissemble my opinion with contrary doings.' 'I constrain not your faith,' said Edward; 'I will you not as a king to rule, but as a subject to obey.' She said nothing, and he went on: 'Your example might breed too much inconvenience.'

To this Mary could only reiterate her desire to withdraw. She was worn out and shaking with agitation. During the rest of that day and the following night she remained in the Palace, too exhausted to move or to see anyone but her ladies. A message came from Edward begging her to stay on; he was deeply concerned for her health. The Lords, following his lead, sent their compliments, and ventured to ask if Her Grace had perhaps changed her mind. To this she made no answer, but consented to receive their emissary, Dr Petre; she told him that she was in no state to continue the discussion, and once more asseverated her love and loyalty to her brother. Edward sent word that she might leave the Palace when she liked, or stay on till she felt better. She decided to go, and did so on the following day.[25]

Edward's diary contains the briefest possible résumé of this discussion; how deeply he felt it is shown by one alteration. 'She was called with my Council into a Chamber,' he wrote, 'where was declared how long I had suffered her Mass *against my will*, in hope of a reconciliation.' Afterwards he struck through the italicized words, thus making it clear that he would have liked to let Mary off, so long as her adherence to the old faith did not create a party that might overthrow the Reformation. This being Mary's hope and intention (she had never for a moment considered hearing her Mass alone) no settlement was possible; and although the Princess might appear, or even pose, as the defenceless victim of Protestant tyranny, she had, in fact, a much stronger backing, both within and without the kingdom, than those who were attacking her. For all her talk of giving her body for her faith, both she and Edward knew that this sacrifice would not be required of her; his dry response to her offer of martyrdom shows his awareness and resentment of her self-dramatization.

In the meantime, the Emperor, by way of a riposte to the assaults made on his cousin, had forbidden Morrison, the resident English Ambassador, to hear the Protestant service: none but Catholic ritual should be held in his dominions. The day after Mary left Westminster the Spanish Ambassadors asked to be received by the Council, to whom they gave their master's ultimatum. If the Princess Mary was not allowed her Mass, he would declare war on England.

Warwick, although apparently forced into an impossible posi-

tion — his negotiations for a French alliance had not yet material-
ized, and the Spanish conquest of England in its present state
would probably have been a matter of weeks — decided to tem-
porize; but he could only preserve his power, and his influence
with Edward, by maintaining his stand as the incorruptible and
fearless defender of the reformed religion.

As soon as the Spanish envoys had withdrawn and he and the
Council were left alone to concoct a reply, Warwick suggested
that this was a matter in which the clergy should be consulted;
no doubt he guessed that Cranmer, Ridley and their satellites
would be over-awed by the Emperor's threats, and that the onus
of yielding would thus fall on them, from Edward's and the Council's point of view.

The bishops asked for a day in which to consider the question.
The form in which it was put threw the whole weight of the decision on Edward. Might the King's Majesty, with a safe conscience, allow the Lady Mary her Mass in these dangerously altered
circumstances? It was then agreed that the subject should be
discussed by a general Council of bishops and peers.

Cecil was now in the habit of priming Edward before the Council meetings with such information as he thought necessary. On
this occasion he was not allowed to do so, and the King was not
summoned to the meeting until the decision recommended by the
bishops and agreed to by the Lords — that the Lady Mary should,
for some further, unspecified period, be allowed her Mass — had
been made.

Lord Darcy was then desired to request the King to attend the
Council without telling him what had happened. He did so in
great haste and agitation — 'as though his realm had already been
upon the sacking'. When Edward entered the Chamber, Paulet,
Marquis of Winchester, then Lord Treasurer, fell on his knees and
implored His Majesty to consider a change of tactics with regard
to his sister's disobedience; as the King stood there, silent and
amazed, the rest of the Council knelt before him, adding their
pleas to Winchester's.

Edward demanded an explanation. Charles V's 'very hot' letter
was read out by the Treasurer, who then said: 'I move Your
Majesty in any wise to agree to the Emperor's request', adding
his own opinion as to the dangers entailed by refusal; the Emperor,

he concluded, had been particularly displeased by the insolent proselytizing of Sir Richard Morrison, who had been so tactless as to give His Imperial Majesty a discourse on Protestantism during a recent audience, and had jocosely referred to the Pope as 'the Hollow Father'.

There was a short pause. Then Edward said: 'How are these perils grown? Why now, more than before?' Receiving no answer he went on: 'How may they be put off?' He was told that the first thing to do was to replace Morrison, and to this he agreed. Another Councillor added that the Lady Mary should be allowed her Mass for a time, at least. Edward said: 'I cannot do it at your advice — nor at any king's or kaiser's, for your entreaty.'

It was now Cranmer's turn to use the precedents of Scripture. 'There were good kings in the Old Testament that suffered ill alterations, and yet were good kings ... ' he began: but was 'roundly' interrupted by his godson. 'As examples are good and have God to allow them,' said the King, 'so are evil examples set out, to warn us.' Edward would have done better to quote to the Archbishop his coronation address; but all his life he had been trained to answer one biblical allusion with another, and his replies came out trippingly. 'Abraham lay with Agar, his maid,' he said; 'David took Uriah's wife to him, and to hide his adultery committed a murder — did they this that we should think it lawful to do it, or doth Scripture make mention of it that any should do as they did?' There was no reply, and he went on: 'My lord, if you will have me grant you this suit, you must show me — by Scripture — that I may do it, and then let me be accounted wilful if I be not as glad to put off all such mischiefs that are like to happen in England as any King that ever lived in England.' Again it was urged that the danger was great, the risk not to be taken — and by the very man who in the most solemn hour of his life had bade Edward take up the sword against the power of the Pope in all his dominions. 'I require you to fear God with me,' Edward burst out, 'and rather to contemn any peril than to set aside God's will to please an Emperor!' Something was said about danger to trade: but the boy stormed on. 'It is not two days since', he exclaimed, 'that we had in our Psalms a complaint against His people, that they had broken His covenant as their forefathers did — when God heard this, He was wroth. He gave His people over to the sword, for He was wroth ... ' he repeated, as if the blankness of the faces around him must be illumined by his own convictions.

No one said anything. Edward adopted the heartening tone that was characteristic of his family in a crisis. 'The Emperor is a man liker to die himself any day than to do us any great harm,' he urged, 'how much soever he mean it. But if he live, and mean us never so much, we must wait upon God's will, and commit the event of things to His wisdom.' Then, as if the thought of being overborne by a foreigner and a papist must rouse his advisers as it had stirred him, he exclaimed: 'If the Emperor speak but in sport to see whether I be knit to my religion or not, I should stain it, and shame myself... if the Emperor mean good earnest, God, I hope, meaneth but to taste us in sport, and will give us stomach to serve him where we ought, and to gratify the Emperor where we may. I know,' he added, reverting to the language of the school-room, 'God is able to defend me against as many Emperors as ever the world had, if they came all at once with as many men as they had in all their whole times!'

The lack of response to this appeal roused his anger once more and he resumed his imperious tone: 'The Emperor is no warrant to you to stir me to that you ought not, nor no discharge to me. I will choose, by your leave' — trying to achieve the correctly courteous manner — 'the surer side, most certain that the Emperor hath no help for me.'

At this point the fearful risks and the possibility of a compromise seem to have been reiterated; but Edward would not be shaken. 'You see,' he said, 'the Emperor himself might learn at the last by his continual disease that there are in him things which God doth reckon better punished than borne withal.' Sure of his own youth and vigour, he went on, with unconscious irony: 'At the least, if he will not learn, let his arms teach us not to fall into God's hands, Who hath made the days of kings a span long — their lives are as nothing before Him.' It was all so simple: those who had God on their side had nothing to fear from the Emperor's battalions; and Edward can have felt no surprise when Cranmer and Ridley, defeated by their own teaching, gave up the argument.

The Lords were not so scrupulous; they renewed persuasion on other grounds — peril to His Majesty's sacred person, as well as to the state — inexorably enough to make Edward feel that his much vaunted prerogative was not, as he had begun to believe, supreme. Even then he stood out, saying desperately: 'I must do as God giveth me in commandment. God would chastise me for breaking His will.' They managed, somehow, to drive him into a corner, and he began to waver, still protesting: 'He that preserved David will preserve me from harm. I would spend my life, and all that I have, rather than agree to what I know certainly to be against the truth.' Someone may have pointed out that his life was not his own to give, and that all that he had was the charge of the realm, for suddenly he broke down, saying: 'I will shed my tears for both.'

Cranmer, seeing him in such distress, tried to make things better by reassurance; but Edward's 'tender heart', says an eye-witness, 'burst out into bitter weeping and sobbing'. The day when as God's Vice-Regent and Christ's Vicar he had given a king's word to see idolatry destroyed and the tyranny of the Bishop of Rome banished from his subjects was now deprived of awe and splendour. 'Be content ... be content ... ' he sobbed. 'Let me alone.'

How the scene closed is not recorded. Cranmer, coming out of the Council Chamber and finding Cheke in one of the ante-rooms, took him by the hand, and said: 'Ah! Master Cheke, you may be glad all the days of your life that you have such a scholar, for he hath more divinity in his little finger than we have in our whole bodies.' There is some self-reproach in the phrase; but the Archbishop used the wrong word: if Edward had acquired less logic and more divinity, he would have accepted compromise as lightly as any of his advisers; indeed, this painfully literal demonstration of all that the pupil had learned was to become an inescapable and treasured memory for his tutor, long after the King's short day had run its span and the invalid Emperor still lived and reigned.[26] Edward's diary sums up the situation in this entry: 'The Emperor's Ambassador came with short message from his master of war, if I would not suffer his cousin the Princess to use her Mass. To this no answer was given at this time.'[27] The bishops' public statement was a masterpiece of prevarication. 'Although to give licence to sin is sin,' it ran, 'yet if all possible haste is observed, to suffer and wink at it for a time may be borne.'[28]

So the inevitable compromise was reached. The Council saved

their faces and a shred of their master's honour by informing the imperial envoys that later on they would have to insist on the Lady Mary's obedience to her brother, as the first of his subjects; while the new English Ambassador, Wotton, managed to placate the Emperor by stressing that aspect of the Princess's duty. Charles replied that Edward ought to respect her beliefs; unofficially, he was assured that she would be allowed to use her Mass, and he became less severe. 'I hope His Majesty will be lenient — I have much affection for him,' he said; 'I would he would return to the faith. I trust', he added, 'that His Majesty will submit to reason.'[29]

For the next few months the brother and sister continued the struggle in a characteristic manner. When another letter from Edward commanding Mary to discontinue the public celebration of her Mass was brought to her by the Chancellor, she received it on her knees, and kissed the superscription before she read the contents. Then she said: 'Rather than use any other service than what was used at the death of the late King my father, I would lay my head upon the block — but I am unworthy to suffer in so good a quarrel. When the King comes to such an age as he may be able to judge these things himself, His Majesty shall find me ready to obey his orders in religion.' Getting up, she went on: 'But in these years of his — though, good, sweet King, he hath more knowledge than any other of his years — yet it is not possible he should be judge of them.' Aware, now, that she had the whip-hand of the Council, she answered their warnings with defiance. 'I know that you desire my death, in spite of your fair words', she said, and, kneeling again, gave Lord Rich a ring for her brother, with her 'very humble recommendation'. She concluded: 'I will die his true subject, and suffer and obey his commandment in all things, except in these matters of religion.'[30]

It was at about this time that Edward's 'princely gravity and majesty' became more noticeable during his public audiences.[31] The Venetian Ambassador described how methodically and quickly he would divide what was said to him under separate headings, answering each in turn.[32] To some of the foreign preachers he was able to speak more naturally. 'How can the Bishop of Rome's authority be made extinct?' he asked Bucer, who replied that the Messiah was not yet come.[33]

Another visiting divine observed that the good Earl of Warwick was always with the King, adding: 'He is like a father to His Majesty — and governs all.'[34]

NOTES TO CHAPTER XI

[1] Harleian MSS, 353; Strype, *Life of Sir John Cheke*, p. 179.
[2] *Lit. Rem.*, vol. II, p. cxxxvii.
[3] Ibid.
[4] Heylyn, pp. 90-1; *Original Letters*, 2nd ser., p. 542; *Lit. Rem.*, vol. I, p. cxl.
[5] Halliwell-Philipps, vol. II, pp. 44-7.
[6] Heylyn, p. 93.
[7] Foxe, vol. V, p. 747.
[8] Ibid.
[9] Strype, *Ecclesiastical Memorials*, vol. I, part 2, p. 388.
[10] Burnet, vol. III, part 1, p. 249.
[11] Privy Council Records, vol. II, p. 129.
[12] Naunton, *Fragmenta Regalia*, p. 14.
[13] Clifford, p. 62.
[14] *Original Letters*, 1st ser., p. 76.
[15] Ibid.
[16] C. Jones, *Recollections of Royalty*, vol. I, p. 241.
[17] *Cal. Span. P.*, vol. X, p. 98.
[18] Ibid., p. 100.
[19] Ibid., p. 209.
[20] Ibid., p. 210.
[21] Holinshed, p. 1031.
[22] Greyfriars, p. 70.
[23] Rapin de Thoyras, vol. VII, p. 67.
[24] Machyn's *Diary*, p. 11; Greyfriars.
[25] *Cal. Span. P.*, vol. X, p. 247; *Lit. Rem.*, vol. II, p. 387.
[26] Harleian MSS, 353; Foxe, vol. V, p. 701; Strype, *Life of Sir John Cheke*, p. 178.
[27] *Lit. Rem.*, vol. II, p. 387.
[28] *Cal. Span. P.*, vol. X, p. 307.
[29] Harleian MSS, 353.
[30] *Cal. Span. P.*, vol. X, p. 247.
[31] Foxe, vol. V, p. 702.
[32] Ibid., p. 700.
[33] Hopf, *Martin Bucer and the English Reformation*, p. 20.
[34] *Original Letters*, 1st ser., p. 99.

CHAPTER TWELVE

THE FRENCH ALLIANCE

FROM the spring of 1551 to that of 1553 Warwick's power was at its height, and one political triumph succeeded another, in spite of the fact that such national prosperity as remained after Somerset's administration was crumbling away. If he had been able to continue his dictatorship Warwick would probably have tried to set in hand the rehabilitation of the country; but he had to consolidate his own position first, and one of the ways in which he did so was by eschewing the outward and official signs of authority, with the result that to those beyond the Court circle he was a shadowy, although sinister, figure. In his letters there is no hint of his personality; neither wit, charm, intellect nor force emerges from a correspondence that reveals colourless efficiency, strict Protestantism, diligent politeness and little else. This refusal to stand in the limelight was of course partly the foundation of his success; it helped to maintain the impression that he was neither self-seeking nor vain-glorious. In private life, his impact on those who knew him as well and saw as much of him as Edward, Somerset, Cranmer and Cheke, was overwhelming. To the end of his reign, Edward believed in Warwick's sincerity; Somerset, even when he became aware of his intentions, did not gauge his ruthlessness; Cranmer partially followed his lead in religious reform; and Cheke lent himself to, while not always approving, his manœuvres to retain Edward's loyalty. This was to some extent ensured by the graces and talents that set off Warwick's serious side, and made him the ideal companion for an intelligent and lively boy. Unlike Somerset, who had been often preoccupied, sometimes irritable and generally over-earnest, Warwick always had time for talks, games, theological debates, for unobtrusive support on public occasions, and for the subtly flattering sympathy and encouragement on which the King grew to depend.

Yet even Warwick, tireless though he was, could not have sustained the part of the perfect friend and adviser without an intermediary. This was John Gates, who was knighted and made

Vice-Chamberlain to the Household and Councillor in April 1551; in fact, he took Fowler's place, thus protecting Warwick from the jealousy and back-biting that would have arisen if he himself had been constantly alone with Edward. Gates reported to Warwick all the trivial and gossiping talk that he heard when the King got up and went to bed. Warwick seldom or never saw Edward alone until everyone else was asleep; then they had long, secret conversations. And in the morning, when His Majesty entered the Council Chamber, his initiative and grasp of detail amazed and sometimes perturbed his ministers.[1]

The fact that these discussions deprived Edward of sleep, alternately over-stimulating and exhausting his energy, was not commented on, possibly because his physicians and tutors did not know about them. Edward himself took a very natural pleasure in this nocturnal coaching, and came to rely on it in ratio to the difficulties and responsibilities that increased with every month of his reign.

Warwick also provided for Edward's distractions and amusements in a characteristically ingenious manner. A week after the King's breakdown in front of the Council, plans were made for him to lead a team of his Gentlemen of the Bedchamber against the same number of noblemen at archery, tilting and running at the ring in a series of matches. In his diary Edward noted the results: 'The first day of the challenge at base, or running, the King won … ' is followed by: 'I lost the challenge of shooting at rounds and won at rovers.' A month later the record of the semi-finals opens with: 'First came the King, sixteen footmen and ten horsemen in black silk coats pulled out with white taffety; then all the Lords, having three men likewise apparelled; and all gentlemen, their footmen in white fustian pulled out with black taffety. The other side came all in yellow taffety; at length the yellow band took it thrice in a hundred and twenty courses.' Then came disappointment — and some private criticism of the umpire: 'And my band touched often, which was counted as nothing, and took never, which seemed strange, and so was of my side lost.'[2] Edward did not report the result of the finals; losing at the ring was what mattered most.

As St George's Day drew near, Edward set himself to reconsider the ceremonial of the Order of the Garter. Here again Warwick's forethought may be perceived. The King's delight in pageantry was overcast by his dislike of 'popish' ritual. It therefore seems as if Warwick suggested that he should reform the service in all its aspects on Protestant lines, and this he proceeded to do. His three drafts for this task, one in Latin and two in English, are evidently the work of many happy hours. He decided that, as to honour a saint was superstitious, St George's Day 'shall no more be so called ... but it shall be called Order of the Garter, or Defence of the Truth wholly contained in Scripture'. The Garter itself was still to be worn below the knee; but instead of the saint and the dragon, a new design was worked out by the thirteen-year-old reformer, of a crowned horseman holding in one hand a sword 'piercing a book, on which shall be written *Verbum Dei* and on the sword *Protectio*, and in the other hand a shield on which shall be written *Fides* — which device shall have a Garter about it, on which shall be written ... ' What? For some time Edward could not make up his mind how revolutionary he was going to be. Finally, as there was no hint of popery or superstition in the famous trope of Edward III, he allowed it to stand; and the strange anomaly of *Honi Soit Qui Mal Y Pense* as a comment on a knight spearing a Bible, was the result. Later on Edward rewrote the ceremony of the oaths, and worked out a scheme of charities for 'maimed or hurt soldiers' from the subscriptions of the members. His final draft was of great length, running into thirty-seven items.[3]

Tactfully — it is to be hoped — the manufacture of His Majesty's new device for the Garter was postponed, no doubt on grounds of economy, and St George and his dragon remained as they are today; some of his alterations in the service were used, and on April 23rd, 1551, he came out of the chapel of Greenwich Palace in a slightly critical mood. Somerset, Warwick, the Lord Treasurer Paulet and a number of other noblemen were with him.

'My lords,' Edward began, 'I pray you, what saint is St George, that we here so honour him?' Silence followed this provocative question. Neither Somerset nor Warwick, who should have taken the initiative, ventured to reply. Then Paulet said, rather lamely: 'If it please Your Majesty, I did never read in any history of St George — but only in the *Legenda Aurea*, where it is thus set down, that St George out with his sword, and ran the dragon through with his spear.'

The picture of a rider drawing a sword with one hand and spearing a dragon with the other was too much for Edward. The majestic gravity that characterized his public manner gave way, and there, in the cloister of the chapel, he burst into peals of laughter; indeed, says an eye-witness: 'he could not a great while speak for laughing' — the elderly Lord Treasurer standing by in respectful but offended silence. At last Edward, having recovered some composure, pursued: 'I pray you, my lord, and what did he with his sword the while?' 'That I cannot tell Your Majesty', Paulet coldly replied. 'And so an end', says the courtier who records this interchange, 'of the question of good St George.'[4]

More important reforms were now being put in hand by Cranmer and Warwick. Tables replaced altars; the clergy were encouraged to preach against the Virgin, the Princess Mary and the popery of Henry VIII; Lenten fasting was allowed only on the grounds of support to the fishing trade.[5] Meanwhile, Cranmer's visitation of the bishoprics revealed that out of two hundred and forty-nine incumbents in one diocese ten could not repeat the Ten Commandments, ten did not know the Lord's Prayer, thirty did not know who wrote it, and twenty-seven could not find it in the Prayer Book; sixty-two did not reside in their parishes, and nearly all were pluralists. As for the bishops themselves, Edward noted that 'some for sloth, some for luxury, were not fit to sit in their places'.[6] Alarmed and disgusted though they were by Warwick's reforms, the more perspicacious Catholic envoys found much to praise in the English administration, in spite of the fact that the late King's arrangements were being rescinded, and that 'everything', according to Barbaro, the Venetian Ambassador, who made a full report in May 1551, 'was going from bad to worse. Nor doth aught remain,' he went on, in that part of his statement dealing with the Council, 'save the reputation of the present King, who is of a good disposition, and the whole realm hopes the best from him, as he is handsome, affable, of becoming stature, seems to be liberal, beginneth to interest himself with public business and in bodily exercises, literary studies and knowledge of languages, appearing to surpass his contemporaries and the standards of his age'. Barbaro did not think that the fall of the government was in question, in spite of its inefficiency, and the 'fickleness' of the English, who 'love their King, and put up with anything to retain him, especially if he keepeth the promises made to them'. But, he added, one could be sure of nothing, in the case of a people 'who do one thing today and another tomorrow', except that on one point all classes appeared to agree: 'whether of the old or new religion, detestation of the Pope is so great that no one can bear to hear him mentioned.' He went on to praise the militia, the navy and the Parliamentary system, but complained that his chaplain was prevented from celebrating Mass and that the foreign heretics were dominating the ecclesiastical administration.[7]

Edward's share in this reorganization was not confined to the religious side. The scene with the Council about his half-sister's Mass had brought home to him the need to strengthen the kingdom through economical reforms; and in addition to his studies on the currency and the foreign markets, he drew up in his own hand new rules for expenditure on dress. No husbandman was to wear any dyed cloth, 'nor leather tanned nor dressed out of the realm'; no one having an income of less than £100 a year could wear satin, damask, ostrich feathers or fur; no one possessing less than £220 a year could buy cambric, or any fur trimming but lamb, or cloth costing more than ten shillings a yard.[8] Many of these rules had been set forth by Henry VIII, and disregarded by his subjects, as they were by Edward's; and when Latimer, who was on the point of retiring, made a final appeal against extravagance and greed, it was ignored, in spite of the fact that he urged frugality and common sense in the King's name and 'for his honour'. The English passion for display was not to be curbed, although their favourite preacher's Christmas sermon combined homeliness and censure in his most persuasive style: 'But I warrant you, there was many a jolly damsel at that time in Bethlehem, yet amongst them all there was no one found that would humble herself so much as once to go and see poor Mary in the stable, and to comfort her — no, no! They were too fine to take such pains ... They had their bracelets and farthingales, and were trimmed with all manner of fine and costly raiment, like as there are many now-a-days amongst us ... I think indeed Mary never had a farthingale ... for in the old time women were content with honest and single garments. Now they have found out these round-abouts — the devil was not so cunning as to make such then ... '[9]

These diatribes drew attention to the grants of land and money and the ostentatious splendour that even the circumspect Warwick acquired with every shift in the political scene. Somerset was the only great noble whose magnificence was not resented by the common people; he was still so popular that his presence on the Council board and his voice in public affairs could not be eliminated without a split that might destroy the whole structure of the government. Herein lay his own danger, and the source of Warwick's enmity. Whatever Warwick did, he could not command the support of those who still called his defeated rival their good Duke, thus implying that Somerset could have done better. The admiration of the foreign preachers and the backing of the extreme Protestant minority compared poorly with the loyalty of a nation.

Warwick therefore began to look for support outside the kingdom through a new French alliance, as being the only way to prove to his critics within it, as well as to the Emperor, that England was indispensable to the balance of power. He reopened the negotiations for the marriage of Edward with Henry II's daughter. Warwick's advances were more cordially received than those of the late King; since 1548 the Emperor's acquisition of the states of Parma and Piacenza and his installation of his son Philip as Sovereign of the Netherlands had caused a breach with Pope Paul III, whose son Pier Luigi, formerly ruler of the Italian provinces, had been murdered during the Germano-Spanish invasion; the Pope had allied himself with Henry II against the Emperor, and both desired English support, considering the domination of Charles V to be more undesirable than the spread of heresy.[10] So the scene was set for Warwick's diplomatic move, of which Edward's marriage was the pretext — one that could in its turn be abandoned if it injured Warwick's jurisdiction at home.

After much correspondence an exchange of honours was agreed on, as the preliminary to discussions about the Princess's dowry. The Dauphin was already Edward's godson; Henry II was now invested with the Order of the Garter: he replied by sending a special mission with the order of St Michael for Edward.

The arrangements for the visit of the ambassadors were at first postponed and subsequently complicated by the continuance of the sweating sickness. In April, rumours that Edward had succumbed made it necessary for him to appear in public for several hours at a time; in full armour he rode through the city and afterwards took part in a military review to which the people were admitted.[11] In July the young Duke of Suffolk died of it; he had been one of the King's closest companions, and his death plunged the whole Court into gloom. It was therefore decided that the French envoys should be received and the investiture held at Hampton Court; those about him hoped that Edward would be distracted by the bustle of preparation. Just before the mission arrived the resident French Ambassador noticed how strenuously Edward practised his tilting and riding, and complimented him on his prowess. But the King's standards, set against those of older and more expert companions, had always been higher than his achievements. 'It is but a small beginning,' Edward said, 'and as time passes I hope to do better.'[12]

The entries in Edward's journal for July 1551 show that his grief for Suffolk and his disappointment about the Princess Mary did not destroy his interest in the preparations. He describes how 'church stuff, [such] as mitres, golden missals and primers ... and relics' was melted down and made into services for the banquets. But, as soon as the Frenchmen landed, 'came the sweat into London, which was more vehement than the old sweat. For if one took cold, he died within three hours, and if he "scaped", it held him but nine hours, or ten, at the most. Also, if he slept the first six hours, as he should be very desirous to do, then he raved, and should die raving. It grew so much', Edward goes on, 'that I removed to Hampton Court with a very few with me.'

Henry II sent over three envoys: Jacques d'Albon (Marshal de St André), François de Rohan de Gyé, and Edward's old acquaintance, de Vieilleville, whose secretary, Carloix, was still in his service, and who left a more detailed account of the celebrations than that of four years before. This time, there were so many guests that they were separately lodged; de Gyé at Westminster, de Vieilleville, as before, at Durham Place, and St André at Richmond Palace. Carloix seems to have circulated between the three; he accompanied the united embassy to Hampton Court, arriving there at nine o'clock on the morning of July 14th.

Here they were received by the Duke of Somerset and twelve other noblemen, who escorted them into the Presence-Chamber, where Edward was seated under his canopy of state. When the Ambassadors had made their reverences, he stood up and said, in excellent French: 'My lords, you are welcome for three reasons — One, thus is confirmed in perpetuity a good peace between my brother of France and myself: Two, it enables me to meet the Grand Marshal, whom I have so long wanted to see: and Three, that you all, being witnesses of the oath of loyalty I shall take towards your King, will remember how it will be kept — for I know that your lordships are so high in his favour that you can make him both love and hate you as you will. *Vous soyez encore, M. le Maréchal, le mieux que très bien venu.*' He then took the letters of Henry II and, after some formal conversation, the guests were conducted to their rooms, where they remained till dinner-time.

After dinner St André had a private talk with the King. He began by asking His Majesty if he was determined to continue in the new religion, to which Edward replied: 'I must consult with my Council before giving your lordship an answer.' St André went on: 'I come not only for delivery of the Order, but also to declare the great friendship the King my master beareth to Your Majesty — I would Your Majesty would think it to be such as a father beareth to his son.' Edward replied that he would so receive it, and the Ambassador continued: 'Although there are divers persuasions — as I think — to dissuade Your Majesty from the friendship of the King my master, yet I trust Your Majesty will not believe them.' (He referred to the Spaniards, who wished to prevent the alliance, and had already made disagreeable comments on the 'meagreness' of Edward's hospitality.) 'As good ministers on the frontiers do great good,' St André added, 'so do ill, much harm.' Having thus delicately brought up the question of the Calais-Boulogne fortresses and the dispute of four years ago, he went on: 'I implore Your Majesty to let no innovation be made on things so long in controversy by hand-strokes — but rather, by commissioners' talks.' According to his custom, Edward replied to each demand in turn. 'I thank your lordship for His Majesty's Order,' he said, 'and also for his love. I will show like love in all points. For rumours,' he added, 'they are not always to be believed. I sometimes provide for the worst, but never do any harm upon a hearing. As for commissioners — I would rather appease their controversies with words than do anything by force.' St André declared himself perfectly satisfied with this answer.[13]

A day passed between this interview and the ceremony of the

investiture. By this time, de Gyé, de Vieilleville and St André were all assembled at Richmond. De Gyé then informed his companions that secret instructions from France had just reached him. He was not to eat any English food; everything necessary was being sent over, via Boulogne and Dover, to the Palace.

Neither St André nor de Vieilleville had received this warning; they pointed out that if de Gyé followed it he would cause great offence. The conclusion, although not stated by Carloix, becomes obvious. If Henry II's government had really believed that his envoys were likely to be poisoned, they would have issued similar instructions to the other two contingents, above all, to St André, who headed the mission. In fact, de Gyé must have heard the usual alarming rumours about English cookery, and had made his arrangements before he left; for, as soon as he and his suite were installed at Richmond, provisions began to arrive from the coast. When asked whether his English attendants were not deeply wounded by these precautions, de Gyé replied that they were envious, merely, of the superior quality of French food, as being so much more delicate and varied than any they could provide. De Gyé was in his turn much annoyed at being asked not to allow his chaplain to celebrate Mass in public during his stay. His gentlemen — among whom was the future resident envoy, M. de Theligny du Bois-Daulphin — continued to feast on their imported diet, regardless of the effect on their hosts. Very soon the talk caused by this discourtesy reached Hampton Court. It was decided to ignore de Gyé's rudeness, although feeling was beginning to run high.[14]

On the 16th the ceremony of investiture took place. The three envoys, preceded by their gentlemen carrying the robes and the Order, entered the Presence-Chamber of Hampton Court to find the English nobles so gorgeously arrayed as to be, according to Carloix, 'unrecognizable'. He describes Edward as 'an angel in human form; for it was impossible', he explains, 'to imagine a more beautiful face and figure, set off by the brilliance of jewels and robes, and a mass of diamonds, rubies and pearls, emeralds and sapphires — they made the whole room look as if lit up'. What with the combined splendour of the French and the English courtiers, *'ce n'était que rayons, étincellement et éclairs, qui éblouissaient la vue des regardants'*.

Edward then proceeded into the chapel, walking between St André and de Gyé, where he received the Communion while they looked on. The Bible was presented to him; laying his hand on it, he swore to be faithful to his oath as Knight of the Holy Order of St Michael. St André hung the Order with its chain of scallop-shells round his neck. To the sound of trumpets and drums, the French and English nobles embraced one another; Carloix observed that many on both sides were in tears.

At last the whole procession passed slowly from the chapel, down the great staircase, to the Banqueting Hall. The banquet was followed by tilting and a concert; then the envoys withdrew. Two days later another feast was held, and a tournament, after which St André attended Edward in his private apartments while he changed his clothes for supper. Next morning he was asked to the King's rising and shown the State Bedchamber — its Holbein paintings, Italian murals and tapestries of scenes from Scriptures. Passing through the Queen's Long Gallery with its heraldically painted glass on either side, the King and his guests came into the courtyard where the horses were waiting. They spent the morning hunting, and then, 'He saw me shoot,' Edward recorded, 'and saw all my guard shoot together.'[15] The dinner that followed was less formal; after it, he played to the ambassadors on the lute; that same evening they all met again for supper.

On July 23rd the final reception was held, during which the new resident envoy was to be presented to the King. This party went on for several hours and Carloix noted that Edward looked tired; nothing was spared him: but he rose to all demands with grace and good humour, speaking Spanish, French, Italian or Latin to each of the foreign envoys, as his nationality required; later on, Carloix and his comrades agreed that His Majesty was over-worked.

Edward was standing with St André, de Gyé and de Vieilleville, when Carloix heard him say to the Marshal: 'Although, to my great regret, you are taking M. de Gyé back to France with you, will you not leave with me M. de Vieilleville in his place?' 'Alas, no, Sire.' 'Who, then?' Edward asked. 'A gentleman named M. de Theligny du Bois-Daulphin. I beg Your Majesty to let me present him.'

Edward glanced towards de Theligny du Bois-Daulphin, who

was standing a few feet away; he was enormously tall and very fat. After a moment's contemplation, Edward drew the three ambassadors aside, and said, smiling: 'You will bring me to shame through this Ambassador — for, *not finding in this country the delicate food he is used to in France*, he will waste away, which will be a constant reproach to me.'

The answer to this little bit of teasing was a burst of laughter, in which Edward joined. He was still laughing when the monumental figure of M. de Theligny du Bois-Daulphin was brought up to him. His Majesty held out his hand to be kissed, Carloix observed, '*avec un visage riant et très joyeux*'. Then they all trooped out into the great courtyard to see the fireworks.[16]

There was a good deal of haggling over the Princess's dowry; when the bargain had been concluded, Edward set down all the negotiations in his journal, adding: 'Thirdly, it was agreed that if I died, she should not have the dote, saying they did that for friendship, without precedent.'[17]

After that, the festivities were resumed at Windsor, where the envoys, having been entertained by Warwick and some of the other nobles in London, came to make their farewells. At their last interview Edward presented St André with two hundred mules; two dozen were harnessed in velvet and leather of different colours with gilt bridles and spurs, 'especially made for us, and quite new', noted Carloix. Edward said to the Marshal: 'I must tell you, my lord, that every year I shall seek to maintain this peace afresh, and I pray your lordship to help me to do so. It will be no new thing — for many other English kings have had this pleasure. And now, we must care for some treaty of trade, that we may benefit both our countries.' Turning to de Vieilleville, he went on: 'I hope your lordship will return. I am sorry you may not tarry.' 'I ask nothing better, Your Majesty,' the envoy replied, 'if I had but the power to remain, I would so do.' In order of precedence, the ambassadors and all their attendants came forward to kiss the King's hand; as Carloix did so he saw a look on the boy's face that he could not get out of his mind; he took it to mean that His Majesty was grieved to see the last of them. As they turned to go, Edward took a diamond ring from his finger (in his diary he noted that it was valued at £150) and putting it on St André's, said: 'This is for your lordship's pains — and also for my memory.'[18]

From Windsor the envoys travelled to Richmond, where Warwick was waiting to escort them to London; he gave St André two
more mules and a couple of hounds, with magnificent trappings
and collars; then they all sat down to a great dinner. They reached
Durham Place next day and went down the river to Greenwich,
whence an escort of English ships accompanied them to Dover.
St André told de Vieilleville that he had been quite overcome by
the kindness and charm of their hosts. They reverted to Warwick's
prescience; how could he have known that in four years Somerset's power would be eclipsed? They had been so taken with the
intelligence and power of this extraordinary man that they forgot
to criticize either his Protestantism or his sharp practice over the
Princess's dowry; in fact, they left England in a daze of benevolence and hope. Edward's gay and tactful tolerance of de Gyé's
bad manners, his generosity, thoughtfulness and intellectual range
remained in Carloix's memory for many years. But it was a pity,
they all agreed, that His Majesty seemed to be living under a
constant strain.[19]

Cheke also had observed the pressure that was being put upon
his pupil, and tried to reduce it by standing between him and the
attentions of the visiting preachers, who were beginning to make
too many claims on the King's time and energy. The tutor asked
a party of them to dinner, and implied that they would do better
to approach His Majesty through him. To an English friend, he
said gloomily: 'The people's esteem of His Majesty will destroy
him — and then his Reformation will be overthrown.' Yet he
could not prevent Edward giving a great deal of thought to these
new protégés; the King insisted on giving one a gold piece for his
birthday, and another a stove, constructed after the German
fashion, because he found English houses draughty. Edward
continued to read and make notes on nearly all the books they sent
him, and listened to their lectures and sermons with the same
interest.[20]

A month after the departure of the French envoys Warwick
defeated Cheke's attempt to lighten Edward's burdens by suggesting that the King should sign all the principal resolutions
passed by the Council, without reference to any of his other advisers; this necessitated Edward's attendance at many more
meetings than formerly; he took up his new duties with immense

enthusiasm. When the Chancellor, Lord Rich, refused to pass some commission without the signatures that usually followed it, the King spoke to him angrily. His signature, his authority, sufficed. Three months later, Warwick told Rich that the Councillors were expected to subscribe to everything that His Majesty approved. The Lord Chancellor began to consider resigning. Long experience of statecraft and intrigue had taught Rich rather to feel than to know when a storm was brewing; on this occasion he was one of the few who managed to take shelter before it burst.

NOTES TO CHAPTER XII

[1] Pollard, *History of England from the Accession of Edward VI to the Death of Elizabeth*, p. 59.
[2] *Lit. Rem.*, vol. II, p. 317.
[3] Ibid., pp. 511-37.
[4] Ibid., vol. I, p. ccclxxx; Foxe, vol. VI, p. 21.
[5] *Ven. S.P.*, vol. V, p. 342.
[6] Strype, *Ecclesiastical Memorials*, vol. II, part 1, p. 79.
[7] *Ven. S.P.*, vol. V, p. 342.
[8] *Lit. Rem.*, vol. II, p. 492.
[9] *Sermons*, p. 84.
[10] Pastor, *History of the Popes*, vol. XII, pp. 371-2.
[11] Machyn, p. 18.
[12] *Cal. Span. P.*, vol. X, p. 288.
[13] Carloix, pp. 106-10.
[14] Ibid.
[15] *Lit. Rem.*, vol. II, p. 332.
[16] Carloix, pp. 106-10; *Lit. Rem.*, vol. II, p. 333.
[17] Ibid., p. 334.
[18] Carloix, pp. 106-10.
[19] Ibid.
[20] *Original Letters*, 2nd ser., p. 652; Hopf, p. 16.

✠

CHAPTER THIRTEEN

THE EXECUTION OF THE DUKE OF SOMERSET

D URING the week of Edward's fourteenth birthday, which was also the first anniversary of Warwick's rise to power, the Spanish Ambassador reported that His Majesty had become very thin and delicate.[1] Some allowance must be made for de Scheyfve's anxiety about the French alliance; naturally he wished to give the impression that the King was no longer a desirable match. And the fact that Edward was now growing fast, and beginning to lose the rounded outlines of childhood, may have contributed towards an apparent fragility that is not borne out by his own account of his activities; he was working and playing with his usual zest. There is no doubt, however, that he was oppressed by responsibility and disappointment. This was shown by a stricter reserve, a more impenetrable self-command. After the burst of tears about the Emperor's threats that sprang from the realization that he was not to be allowed to do his duty, he did not again give way in public; he may have done so when he was alone with some confidant; there is no record of it. And in the weeks that followed his fourteenth birthday, it became more necessary than ever for him to control, if not to conceal, his deeper feelings. As for entrusting them to his journal, that was now quite out of the question.

It is, therefore, impossible to assess what Edward felt about his uncle Somerset at this time; absorbed in new duties, marriage plans, and civil and religious reforms, he may well have ceased to think of him, except as part of the machine that he himself, with Warwick's help, was controlling. Four years had passed since he had said to Thomas Seymour that it were better the Duke should die — a judgment made in panic and confusion of mind. Since then, Somerset had again alarmed him, and again reinstated himself; so that what lay beneath Edward's acceptance of his former guardian as adviser, courtier and companion must remain a matter of conjecture. Thomas Seymour had sown the seeds of mistrust: Somerset himself had fostered them by the attempted *coup d'état* of December 1549; it now remained for Warwick to reap the harvest; he came to the conclusion that he must do so quickly, or not at all.

For many months Warwick had looked vainly for a weak spot in the Duke's defences. As long ago as June 1550 it had been found for him by a new agent, Richard Whalley, a member of the House of Commons, who in the preceding February had been committed to the Fleet for 'conspiring' against the Council on behalf of Somerset. In March, Sir Ralph Vane was arrested on the same grounds and joined Whalley in the same prison. Somerset had been able to prove himself completely innocent of the charge. During the next three months it was made clear to Whalley — possibly by Cecil — that he could only obtain his freedom by informing on the Duke.

On the night of June 25th, 1550, Whalley had been admitted to Warwick's London house, where they had a long, private conversation; next day, Whalley's report of this talk reached Cecil, who in his turn reported its content to the Council. [2]

Whalley described, in moving terms, the noble Earl's anxiety about the dangerous behaviour of Somerset 'in sundry things ... He is', Whalley declared, 'a most dear and faithful friend unto my Lord's Grace.' Warwick began by saying how alarmed he and the Council had been by Somerset's attempts to liberate Gardiner from the Tower. Not only so, but the manner in which the Duke had urged his release was peremptory and harsh: quite frightening, in fact. 'Alas! Mr Whalley,' Warwick exclaimed, 'what meaneth my lord in this wise to discredit himself — and why will he not see his own decay herein?' Here the Earl shed a few tears; then he resumed: 'Thinks he to rule and direct the whole Council as he will, considering how his late governance is yet misliked? Neither is he in that credit and best opinion with the King's Majesty, as he believeth — and is, by some, fondly persuaded.' (This was a hit at Cheke and Cranmer, who were still on friendly terms with the Duke.) Warwick added mournfully: 'Truly, Mr Whalley, as by discreet and orderly suffering with the Council, he may assuredly have the King his good lord, and also all things else that he can desire — by the contrary, taking perilous ways by himself, he will so far overthrow himself as shall pass the power of his friends to recover.'

Warwick continued to deplore the criminal folly of his old comrade; he had done so much for him! He spoke warmly of Cecil's loyalty; then, resuming his pose of the humble servant of the Council, begged Whalley to help him by combining with Cecil to restrain Somerset from his fatal endeavours to reinstall Gardiner, and regain his former position as Protector. Warwick himself was, of course, anxious to save His Grace if he could do so without betraying his trust: but it looked as if the Duke was bent on his own ruin; Warwick parted from the virtuous Whalley with another burst of tears.[3]

Unfortunately, all this weeping and complaining had led no-where; whatever Somerset secretly thought or desired — and he was an embittered and ambitious man, to whom security and position meant little without power — he behaved impeccably during the following year, carrying out his duties, punishing malcontents and rebels and accepting his defeat over the liberation of Bishop Gardiner. In September 1551, however, he was so rash as to attempt a more tolerant treatment of the Lady Mary. During an interview with de Scheyfve, he and Warwick disagreed at a meeting of the Council that Edward did not attend.

The ambassador asked that the Princess's chaplains should be released. Warwick replied that this was impossible without Edward's consent; and, oddly enough, His Majesty was elsewhere. De Scheyfve said that that was not necessary. Warwick replied smoothly: 'His Majesty is now so old that he wisheth to concern himself with all the affairs of the kingdom.' The ambassador countered this excuse with a few polite remarks about Edward's intelligence: 'I hope it may yet improve with age', he added significantly. 'His Majesty', Warwick said, 'is, I hold, as much of age as if he were forty.' De Scheyfve, who thought this ridiculous, said nothing. Then the Marquis of Northampton struck in: 'Your lordship should not call the Lady Mary Princess of England, but the King's sister,' he said pompously; and Warwick added: 'To give her that title would be to wrong the Lady Elizabeth, who is also the King's sister'. De Scheyfve replied: 'I hold the Lady Mary to be the Princess of England because the King her father hath so held her — your lordships well know the difference', he went on, 'between the Lady Mary and the Lady Elizabeth.' 'She is Princess,' said Warwick, 'but not Princess of England.' The envoy then reverted to the Lady Mary's Mass. Somerset suggested that the resolution made by the Council a few months earlier — to which Warwick himself had subscribed — should be kept. Warwick turned upon him and said: 'The Mass is either of God or of the devil. If it is of God, it is but right that all our people should be allowed to go to it; but if it is not out of God, as we are taught in the Scriptures, why then should not the voice of this fury be proscribed to all?' No more was said; later on, a full report of all that had passed was given to the King. Scheyfve was told by his master that, in view of the French alliance, the Lady Mary could no longer expect active help from abroad. [4]

The foreign clergy were delighted to hear of their great patron's demonstration of his beliefs, and their distrust of Somerset increased; the Duke was still 'King of the King', they said, and the sooner he was removed from his place the better. [5] They were partly responsible for fresh gossip about Edward's marriage; Somerset, it was believed, had been working against the French alliance, and planned to contract the King to his third daughter, Lady Jane Seymour, in order to regain his power. [6] During August and September, the impression that the Duke had again overreached himself and was on the edge of disaster spread beyond London to the countryside. Mrs Woocock of Poole, in Dorset, told her neighbours that 'a voice followed her, saying, "He whom the King did best trust will deceive him and work treason against him"'. This was reported to the magistrates, who sent her up to London to be examined by the Council; when she appeared, Somerset was not present; they reproved her, and she set off home; she had got as far as Wimborne when she again heard the voice, saying the same words, and she asked the advice of Mr Hancock, the local parson, who wrote down what she told him and reported it to Somerset.

In the last week of September the Duke sent for Hancock and interviewed him at Sion House. 'Have you a note of her words?' he said, when Hancock had repeated the prophecy, and on receiving it, remained silent a long time. Suddenly it dawned on him what the Council had done; he exclaimed: 'Ah! sirrah — this is strange, that these things should come before the Council, and I not hear of it! I am of the Council also', he went on, flying into one of his terrifying rages. 'Before whom was it brought?' Hancock was not sure. 'Who do you suppose?' Somerset persisted; the parson muttered something about Paulet, the Lord Treasurer. 'It is likely to be so ... ' said Somerset, and sent him away.'

The Duke did not return to London till October 4th; there had been two cases of sweating sickness at Somerset House, and he was waiting for it to be cleansed. His suspicions must have been strengthened by the fact that nothing was said of Mrs Woocock, and that the Lords had agreed with the King to confer honours on a number of persons without consulting him. Cheke, Cecil and Henry Sidney were to be knighted, Paulet to be created Marquis of Winchester, and Dorset to receive the recently extinct dukedom of Suffolk. Warwick was to be created Duke of Northumberland.

Warwick's plans were nearly complete. On October 7th he was visited by another agent, Sir Thomas Palmer, and they had a long talk in the garden of Warwick's house. Palmer had distinguished himself under Warwick and Somerset in the French and Scottish campaigns; now his fighting days were over, and he was looking for a Court post and a pension.

On the 11th the investitures took place. Warwick's supporters throughout the splendid and elaborate ceremony were Somerset and Paulet. Every member of the Warwick faction was now rewarded — Cecil, Dorset, Paulet and Herbert, who received the earldom of Pembroke. The new Duke, now in his forty-eighth year, had come farthest of any: Dudley — Lisle — Warwick — Northumberland: the penniless son of a shady lawyer had climbed from the middle class to a viscounty, then to an earldom, and so to one of the four dukedoms of England, through the revival and, as some thought, the vulgar aggrandisement of the Percy title; the ancient earldom of Northumberland had become extinct in 1537. Now the Percy family 'had the mortification', according to an eighteenth-century genealogist, of seeing the title of Duke of Northumberland conferred on an upstart. But Northumberland carried his honours with distinction, for he had most of the graces, if few of the qualities, of a gentleman. His private life had always been well conducted (he had no time for dissipations) for he trained his wife and his seven children as a skilled general trains his staff, directing, relying on them, allotting each a part in his schemes, and rewarding them without favouritism or caprice.

Somerset's suspicions rose to anxiety and then to alarm at this strengthening and ennobling of Northumberland's faction. Believing that Cecil, who had been in his service for a decade, and for whose career he had been mainly responsible, would not fail in gratitude and loyalty, he sent for him, said 'I suspect some ill ... ' and asked for his advice. The new knight at once made their positions clear in the succinct and businesslike manner that was to characterize his long and famous administration. 'If your Grace be not guilty, you may be of good courage,' he said; 'if you are, I have nothing to say but to lament you.'[8]

Guilty of what? the Duke might have replied: a coward would have done so. Somerset knew himself doomed; he resolved to meet disaster as became a soldier and a statesman. He had not long to wait.

On the night of October 13th the Duke of Northumberland had a long interview with Edward, in which he told him everything that Sir Thomas Palmer had discovered about Somerset. What actually passed between Palmer and Northumberland on the evening of the 7th will never be known. Northumberland produced his own version for Edward, who believed every word and noted it in his diary.

According to Palmer, Somerset's conspiracy against the state had been set in hand on St George's Day, six months before. Palmer, who had been a party to it, had all the information; his change of heart enabled him to pass it on in detail. Lord Grey was to 'raise the people' against the Council in order to reinstate Somerset as Lord Protector, who was then going to ask Northumberland, Suffolk, Northampton and several other of the Lords to a banquet, where they were to be assassinated; he would then break up the French alliance, marry the King to Lady Jane Seymour and resume the dictatorship of the country. This *coup d'état* would be enforced by 2000 soldiers under the command of Sir Ralph Vane; Sir Thomas Arundel was to hold the Tower, while Sir Miles Partridge 'raised London', seized the Great Seal and rallied the apprentices. Lord Arundel, a leading Catholic, was to be Somerset's second-in-command. A general massacre of the city militia would follow unless they deserted to Somerset and his fellow-conspirators, of whom thirty-nine were named; among them were the Duchess of Somerset, her children and several upper servants in the Somerset household.[9]

After Edward had set down these facts in his diary and put it away, it was taken from his desk. Above the entry beginning 'Sir Thomas Palmer' these words were inserted in another hand: 'hating the Duke [of Somerset] and hated of him'. When Edward reopened his diary and came upon this sentence, he appears to have struck it through, but it can still be seen. The handwriting is that of a contemporary, and may have been disguised. This tampering with his private record was perhaps an attempt to warn Edward against Palmer, as being the instrument of Northumberland's machinations. The King ignored it.[10] Northumberland had warned him first, against Somerset, in those secret midnight conversations. Not only did Somerset desire Northumberland's death: he was planning to overthrow the Reformation, and return to the Six Articles and the popish regime. His support of the Princess Mary was proof of that; that he was capable of violent and tyrannical action had been shown by his kidnapping Edward and rushing him from Hampton Court to Windsor in the middle of the night under the pretence that he himself was in danger, although he had received no worse punishment than a fine and the loss of the Protectorate. The whole case against Somerset was, from Edward's point of view, utterly convincing. The fact that from April till October the Duke had been in constant attendance on him, and doing his usual work as Minister and Councillor, was overshadowed by Northumberland's insinuations. Once, for a few moments, within an hour of Somerset's execution, Edward wavered in his belief of his uncle's guilt: then, never again.

On October 16th Somerset arrived late at the Council meeting. They sat till midday, then rose for dinner. As he took his seat the Lord Treasurer stood up and accused him of high treason. All was in readiness; the guards were waiting; Somerset was taken to the Tower. A few hours later his wife and children arrived there. Beyond the fact that he had been formally accused, he knew nothing.[11]

That same day a proclamation was sent out to all the judges and magistrates in the kingdom, describing Somerset's long-planned scheme to murder the Council and seize the government of the realm. During the next few weeks the witnesses for the prosecution were assembled, their statements collated and a questionnaire was made out to be answered by Somerset *in camera*.

Until this moment the pace of Northumberland's campaign had been extremely rapid; now it slowed down, owing to the difficulties caused by the variations in the evidence and the number of witnesses. As one followed another into the Tower — and as each version of Somerset's plot so differed as to contradict what had already been taken down — it became clear that several weeks must pass before the case could come up for trial. As most of the prisoner's statements were destroyed after the Duke's execution, a retrospective analysis is impossible; but from what seems to be a verbatim account of Lord Arundel's examination by Northumberland, Pembroke and two other Lords, it appears that Somerset had at one time considered 'apprehending' Northumberland in order to reform the administration. Very foolishly, he had discussed this with Arundel; then he decided to take no action. 'We determined', Arundel said, 'to have apprehended you — but by the passion of God! for no harm to your bodies.' When asked: 'How often did you and my Lord's Grace meet together about these matters?' he replied: 'But once.' He was told that Somerset had already confessed to several meetings at Sion House for that purpose; at this, he threw up his hands, exclaiming: 'You know all!' — whether ironically or not, is uncertain. Accused of conspiring with the Duchess of Somerset, he denied it; further pressed, he admitted to warning Somerset against Northumberland's faction.[12]

Although Arundel stood out against the brow-beating of the Council, the other witnesses were not so bold; many were bent on obtaining their liberty through any evidence that suited their inquisitors; one or two (the most useful was Sir Thomas Palmer) saw a means of establishing themselves for life through the incrimination of the Seymour family. Lord Rich, who had managed so far to keep himself apart from both the winning and the losing side, perceived that he could not hope to remain unmolested if he continued in the Chancellorship; before he gave in his resignation to the King and Council, he decided to do what he could for Somerset. He sent him a letter describing all that he had been able to discover about Northumberland's preparations, addressing it, simply, 'to the Duke'. He had forgotten that there was another Duke imprisoned in the Tower: Norfolk, who had been there since his arraignment in 1547. The Lieutenant of the Tower took the superscription to mean the senior Duke, and it was brought to Norfolk by Rich's servant.

Norfolk, who had lost his position and his freedom through Somerset's influence, was his bitterest enemy. Before Rich's servant could stop him, he opened the letter and, taking it to the window, began to read. Then he smiled.[13] The servant stood appalled; he managed to get out of the cell without delay and rushed back to the Lord Chancellor. Meanwhile, Norfolk handed over the letter to Northumberland, who at that moment was coaching his witnesses for the prosecution. The unfortunate Rich, seeing that his own arrest must follow within an hour or so, hurried to the Palace and obtained an audience with the King, although Edward had not yet risen. Falling on his knees by the bed, Rich implored His Majesty's leave to retire to the country; he could not wait to give in his formal resignation.

Edward demurred: he did not care to settle such a matter in this helter-skelter fashion. Rich cried out that he was old — ailing — dying — he must go to his Essex estate to 'attend to his devotions', and prepare for death. It was not in Edward's nature to resist such an appeal: he consented, and Rich left London just in time.[14]

Somerset's arrest had been made in secret, and the public knew nothing of it till the proclamation of his guilt reached the magistrates. Unfortunately for Northumberland, this coincided with the issue of the new coinage, on which Edward was shown crowned and holding a sword with a lion in the background: or what looked like a lion: the design was not very clear. A rumour started that this was not the royal lion of England, but the bear and the ragged staff of the Warwicks, the cognizance that Northumberland had taken from the ancient house of Warwick the King-maker when he received his earldom on Edward's accession. As the new coin began to circulate, the belief in this outward transference of power — highly uncharacteristic of Northumberland's technique — prevailed, in spite of the fact that those who spread it were arrested and fined. Thomas Holland of Bath, visiting Mr and Mrs Cotton in London, showed them a new shilling, declaring that the bear and the ragged staff were plain to see. 'It is no other than a lion', said his more sophisticated host. 'Tush, tush, hold thy peace, fool!' Holland replied. 'Thou shalt see another world ere Candlemas. The Duke of Somerset shall go forth from the Tower, and the Duke of Northumberland shall go in.' Less than two years later this prophecy was fulfilled.[15]

The gossip about the coinage was the first sign of Northumberland's unpopularity, one that he could afford to disregard. A more serious set-back was Edward's sudden and unexpected recalcitrance over signing certain documents, of which the content has not survived, presented to him by the now submissive Council. It must have come as a shock to the new Duke that his apparently docile pupil was forming his own judgments and using independently the authority that Northumberland had provided for the establishment of his personal power. As the weeks went by and the reports of the evidence collected against Somerset reached the King, he realized that this time his uncle's downfall was to end in death. He tried to stop the course of what was represented to him as justice; when petitions were put before him asking for the supreme penalty for all the conspirators, he refused to grant them. And then, for the first time, Edward saw Northumberland lose his temper, just as Somerset had. The scene took place behind closed doors; but hints of it reached the French and Spanish Ambassadors. De Scheyfve said cynically: 'His Majesty is supposed to grieve for his uncle's arrest, but that I do not believe. His mind is poisoned against him.' De Noailles thought that the King had pleaded for Somerset's life.[16]

This temporary split between Northumberland and Edward may have partly caused the delay in bringing Somerset to trial; when some of those in his household persisted in their asseverations of his innocence, torture was used, and the evidence reassembled; even then, Arundel's obstinacy and defiance — 'None of my race have been traitors, but all know who have', he said to Northumberland — seemed likely to spoil the symmetry of the case. And the increasing resentment of the people made the organization of the trial a complicated business.[17]

By the end of November the arrangements were complete. Under cover of darkness — at five o'clock on the morning of December 1st, 1551 — the Duke of Somerset was brought by water from the Tower to Westminster Hall. A few hours later

THE DUKE OF SOMERSET

Palace Yard was crowded with people calling for justice for the Duke, and a thousand men-at-arms surrounded the building. At six o'clock the peers took their places. Yells and curses against Northumberland and the Council were heard from outside as Somerset came to the bar and faced his judges.

The setting of that scene has not changed in six hundred years. Still the golden angels seem to fly upwards from the hammer beams; still the vaulted ceiling holds the shadows and throws back the echoes; already, then, as Somerset stood there alone to conduct his own defence those shadows were haunted and those echoes muffled and heavy with the tragedies, triumphs and degradations of the historic past. And as the hours went by, the procedure became curiously repetitive: idealism knelt to expediency: justice was mocked: truth and mercy were thrust aside. The phantasmagoria of old cruelties, forgotten hatred and dead revenge was re-created as Somerset looked across the hall at the men he had worked and fought with, gathered there to destroy him; Paulet, Marquis of Winchester, as Lord Treasurer and Steward of England sitting under the canopy of state — and behind him Northumberland and twenty-six of his peers.

The indictments were read out; the depositions were then put by the judges to the prisoner, who answered each point as it arose; he had the right to question personally two of the witnesses and refute their evidence in cross-examination.

Somerset was charged on five counts: with having treasonably collected a number of persons in order to kill the Duke of Northumberland; with having planned the assassination of the Council; with devising a revolution in the City of London; with the intention of resisting arrest; with having schemed to break the French alliance and marry his daughter to the King. The first two counts were treasonable, the other three felonious. The principal witness was Crane, a member of his household; the second, Palmer. When the prisoner asked to be confronted with Crane, this was refused, and Palmer substituted. Then Somerset's pride rose with his awareness of the travesty in which he was being forced to plead for a life already forfeited. He refused to cross-question Palmer, whom he described as a worthless villain, and confined himself to denying, categorically, all the charges except that of wishing to alter the administration and having discussed doing so with others

besides Arundel; he had planned nothing. As proof of his innocence he cited his past services and his conduct during the months
of his supposed conspiring. He was heard courteously, patiently,
without bullying or interruption; all the forms of equity and
fair dealing were scrupulously observed.

The Lords then withdrew to consider the verdict. Somerset's
defence had been well sustained; they debated for six hours. The
charges of treason — those of planning to murder Northumberland
and the Lords — were not pressed, at Northumberland's particular
request. He modestly said that he would not have an attempt on his
own life dignified by such a name (this was what he afterwards
told Edward); he desired mercy for his old friend and ally. 'So',
says Edward, recording Northumberland's version of the debate,
'the Lords acquitted him of high treason and condemned him of
treason felonious.' Describing the trial in greater detail — and
with less danger of supervision — in a letter to Barnaby Fitzpatrick, Edward said that his uncle 'very barely' answered the
charges of felony, 'which he seemed to have confessed'. The
phrase is ambiguous: even in a private letter the King would not
commit himself to more than this one implication of doubt and
distrust. In his journal he says that Somerset confessed to having
planned the assassinations. Edward's record of this supposed
avowal has been copied by a number of historians in default of
other contemporary data. But in a letter written by Paulet to
Admiral Clinton the day after the trial and describing the
evidence in full, there is no mention that Somerset admitted the
intent to murder; and Paulet, as Northumberland's ally and
Somerset's enemy, wrote to Clinton in order to incriminate
Somerset and justify his condemnation, as the content of his letter
shows; it is therefore obvious that this statement was never made
by Somerset, but invented by Northumberland for Edward's
benefit.[18]

When the Lords returned and Somerset was again called to the
Bar, he was pronounced not guilty of treason. As the custom then
was, the Sergeant-at-Arms who had preceded him into the hall
carrying the axe, was dismissed. As he came out, the waiting
crowds set up a shout of rapture — the Duke was innocent! The
good Duke was free! As the news spread from Palace Yard down
the riverside and along the Strand, they cheered and wept and

embraced, throwing up their caps in delirious ecstasy. 'The people, knowing not the matter,' Edward records, 'shouted ... so loud, that from the Hall door it was heard at Charing Cross, and plainly, and rumours went that he was quit of all.'[19]

Somerset was not deluded by this masquerade of leniency and fairness. Felonious intent called for the penalty of death. The Lord Treasurer stood up and pronounced sentence.

In accordance with the etiquette of the day, Somerset knelt and thanked the Court for his trial, asking mercy for his wife and children. In his diary, Edward noted that his uncle 'made suit for his life' — and here is another mystery. In this entry the last word is inserted above the line; without it, the sentence reads 'made suit for his wife and children'. And in Paulet's letter to Clinton, there is no mention of the other appeal.

Then followed the final irony. Northumberland rose; and for the last time in the world of the living, the two men faced one another. Northumberland said: 'O! Duke of Somerset, you see yourself brought into the utmost danger, and that nothing but death awaits you. I have once before delivered you from a similar hazard of your life; and I will not now desist from serving you, how little soever you may expect it. I desire you therefore to appeal to the royal clemency, which I doubt not will be extended to you.' After a pause, he resumed: 'As for myself, I shall willingly forgive you everything, and will use every exertion in my power that your life may be spared.'[20]

Somerset's pride and dignity sustained him through this histrionic exploitation of his defeat, as it was to sustain him in the last ordeal. As he was conducted back to the Tower the people, realizing their mistake, watched him in mournful silence, too crushed by disappointment to protest.[21]

There was an interval of seven weeks between Somerset's trial and his execution; untroubled by hope or suspense, he spent it calmly, preparing for the end. While some believed in the supplementary confessions of his guilt — Edward was told that his uncle had admitted to hiring foreign mercenaries for the murder of Northumberland — others suspected that the King was trying to save him. It is not clear whether Northumberland arranged for the delay between condemnation and execution in order to destroy Edward's scruples, or whether he submitted to it under pressure, in the hope that public feeling would die down. What Edward believed is also uncertain; in any case, he became very depressed, and it was necessary to organize every kind of distraction for the Christmas festivities; masques, jousts, banquets and challenges for tilting and running at the ring succeeded one another in the weeks that followed.[22] When Edward appealed for Somerset's life, Northumberland was sympathetic — even cooperative. He himself, he said, would wish the sentence commuted to imprisonment: but the risk was too great; Somerset's designs were so dangerous, his potentialities, even as a prisoner, so hostile, that there would be no hope of peace for England or security for the Protestant faith while he remained alive. Edward was at last persuaded to believe this; even then, he could not bring himself to give the final orders. Meanwhile, Northumberland saw to it that he was never approached by such friends of Somerset's as were bold enough to remain at Court; and he began to work on the feelings of the French Ambassador, hinting that, if Somerset was spared, the marriage contract might be broken, with the result that de Noailles urged the King 'to make an example in so serious a matter'.[23]

Finally, in the third week of January 1552, Edward decided to reconsider his uncle's case at a Council meeting; he may have hoped to find a loop-hole; whatever he secretly desired, or had made up his mind to, was known to Northumberland, who was now ready to circumvent any attempt to save his victim. On January 18th, two days before the Council meeting, the King, as his custom was, drew up an official memorandum of the agenda for the next day that ran as follows: 'Certain points of weighty matters to be immediately concluded on by my Council ... ' (Then followed notes of the usual business.) He goes on: 'The matter for the Duke of Somerset's confederates to be considered, as appertaineth to our surety and quietness of our realm, that by their punishment example may be showed to others.' This he signed, and it was given by Cecil with a covering note to the Council on the 19th. Between the 18th and the 19th this memorandum was partially erased, and so interlined that it read: '... that by their punishment *and execution according to the laws*, example may be showed to others'. Later investigations seem to indicate that the interpolations were forged; the trick was not then, and cannot now, be proved. But it was done. Edward had commanded Somerset's execution.[24]

Three days passed between the presentation of this document to the Lords and the execution. During that time Edward was again approached by Northumberland, who made a final appeal to him as responsible for the welfare of the kingdom and the establishment of the faith. At last Edward was overborne. He said: 'Let the law take its course' — and the writs containing the necessary instructions for the Lieutenant of the Tower and the City sheriffs were made out and signed by the King.[25] A few days later, at another Council meeting, he was asked for a reprieve for one of the other prisoners. If a contemporary chronicler is to be believed, Edward said — 'very deliberately': 'How is this, my Lords? There was no one to beg for mercy for my uncle — and for this man you all come. My command is that the law's behest be carried out.'[26] Northumberland had done his work well.

At eight o'clock on the morning of January 22nd Somerset, escorted by a strong guard and attended by Edward's old tutor, Dr Cox, came out on Tower Hill. A proclamation had been issued commanding the people to keep themselves and their families within doors; no one dreamed of obeying it; streets, roof-tops, walls and courtyards were thronged, not only with angry Londoners, but with the country folk who had come for many miles to see the last of their beloved Duke and to hear what he had to say. If the Council had dared, they would have forbidden Somerset to speak, or ordered his voice to be drowned by a roll of drums; but the temper of the people was so fierce, their behaviour, long before Somerset appeared, so turbulent and threatening, that the Lords could only arrange for the scaffold to be encircled by a triple ring of soldiers to prevent any attempt at the rescue of which the Tower officials had been warned.

As Somerset appeared, stately and serene, in a magnificent Court dress with all his orders, the shouts that greeted him were echoed beyond Tower Hill, and the people standing nearest the men-at-arms began to sway to and fro. Sir Thomas Arundel, whose release through his turning king's evidence had enabled him to ride in the procession to the scaffold, said to another nobleman: 'His blood will make my Lord of Northumberland's pillow uneasy.'[27] Neither Northumberland nor any of those he now

237

directed need have concerned themselves. Somerset had not known how to rule; but he knew how to die, and he had made up his mind to do so.

As he stepped on the scaffold, silence fell. He knelt and said a short prayer. Then he came to the railings, and in the strong, sonorous voice that had dominated so many gatherings, he began: 'Masters and good fellows — I come hither to die — but a true and faithful man as any was unto the King's Majesty, and to his realm. But I am condemned by a law whereunto I am subject, as we all, and therefore to show obedience I am content to die. For, as I am a man, I have deserved at God's hand many deaths; and it has pleased His goodness, whereas He might have taken me suddenly, thus now to visit me and call me with this present death as you do see, where I have had time to remember and acknowledge Him, and to know also myself, for which I do thank Him heartily. And, my friends, more I have to say to you concerning religion; I have been always, being in authority, a furtherer of it to the glory of God, to the uttermost of my power; whereof I am nothing sorry, but rather have cause and do rejoice most gladly that I have so done, for the greatest benefit of God that ever I had, beseeching you all to take it so, and to follow it on still — for if not, there will follow a worse plague.'

As if he were prophetically inspired, a noise was heard — of marching men. The crowd began to heave and murmur: the ranks of men-at-arms wavered and shifted. From beyond the scaffold voices rose crying 'Away! Away!' — and panic, rather than hope, seized the people; afterwards, many declared that they had seen a concourse of ghostly horsemen descending to destroy the wicked and save the innocent. What had actually happened was that a body of soldiers, commanded at the last moment to support their comrades, had set off late and were now running down a side-street towards the gates of the Tower. Shouts of 'A rescue!' went up, and the confusion became desperate in the struggle between those nearest the soldiers and the larger number beyond who were making way for the others; these appeared to be led by a rider forcing his way towards the scaffold; some recognized him as Sir Anthony Browne, the Master of the Horse — and there were cries of 'Reprieve! Reprieve!' In another few seconds, the guards would have been compelled to turn upon the people, who were trying now to tear Somerset from the scaffold and carry him away.

Standing high above them, he saw what was going on. He leant forward and called out: 'There is no such thing, good people — there is no such thing'— and gradually quiet fell once more. Somerset said: 'Dearly beloved friends — there is no such matter here in hand, as you vainly hope or believe. I pray you all to be quiet and contented with my death, which I am most willing to suffer. For I have often looked death in the face, upon great adventures in the field, he is now no stranger to me. And among all the vain mockeries of this world, I repent me of nothing more than in esteeming life more dear than I should.'

He paused. The silence was now complete. Then he went on: 'I have endured the hate of great persons — so much the more dangerous because unjust. I have incurred displeasure from inferiors, for giving way to the faults of others — and now, being constantly resolved, I neither fear to die, nor desire to live. Let us now join in prayer to the Lord for the preservation of the King's Majesty, to whose Grace I have always been a faithful, true and most loving subject, desirous always of his most prosperous success in all his affairs, and ever glad of the helping forward of the commonwealth of this realm.'

At this point his voice was drowned by shouts of 'Yes! Yes!' Someone called out above the rest: 'This is now found too true.'

'If there are any that have been offended and injured by me,' the Duke resumed, 'I most humbly ask him forgiveness — but especially Almighty God, Whom throughout my life I have most grievously offended. And all others, whatsoever they be,' he added emphatically, 'I do with my whole heart forgive them.' Shouts and curses against Northumberland and the Council arose. Somerset called for silence, saying: 'I once again require you, dearly beloved in the Lord, that you all keep yourselves quiet and still, lest by your tumult you should trouble me. For albeit the spirit be ready and willing, the flesh is frail and wavering — and through your quietness I shall be much more quieter.'

No one moved or spoke. His voice rang out again: 'I desire you all to bear me witness that I die here in the faith of Jesus Christ — desiring you all to help me with your prayers, that I may persevere constant in the same.'

Once more he knelt to pray. As he rose Dr Cox gave him a

paper; this was Cranmer's newly composed General Confession, which he read aloud. He shook hands with the sheriffs and the Lieutenant of the Tower, thanking them for their courtesy and patience. He took off his collar, and his orders: then he stood still. The executioner approached and asked him to remove his doublet. Somerset roused himself to do this, and to give the man the usual fee. As he knelt and put his head on the block his face became crimson. Three times he said in a loud voice: 'Lord Jesu, receive my soul!' His head fell at the first stroke. Then, at last, the people burst through the ranks of the men-at-arms, those nearest dipping their handkerchiefs in Somerset's blood. [28]

That the Duke had refused to attempt to escape was, for many, a source of passionate bewilderment and grief. But although he had spoken in the set terms required by the occasion, it may well have been that this deeply religious man, whose God was the jealous God of the Old Testament, felt himself to be expiating his brother's death. And Somerset knew, none better, that escape would have been momentary. Behind the crowds and the guard and the friendly, sheltering houses his destroyer stood, between Edward and himself. He was in the grasp of one who never forgave.

The tumult of the enraged and miserable people surging back from Tower Hill through the City and along the river penetrated at last to the Palace of Westminster. Edward, who was with the Spanish Ambassador, asked what was happening. When de Scheyfve told him, he remained silent for a long time. Then he said: 'I would not have believed that he would have been a traitor.' In his diary for that day he made a single entry: 'The Duke of Somerset had his head cut off upon Tower Hill between eight and nine o'clock in the morning.' [29]

Nineteen months later, Northumberland, Sir John Gates and Sir Thomas Palmer, waiting to be executed on the same spot, solemnly declared, within a few moments of their deaths, that the Duke of Somerset had been falsely accused in evidence set out and provided by themselves. [30]

NOTES TO CHAPTER XIII

[1] *Cal. Span. P.*, vol. X, p. 386.
[2] This letter has been wrongly dated by Tytler as written in 1551 instead of 1550.
[3] Tytler, vol. II, p. 21.
[4] *Cal. Span. P.*, vol. X, p. 384.
[5] *Original Letters*, 2nd ser., p. 636.
[6] Strype, *Ecclesiastical Memorials*, vol. III, part 1, p. 380.
[7] Ibid.
[8] *Lit. Rem.*, vol. II, p. 354.
[9] Ibid., p. 355.
[10] Ibid., p. 353.
[11] Tytler, vol. II, p. 37.
[12] Ibid., p. 43.
[13] *Lit. Rem.*, vol. I, pp. 378-80.
[14] Lloyd, pp. 223-4; De Thoyras, vol. VII, p. 81.
[15] Greyfriars, p. 72.
[16] *Cal. Span. P.*, vol. X, p. 389; *De Noailles*, p. 184.
[17] *Cal. Span. P.*, vol. X, p. 389.
[18] Tytler, vol. II, p. 97.
[19] *Lit. Rem.*, vol. II, p. 374.
[20] Ibid.; *Original Letters*, 2nd ser., p. 441; Cobbett, *State Trials*, vol. I, pp. 483-506.
[21] Hayward, p. 316.
[22] Heylyn, p. 117.
[23] *Cal. Span. P.*, vol. X, p. 389.
[24] Tytler, vol. II, p. 69; Pollard, *England Under Protector Somerset*, p. 64; Burnet, *History of the Reformation*, vol. III, part 2, p. 271.
[25] Hume, p. 218; Rymer, *Foedera*, vol. XV, p. 295.
[26] Hume, p. 219.
[27] Godwin, p. 251.
[28] Cobbett, *State Trials*, vol. I, pp. 183-506; Hayward, p. 338.
[29] *Cal. Span. P.*, vol. X, p. 407; *Lit. Rem.*, vol. II, p. 390.
[30] Von Raumer, vol. II, pp. 79-80.

CHAPTER FOURTEEN

THE PROGRESS AND THE PRAYER BOOK

EDWARD's formal education was supposed to end with his fourteenth birthday: although by that time his administrative duties so encroached on his hours of study as to prevent his doing any written work, he continued his classical reading with Cheke; this included history, geography, philosophy, poetry, rhetoric and Roman law. His range of subjects was not really taxing; the entries in his diary relating to athletics show that he spent several hours a day out of doors doing whatever he liked; he was often reported as having 'gone out to play' by ambassadors desiring audience; they sometimes had to pursue him into the tennis-court or the tilt-yard in order to find out when they might interview him officially.[1] The brevity of his notes shows that he cannot have spent more than a couple of hours a week over his diary; his plans for the improvement of the administration, although lengthy and detailed, are few, and give the impression of being worked at intermittently over long periods of time. He was what is now called a natural writer; his private correspondence was one of his relaxations, as was his delight in the masques and concerts in which he sometimes took part; he does not seem to have cared for indoor games. In fact, his routine was strenuous, but well regulated; it bore no relation to the constant pressure exercised on brain and spirit that his prerogative and his temperament combined to intensify with every month, every week, of his reign. Yet those who saw Edward daily, from his fourteenth to his fifteenth year, make no mention of his appearing over-worked; in his country palaces, at Greenwich especially, his life was easy, informal and free; almost that of a country gentleman.

In the 1550s the structure – it could hardly be called a design – of the Palace of Greenwich, was so irregular as to give the effect of an unfinished Gothic manor-house. Edward IV had enlarged the two-storeyed façade that now rambled along the river front, its outline broken by square mullioned windows and small towers.

Henry VIII, whose birthplace it was, had added a chapel of four storeys at one end and a three-tiered oratory that jutted out into the water, thus intensifying an architectural confusion that must have been rather pleasant in summer, when the trees at the back hid the squat cottages beyond the gardens. In such a setting it would have been impossible to keep up great state, or move processionally from one wing to another; personal access to the King was no doubt correspondingly casual. As at Hampton Court, one or two old servants, among them Sibylla Penn and Will Somers, had their own rooms; honoured and pensioned, the fool and the nurse lived among their memories and for the visits of the King and his circle of intimates: Cheke and Sidney, both Gentlemen of the Bedchamber now; Throckmorton, whom the Duke of Northumberland was trying to remove; handsome Robert Dudley, Carver to His Majesty; and the 'dearest and most obligingest' of all Edward's friends, Barnaby Fitzpatrick, who became his private agent at the French Court in December 1551, and to whom he wrote rather sketchy accounts of his daily life with detailed instructions about Barnaby's expenditure, dress and sight-seeing. Edward's letters give the impression that his Irish emissary, although intelligent and adaptable, was scatter-brained and too easily led; otherwise, there would have been no need for the King's anxious forethought, his arrangements for every contingency.

Of course, Barnaby was to perfect his French and fittingly represent the graces of the English Court; Sir William Pickering, the resident Ambassador, would supply him with money and anything else he wanted, and look after him when he joined the army for the winter campaign against the Spaniards; but his friend must be reminded, Edward told Pickering, 'to behave himself honestly, more following the company of gentlemen than pressing into the company of the ladies there; and his chief pastime shall be hunting and riding. Also his apparel ... shall be comely, and not too much superfluous'. When Barnaby wrote enthusiastically about the good time he was having, and added that he had been asked to accompany some of Henry II's courtiers on a pilgrimage to some shrine, Edward replied with advice as firm as it was tactful. Such an expedition was highly undesirable, but Barnaby must on no account offend the French King 'because you have been so favourably used'. He must therefore throw the burden of his refusal on to Edward, saying that 'you cannot do any such thing, being brought up with me, and bound to obey my laws. Also that you had commandment from me to the contrary. Yet, if you be vehemently procured, you may go on waiting on the King ... so you look not on the Mass ... If the King command you, you may sometimes dance, so measure be your mean.' (Was Barnaby apt to overdo things?) 'Else, apply yourself to riding, shooting or tennis, not forgetting, some time, when you have leisure, your learning, chiefly reading of the Scripture.' As if aware that he was being over-solicitous, Edward added: 'This I write, not doubting but you would have done so, but to spur you on.' Barnaby replied that he would frequent no other ladies but those of the Court, and this seemed to satisfy Edward, who, in the last week of January 1552, described his own Christmas and Twelfth Night festivities as 'well and merrily passed', at Greenwich. [2]

No one could be sure how deeply Edward felt the execution of his uncle. Probably his mood varied, bewildering himself; there is no doubt of his enjoyment in the Twelfth Night entertainment that began with a duologue 'between one that was called Riches and the other Youth, whether of them was better. After some pretty reasoning,' he goes on, 'there came in six champions of either side ... '[3] He then gives their names and disguises, but of the masque that concluded the festivities in which he himself took part he says nothing, perhaps because it gave great offence to some of his foreign guests. George Ferrers, Edward's Lord of Misrule for that year, had been given a free hand, and some crude mockery of Catholicism was the result. The Venetian and French Ambassadors showed their disgust: the Spanish envoy maintained an icy silence, sending an embittered account of this tactless horseplay to his master. A few days later he sought Edward out in order to speak to him privately about the Princess Mary's Mass. Approaching Edward in the tilt-yard, de Scheyfve got a courteous reception. 'Where is His Majesty?' Edward asked. 'At Innsbruck, sire.' 'Will he tarry there?' Edward went on. Just as de Scheyfve was going to lead the conversation into the desired channel a match began, in which the King became so absorbed that no further talk was possible. After dinner de Scheyfve managed to see him alone: his request was set aside. 'His Majesty the Emperor hath commanded the strictest observance of his statutes and ordinances in his realm, and I will do the same', Edward said. De Scheyfve pleaded that no official promise had been made — could not the Princess be allowed her Mass till His Majesty was of age to judge for himself? Edward referred him to the Council, who put him off with vague assurances. A few days later de Scheyfve tackled Edward again; this time Northumberland was with him. Edward listened patiently, and then said: 'It would be against my conscience to allow the Mass, but in other matters I will treat the Lady's Mary's Grace as my good sister. My ministers know of no promise made.' De Scheyfve began to protest. Edward interrupted him: 'I would not argue with Your Excellency on religion — if you have aught to say, go to the Council. I know of no promise.' 'I would never think of so far forgetting my duty as to argue with Your Majesty — but I would you should know what hath passed', said the envoy, going on to plead again for the Princess and stressing her loyalty to Edward, who said simply: 'I am sure of that.' De Scheyfve then repeated all that he had said before; in the middle of a sentence Edward interchanged glances with Northumberland, and dismissed him. 'His Majesty', the envoy concluded in his report to the Emperor, 'is an intelligent lad, of quick, ready and well developed mind, remarkable for his age. If he were well taught, he would be a very noteworthy prince. The Duke of Northumberland — whom he seems to love and fear — is beginning to grant him a great deal of freedom in order to dispel the hostility felt for himself and to cause the King to forget the Duke of Somerset as quickly as possible.' Edward, weary of these repetitive discussions, merely noted that the 'Emperor's Ambassador moved me several times that my sister Mary might have Mass, which, with no little reasoning with him, was denied him'. [4]

The wrangle over the Princess's Mass had become secondary since Edward's betrothal to Madame Elisabeth made it impossible for the Emperor to do more than protest on his cousin's behalf. The problems that Edward now turned to were set out in his memoranda for the Parliament of 1552 in twelve 'bills'. His solutions, although perhaps over-simplified, were eminently practical; but they amounted to an administrative reorganization that would certainly have ended Northumberland's dictatorship and might have caused a revolution. In fact — this was not realized by Edward — the religious and economic abuses he wanted to put right were inextricably intertwined and only remediable on a long-term basis. It may have been for these reasons that Parliament rejected all his suggestions; although one, '*A Paper concerning a Free Mart in England*', under eight heads subdivided into fifty-one sections, could have been attempted without disrupting vested interests or further confounding the confusion that already prevailed. [5]

It was not to be. Northumberland and his satellites were in control. Yet the Duke's hold over Edward was so subtly persuasive, so tactfully reassuring, that although, as de Scheyfve had observed, there were moments when the King was over-awed, perhaps even terrorized, his response to this minister's advice was that of the pupil whose trust is unwavering. How Northumberland managed to reconcile his own management of the kingdom with the unobtrusive shelving of all Edward's laboriously worked out plans will never be known. From January till November of this year Edward's suspicions were easily lulled, perhaps by promises of future endeavour; so, disappointed at the failure of his trading scheme, the King fell back on a reorganization, under nineteen heads, of the Privy Council — 'for the better, quicker and more orderly dispatch of causes' — which he dictated to Cecil and corrected with his own hand, and which seems to have been adopted, in part, at least; these improvements would not have affected Northumberland's domination and might indeed have strengthened it; they gave Edward the credit and show of beneficent government without the reality of power.

Such a reform was enough to appease, temporarily, a boy of fourteen; the few men of integrity and experience who were in a position to speak out were not so easily set aside. Of these, Ridley was one, and John Knox, recently a refugee from Scotland and now chaplain at Court, another. Ridley's province was more limited — Knox took the whole of what he called Christendom for his — and his correspondingly practical suggestions more acceptable.

Towards the end of February 1552 Ridley preached before the King at Westminster. Resuming, as it were, where Latimer had left off, he began his sermon with a diatribe against the wealthy, voracious and stony-hearted men in high places, going on to describe the miseries of the poor throughout the country; he added that there was greater suffering in London than anywhere else; crime, starvation and disease raged, unheeded, at the doors of the nobles' palaces, in the filthy alleys and dens that surrounded their gardens, in the ruins of the monasteries and churches they had despoiled. Ridley concluded by appealing over their heads to the King, the fount of all goodness, the tender and compassionate father of his people. 'As Your Majesty is entirely beloved of your subjects, so with the like affection your Majesty loves them again ... ' he wound up, with what may have been a challenge in his tone. ⁶

The service was over and Ridley about to leave the Palace when a messenger came running after him; he was not to go until he had seen His Majesty. He returned, and had to wait several hours before he was ushered into the Great Gallery. Here two chairs were set out. The room was empty: no halberdiers, no gentlemen in waiting, not a single page or Yeoman of the Bedchamber, were to be seen. Standing there in some trepidation, Ridley saw Edward come in alone, and sank on his knees. The King told him to get up and put on his cap. Amazed, a little distrustful perhaps, the Bishop refused. Edward insisted; then he sat down and told Ridley to do the same. He said that they were alone at his command, and that no formalities were to be observed.

Edward began by thanking Ridley for a good sermon. He then read out some of the notes he had made of it: they were lengthy and detailed. Still the Bishop was at a loss. 'I thank your lordship', Edward went on, 'for what you said concerning the poor.' After a pause, he added: 'But, my lord, ye willed such as are in authority to be careful thereof, and to devise some good order for their relief, wherein I think you meant me — for I am in highest place, and therefore am the first that must make answer to God for my negligence if I should not be careful therein.' The simple immediacy of this response to his appeal silenced Ridley. Edward seems to have felt that he had not made himself clear, for he resumed: 'I know it to be the express commandment of Almighty God to have compassion on His poor and needy members, for whom we must make an account unto Him.' Still Ridley found himself unable to speak. Edward said: 'Truly, my lord, I am before all things most willing to travail that way — and I doubt nothing of your long and approved wisdom and learning, who, having such good zeal, wisheth help unto them — but also that you have had some conference with others what ways are best to be taken therein — the which I am desirous to understand. And therefore I pray you, say your mind.'

There followed a very long silence indeed. The dearest wish of Ridley's heart was apparently to be granted; but the suddenness, the direct and business-like manner of the King's approach had so taken him by surprise that to speak his mind was almost impossible. So the slight, fair boy and the bearded, elderly man sat looking at one another in the vast empty room without speaking. But Edward knew how to wait; he had often sat thus, deliberating, at Council meetings, till his turn came to give his opinion. At last Ridley put his into words.

The worst evils, he began, were to be found in London, where over-crowding, dirt and disease had increased with appalling rapidity since the dissolution of the monasteries had closed the city hospitals. Of its administration he knew little; nor had he any official authority. The most practical plan, therefore, would be for His Majesty to write to the Lord Mayor outlining a scheme for the charitable and reformatory organizations that Ridley had already considered and that he now briefly outlined. Edward listened without comment; then he said: 'I agree with your lordship', sent for a secretary and dictated a letter commanding the Lord Mayor's immediate attendance; he gave orders that it was to be delivered at once. Then he got up and held out his hand.

That same evening Ridley had a long interview with Sir Richard Dobbs, the Lord Mayor, and between them they worked out a scheme for hospitals, orphanages, schools and the division of persons in need. A committee of aldermen was elected, who were to share in Dobbs's discussions with the King. 'Truly, truly,' Ridley burst out, 'I could never have thought that excellency to have been in His Grace that I saw in him.'

After a series of committee meetings Edward, Dobbs and the chief aldermen had their plan — device for the poor, was the King's phrase — drawn up ready for engrossing; its subdivisions are characteristic of Edward's methods. There were (1) the poor by impotency (subdivided into three kinds); (2) the poor by casualty (similarly subdivided); and (3) the poor by thriftlessness, more sternly subdivided into '(*a*) the rioter that consumeth all, (*b*) the vagabond that will abide in no place and (*c*) the strumpet and other'. Edward headed the list of subscribers with the gift of the Palace of Bridewell, that became known as Christ's Hospital and was first instituted as a 'place of correction for the idle and vagabond', later becoming an orphanage.⁷ St Thomas's, long un-repaired and almost uninhabitable, was to be rebuilt and re-endowed: Grey Friars, intended for poor relief by Henry VIII, was similarly treated, it was hoped that all three would be ready for use by the end of the year.

There is no mention of these plans in Edward's diary: this had now become a record of foreign and military affairs; the entries relating to religion, amusements and Council meetings are generally confined to a single sentence. His first letters to Barnaby Fitzpatrick show his concern for the French alliance and are inter-spersed with accounts of tilting matches ('six to six — very well run ... eighteen to twenty, very well accomplished'), the floods in East Anglia and the rise of Protestantism in the German pro-vinces. In February Edward replied to his friend's request (from Paris) for a larger allowance and some mules, with permission to buy these in France, and, while granting him a further sum, desired him 'not to live too sumptuously, as an ambassador, but so as your proportion of living may serve you, we mean, because we know how many will resort to you, and desire to serve you. I told you how many [servants] I thought convenient you should keep'. When Barnaby joined the French armies at Nancy he sent his master an account of their organization, to which Edward replied with further inquiries: 'And to the intent you might be better instructed how to use yourself in these wars, we have thought good to advertise you of our pleasure therein. First, we would wish you, as much as you may conveniently, to be in the French King's presence, or at least in some part of his army where you shall perceive most business to be, and that for two causes; one is, because you may have more experience in the wars, and see things that might stand you in stead another day; the other is because you might be more profitable in the language; for our Ambassador who cannot wear harness [armour] cannot well come to those places of danger, nor seem so to serve the French King as you may; and so you shall be more acceptable to him, and do yourself much good. We doubt not also but of such things as you see there done you will not fail to advertise us, as you have well begun in your last letters ... We shall be nothing wearied with often advertising, nor with reciting of particularity of things. And to the intent we would see how you profit in the French, we would be glad to receive some letters from you in the French tongue, and we would write to you again therein.'⁸ Although there was a second request for letters in French, Barnaby did not respond to it; and Edward, having a great many other matters on his mind, did not press the point.

Edward's relations with the Princess Mary were now too strained for them to see much of one another; Elizabeth, with whom he exchanged letters and presents, rode through the City in state to visit him, and with her ladies was received at St James's. No doubt she would have spent some time with her brother: but on April 2nd he developed a rash and high fever; for a week he was seriously ill.⁹

This attack was diagnosed as measles and smallpox — a combination that would almost certainly have killed him. Such information as survives about its after-effects seems to indicate a bad bout of measles; and though Edward's life was not in danger, certain weaknesses remained that may have made him more susceptible to the consumption of which he died fifteen months later. His physique now became that traditionally — and wrongly — ascribed to him throughout his life; he looked, and was, frail, although he would never admit to fatigue. Yet until April 1552 his health had been so good (he had not had a day's illness since his recovery from malaria in his fifth year) that in a fortnight he threw off the worst of the disease. On the 23rd he was well enough to attend the St George's Day celebrations in Westminster Abbey in his Garter robes, and on the 28th the Spanish Ambassador reported him as completely recovered and in excellent spirits; four days after that he wrote to Barnaby Fitzpatrick that he had been 'a little troubled with the smallpox, which hath letted us to write hitherto, but now we have shaken that quite away'.¹⁰

While Edward was convalescing at Greenwich, Paget, who had managed to avoid being implicated in Somerset's downfall, received the reward of his treachery of 1549. He knew too many of

Northumberland's secrets, with the result that on April 22nd he was accused of peculation and the embezzlement of Crown property. His Garter was taken away and given to the Duke's eldest son, John Dudley, and he himself imprisoned. A less astute politician would not have escaped with his life: Paget contrived to remain unmolested until his reinstatement in Mary's reign.

Edward remained at Greenwich during the whole of May and the first fortnight in June; in order to reassure the people about his health, he rode at the ring at Blackheath and afterwards held a military review.[11] Then Mary visited him; she was followed by de Scheyfve, who this time was tactful enough not to raise the question of her Mass. Edward was out when he called; after a long wait he and the envoy had what de Scheyfve described as a general and friendly conversation.[12]

Then came a time of great anxiety for Edward. Cheke, who had been using his pupil's holiday to add to his library and install Ascham as his librarian, fell ill of the sweating sickness: the attack was severe and prolonged: finally, the physicians had to break to the King that there was no hope. Edward had prayed every day for his tutor's life, and every day his inquiries were greeted with darker news. He said: 'I shall continue to pray for him ... ' and the physicians withdrew. Next day Cheke's condition was the same, and the doctors reiterated that he could not live. Edward said: 'No — Cheke will not die this time — for this morning I begged for his life in my prayers, and obtained it' — an answer highly characteristic of the Tudors. This was one of the few prayers that Edward's merciless Protestant God granted without reservations. Cheke began to get better; in a few weeks he was able to go to Cambridge for change of air.[13] It is an indication of how entirely impersonal Edward's diary had become that there is no mention in it of his tutor's illness.

With Cheke's recovery began the last pleasurable months of Edward's life. Northumberland had decided that he should make an extended progress through Sussex, Hampshire, Wiltshire and Dorset, and preparations for the departure of the whole Court were set in hand. Some said that Northumberland had planned this tour in order to distract Edward from thinking about Somerset; but the Duke's influence was now so well established, and his relations with Edward so happy, that this may be discredited.

Edward did not forget his uncle; but from a remark that he let fall at this time, he appears to have accepted the fact of Somerset's treachery; indeed, if he had not, his situation would have been unendurable. He was shooting at the butts with Northumberland and some of his gentlemen, and hit the white. Northumberland called out: 'Well aimed, my liege!' Edward turned and said: 'But you aimed better when you cut off the head of my uncle Somerset.'[14] This retort has been quoted as proof of the King's remorse for Somerset's treatment, and as an indication that he was beginning to turn against Northumberland. Contemporary evidence shows that he was not speaking ironically; the entries in his diary relating to the trial and execution of the other supposed plotters make it clear that he believed Northumberland had saved him from a dangerous enemy. Meanwhile, from within the Tower, where Somerset's family were to remain until Mary's accession, a single protest was heard. Mrs Elizabeth Huggons, one of the Duchess's maids, burst into abuse of the King as 'an unnatural nephew — I wish I had the jerking of him', she exclaimed, adding: 'Have at the crown, with your leave', and shaking her fist. Summoned before the Privy Council, she denied everything, and was sent back to her cell.[15]

As his remaining doubts about Somerset vanished — as he felt his strength return — as he began to look forward to what he believed would be the first of many progresses through his kingdom — Edward's vitality soared; he was never again to appear so lively or so gay; and his intellectual grasp had reached its highest point. Just before his departure he received a request for help against the French from the Emperor. When de Scheyfve approached him about it, many of the Council, including Northumberland, were away; the remainder did not care to take the initiative, and replied to the envoy's suggestions with the old excuse of Edward's youth. De Scheyfve's irritation exploded. 'Although His Majesty is very young, he is very able, and quite capable of understanding the matter', he said, and asked Edward to call a full meeting. This took place at Hampton Court, where the envoy presented his master's letters of protest about the hostile activities of Henry II's armies in the Low Countries. Edward, who was receiving weekly reports of these from Barnaby Fitzpatrick, would not permit the Emperor's letters to be read out in front of the Council as usual, but went through them himself; de Scheyfve noticed that he stopped several times as if his eyes were troubling him; he said that the Emperor's hand-writing was difficult to read.[16]

Then followed a short discussion in which Edward took the lead, noting certain points from the letters, and asking after the Emperor's health. Not until he had done this did he turn to the Council and give them the gist of Charles's complaints, desiring their opinions courteously but, de Scheyfve thought, as a matter of form; it was obvious that he had already made up his mind. To the Ambassador he said that his reply to his good brother and cousin would be forthcoming in a day or two. Impressed in spite of himself, de Scheyfve withdrew — only to find that he was not able to approach the King again before he left Hampton Court for Oatlands, the first stop on his progress. All the envoy could do was to send one of his gentlemen in Edward's train; and all the agent did was to produce a few sketchy and useless reports of Edward's activities.[17] So the Emperor's demands for help remained as Edward had intended they should, unanswered, although not so ignored as to cause inconvenient pressure. The entry in Edward's diary for July 10th shows the diplomatic methods of his family at their most evasive: 'It was appointed here' (i.e. on his journey from Oatlands to Guildford) 'that if the Emperor's Ambassador did move any more for help or aid, this answer should be sent him by two of my Council, that this progress-time my Council was dispersed, I would move by their advice, and he must tarry till the matter were concluded, and their opinions heard ... How I had amity sworn with the French King which I could not well break; and therefore if the Emperor thought it so meet, I would be a mean for peace between them, but not otherwise. And if he did press the treaty [of 1542] ... that the treaty did not bind me which my father had made, being against the profit of my realm and country; and to desire a new treaty to be made between me and the Emperor ... '[18] When Charles protested again, Edward blandly put off a decision on the grounds of his 'young years' — a retort that infuriated the potentate who had so often told him that he was not old enough to judge for himself. The French alliance had put Edward in the ascendant; he must have enjoyed turning this attack with the Emperor's own weapon.[19]

Having thus temporarily disposed of foreign affairs, Edward began his progress — without Northumberland; the Duke's excuse was that he had to inspect the fortifications on the Border; he was probably aware that his unpopularity with the people would have become so apparent as to lower Edward's opinion of him, and might have caused disagreeable scenes. The success of the tour was much enhanced thereby; for Northumberland's personality was apt to over-shadow the King's. From the reports of those who saw them together it becomes clear that Northumberland, whether intentionally or not, curbed Edward's natural exuberance, and, while flattering and encouraging, dominated him. When the Duke was there, Edward subordinated himself to the pattern of kingship that Northumberland had imposed from without, instead of following that in which he had been trained.

Edward therefore set out in the highest spirits. He had no time to write down anything that he saw until he reached Petworth on July 20th, where it was decided that his entourage should be cut down from four hundred to a hundred and fifty; their train of horses had been enough, he noted, 'to eat up the country, for there was little meadow nor hay all the way I went'.[20] On the 25th he left Petworth for Cowdray, Sir Anthony Browne's mansion, then one of the most splendid private houses in England, famous for its vast Buck Hall, so called because of the eleven life-size stags (brow, bay and trey) in carved oak that stood on brackets above the wainscoting. The richness of the entertainment was a little overpowering for a boy who had just been ill and was used to a comparatively simple diet. Edward seems to have over-indulged himself and regretted it, for, he wrote to Barnaby Fitzpatrick, 'at that goodly house ... we were marvellously, nay rather excessively, banqueted'. The thought of his friend's privations saddened him a little. 'Whereas you have all been occupied in killing of your enemies, in long marchings, in pained journeys, in extreme heat, in sore skirmishings and divers assaults, we have been occupied in killing of wild beasts, in pleasant journeys, in good fare, in viewing of fair countries, and have rather sought how to fortify our own than to spoil another man's.'[21]

Passing from Sussex into Hampshire — spending a few nights at Havernaker, Warblington and Waltham respectively — hunting most of the day and sitting up late — Edward was still enjoying himself far too much to be aware of fatigue; but on August 8th, when he reached Portsmouth, where he stayed longer and was seen by more people, it was observed that he looked very frail, and 'general pity', according to one eye-witness, was felt for him.[22]

Edward himself would have been surprised and irritated by such a reaction; for at Portsmouth he was joined by Cheke, whose company, next to Barnaby's and Henry Sidney's, he enjoyed above all others. He stayed there several days, inspecting the fortifications and dockyards, which were badly in need of modernization. With characteristic energy Edward gave orders for this to be set in hand, going into and noting all the details of the work; the main fort must have new bulwarks, for the old ones, he wrote to Barnaby, were 'chargeable, massy, well repaired but ill fashioned, ill flanked and set in unmeet places, the town weak in comparison of that it ought to be, too hugely great (for within the walls are fair and large closes and much vacant room) the haven notable great, and standing by nature easy to be fortified. And for the more strength thereof, we have devised two strong castles on either side of the haven, at the mouth thereof. For at the mouth, the haven is not passed ten score over, but in the middle almost a mile over, and in length ... able to bear the greatest ship in Christendom'.[23] Having arranged for these improvements, and for 'a great rampier to be made within the wall, a great ditch within that, another wall within that, with two other slaughter-houses, and a rampier within that again', Edward went on to stay with the Earl of Southampton, at Titchfield; on the way there he lost a large pendent pearl from his gold collar: this was found before nightfall.[24] At Southampton, he wrote to Barnaby: 'the citizens had bestowed for our coming great cost in painting, repairing and ramparting of their walls. The town is handsome,' he added, 'and for the bigness of it, as fair houses as be in London. The citizens made great cheer, and many of them kept costly tables'. Edward was staying at the Castle in the midst of all this display, when he was told that an old friend of his father's, Bishop Bale of Ossory, had come from the next parish to see him. The King was standing at the window when he saw the Bishop come into the courtyard; he sent one of his ushers to escort him across; leaning out he began to ask him about his recent illness, congratulated him on his recovery and told him not to do too much, in what Bale afterwards described as 'a very fatherly and earnest' manner. Edward went on to inspect the shipyards of the city, and thought them overstaffed compared with those of the Thames; he gave orders that a number of local carpenters were to be temporarily transferred to work on his new men-of-war in the Port of London.[25]

By this time it had become obvious that he was exhausting himself and, while he rested at Beaulieu, it was agreed to curtail the progress on the grounds of economy. Edward was told that his courtiers were making a great fuss about the expense and discomfort they had to put up with, and something was said about a local recurrence of the sweating sickness. He agreed to cut down his programme, but thought the rumours of illness absurd. 'The most part of England', he told Barnaby, 'is (thanks be to God) clear of any dangerous or infectious sickness ... I hear of no place where any sweat or plague hath reigned, but only in Bristol, and the country near about. Some suspected it to be among a few in the town of Poole ... but I think rather not ... for I was within three mile of it, and less, and yet no man feared it. And thus God have you in his keeping.'[26] At last he came to Wilton, where the Earl of Pembroke entertained him over a period of several days with a magnificence that surpassed even that of Sir Anthony Browne. At Edward's table the vessels were of beaten gold, at those of the Councillors of silver-gilt; 'all the members of his household, down to the very least, ate off solid silver'. When Edward left, Pembroke gave him a travelling bed decorated with pearls and precious stones made to fold up and be carried by mule.[27]

At Wilton the hunting-parties were many and prolonged — too much so, perhaps; but although Edward did not believe himself in the least tired, he never had time to write to Barnaby. The memory of his Wiltshire visit lived on among the people. One day, galloping over the downs, Edward lost sight of his gentlemen and found himself cut off from everybody in a lane near the village of Bowerchalk; the only person he met was a little girl of six, whose name was Dew. Still alive in 1649, at the age of a hundred and three, she was something of a phenomenon, and people came to see her from many miles away. Then she would tell them how she once saw the beautiful young King in Felstone Lane: how he rode past her, all alone, and she stood staring after him.[28]

Passing through Salisbury, Winchester, Newbury and Reading, Edward reached Windsor on September 15th — 'in good health', he assured Barnaby, who may have heard some disquieting rumours.

Perhaps because he was really very tired, and found the resumption of his daily routine an effort, Edward began to miss his friend; Barnaby had been away now for nearly a year, and it was time, the King wrote, 'for divers other causes ... which you shall the perfectlier know at your coming hither', that he came home, 'with as much expedition as, with your ease, you can conveniently make ... Considering', he went on, 'the dead time of the year for wars draweth near', Barnaby had better ask leave of absence from Henry II, 'declaring that for your part you will at any other time when he shall have need, with leave of your master, serve him with all you can make ... '[29]

With great respect, Barnaby objected. A new army, in which he had been given a commission, was being put into the field: it would not look well if he were to ask for leave: he might appear lazy, or even afraid. Edward answered at once: 'We like your opinion very well ... Nevertheless, as soon as this business is once overpast, you ... may take some occasion to ask leave for this winter to come home ... in such manner and form as we have written in our former letters ... Therefore, we commit you to God.' So it was arranged that Barnaby should return in December; by that time the new campaign would be at a standstill.[30]

No one but Cecil seems to have been aware that, through Barnaby, Edward was in close touch with the Franco-Spanish campaign. Certainly the Spanish Ambassador did not; when he was received by Edward in October, he replied to His Majesty's inquiries about the war with a satirical account of the behaviour of the French King and his allies in the Low Countries; de Scheyfve told the Emperor that Edward had laughed at his jokes, and promised to stand godfather to his newly born son; the envoy was hurt and annoyed when the King told him that he would give the child a present, but that his coronation oath forbade his attending the christening. De Scheyfve thought this absurd and discourteous — surely His Majesty could have made an exception? Edward remained firm. The Ambassador went into a pet, and then into a sulk, and some for weeks absented himself from Court.[31]

A day or two after this disagreement Northumberland, who had joined the Court at Salisbury, became aware of the change in Edward. It alarmed him; whether he consulted the King's physicians or overrode them, is not clear; he and the Council decided that an expert should be summoned to report on him, and, if necessary, cast his horoscope. It so happened that Girolamo Cardano, the celebrated Italian doctor and mathematician, had just concluded a visit to the Bishop of St Andrews, whom he had cured of asthma, wrongly diagnosed as consumption. Cardano was therefore summoned to London, where he visited Edward towards the end of October. His account of the King is the most detailed and unbiased that exists.

Aged fifty-one and at the height of his fame, Cardano was what is now called an eccentric; in his autobiography he claims to have effected a hundred and eighty cures and actually killed only three of his patients; he combined the study of medicine and mathematics with astrology and necromancy, and had achieved success in all four sciences, in spite of early poverty, a stammer, poor health, and the refusal of the Milanese College of Physicians to admit him on the grounds of his illegitimacy. As a doctor, he was in advance of his age; his treatments were based on observation and common sense rather than on the terrifying combinations of drugs then used by most of the faculty. In London he stayed with Cheke, whose horoscope he cast — wrongly — and through the tutor got leave to dedicate his forthcoming book, *De Varietate Rerum*, to the King. Realizing that if he could cure Edward of a serious illness, his reputation would become unassailable, he decided to help his stammer before they met by 'cutting the band under his tongue'. He was then escorted by Cheke to the Palace of Westminster.

It was not then customary for doctors visiting patients in these circumstances to examine them or to ask questions about their symptoms. In Edward's case the situation was complicated by the fact that his weak — but not, at that time, dangerous — state of health was not admitted by himself, and must be concealed from the public and from all but a few of his courtiers. Cardano's interviews were therefore conducted on the assumption that he was being received as a scientist and a man of letters; he could only guess at Edward's condition, record what he saw and advise accordingly. His account was not written in full till some years after Edward's death; as he was both truthful and modest, it bears little trace of being wise after the event.

All their conversations were in Latin; the first opened with the usual compliments, followed by Cardano's praise of Cheke. 'Yes,' Edward said, 'I have two masters, Diligence and Moderation' — the second substantive was presumably a description of Cranmer. He went on: 'What is there in these rare books of yours, on the Variety of Things?'

By this time Cardano had received a superficial impression of Edward, whom he describes as 'of a stature somewhat below the middle height, pale-faced with grey eyes, a grave aspect, decorous and handsome. He was rather of a bad habit of body, than a sufferer from fixed diseases. He had a somewhat projecting shoulder-blade: but such defects do not amount to deformity'.

To the King's question, Cardano replied: 'In the first chapter I show the cause of comets, long sought for in vain.' 'What is it?' Edward asked. 'The concourse of the light of the planets', said Cardano. Edward — who, like many of his contemporaries, had confused astrology with astronomy — pursued this point. He said: 'How is it, since the motions of these are different, that it [the light] is not dissipated, or doth not move in accordance with their motion?' Cardano replied: 'It doth so move, only much faster than they, on account of the difference of aspect, as the sun shining through a crystal maketh a rainbow on a wall. A very slight movement of the crystal makes a great change in the rainbow's place.' Edward persisted. 'And how can that be done', he asked, 'when there is no *subjectum*? For to the rainbow the *subjectum* is the wall.' 'It occurs as in the Milky Way,' Cardano told him, 'and by the reflection of lights.'

During this part of their talk Cardano noticed that Edward was short-sighted and a little deaf; the latter impression may have been created by the King's difficulty in understanding his pronunciation of Latin; he adds that Edward spoke that tongue quickly and easily. Thereafter they met again several times and, although Cardano has left no further record of their talk, he was increasingly impressed by the King, and very sorry for him. 'This boy', he says, 'filled with the highest expectation every good and learned man, on account of his cleverness and sweetness of manner. When a royal gravity was called for, you would think it was an old man you saw, but he was friendly and companionable as became his years. He played upon the lute, took trouble over public affairs, was liberal of mind, and in these respects emulated his father ... He was well trained in philosophic studies.' During a final interview — when Edward seems to have appeared very tired — Cardano observed that 'in his humanity he was a picture of our mortal state; his gravity was that of kingly majesty, his disposition worthy of so great a prince. This boy of so much wit and promise was nearing a comprehension of the sum of things. (I do not here adorn the truth with rhetoric, but speak below the truth.) And there was the mark in his face of death that was to come too soon. Otherwise, he was comely, because of his age and of his parents, who had both been handsome'.

When the Council interviewed Cardano and asked him for Edward's horoscope and a diagnosis of his condition, the doctor was in a quandary. He tried to avoid giving either; he disliked all the King's ministers, Northumberland especially, finding them corrupt, hard, and, from his point of view, bullying and unscrupulous. In fact, he dared not express his real opinion, partly because it had become clear to him that he would have been punished for it, partly because it was difficult to make a more definite statement about the King than that he was liable to die young, but not necessarily doomed to do so. Also, although the English courtiers spoke Latin and Italian fluently, their pronunciation made his talks with them very difficult, 'for they inflected the tongue upon the palate, twisted words in the mouth, and maintained a sort of gnashing with the teeth'.

At last Cardano came to the conclusion that there was nothing for it but to produce a false horoscope, warn Cheke — and through him, Edward's jealous physicians — about over-fatiguing the boy, and so depart. 'I saw', he says cryptically, 'the omens of a great calamity.' In the horoscope he permitted himself to predict 'much ill health' for His Majesty, but added that he would live till the age of fifty-five; Cardano's circumstances made it impossible for him to put the full procedure of prophecy in hand, for this would have kept him at Court and subject to constant interference and worry for four days and nights. From Edward he received a hundred gold crowns and the memory of 'a boy of wondrous hope, who, if he had lived, would have done much for the betterment of his kingdom'. His final summing-up is strange and melancholy. 'It would have been better, I think, for this boy not to have been born, or if he had been born, not to have survived — for he had graces.'[32]

If Cardano had been able to prescribe for Edward, his remedies would probably have been ignored. Soon after he left England the King's energies were further taxed by the controversy about the Prayer Book of 1552. In October, Knox, preaching before Edward at Westminster, burst into a passionate protest against kneeling to receive the Sacrament; this he described as the Table Gesture. His objections carried weight with some of the bishops, Hooper among them; more important still, Knox was one of Northumberland's protégés, for the Duke was using this preacher's vogue in England to push the Calvinistic puritanism that screened other activities — one of these being the discrediting of Cranmer, who was responsible for the Second Prayer Book, although he had inserted a number of concessions to the Zwinglian doctrine about the Sacrament. (Zwingli maintained that it could not be proved from Scripture that Christ's Body and Blood were actually present in the bread and wine: His Presence could only be received by faith, and the rite was a pledge through which the communicants' redemption was renewed.)* In his reply to Knox's attack, Cranmer insisted on kneeling to receive the Sacrament — not as savouring of idolatry or adoration, but in reverence and humility. Knox's sermon had created two parties; and as the Second Prayer Book was already in the press, an extremely awkward situation arose. Northumberland, Hooper and a few of the clergy supported Knox: Edward, Cranmer and the majority of the bishops were against him.

This Prayer Book was Edward's special care, in which he had himself made several alterations and amendments. Now he was

---

* The divergence of modern expert opinion on Cranmer's final phase is interesting. A Catholic theologian (the Abbé Constant, writing in 1934) says that it was uncompromisingly Zwinglian. A Church of England historian (Dean Carpenter, 1957) finds him semi-Zwinglian. Of the lay authorities, Pollard (1905) describes him as rejecting both the Roman and Lutheran doctrines of the Sacrament, 'without descending' to the Zwinglian view; and G. R. Elton (1955), apparently agreeing with Pollard, adds that the Second Prayer Book is a compromise between the Lutheran, Zwinglian and Calvinist attitudes. Cranmer has also been described as a Dynamic Receptionist. Surely he would have delighted in these variations.

faced with an attack on one of its most vital passages that might result either in its postponement or in general dissatisfaction and bewilderment when it did appear. The dispute — in which Knox took a leading, and, from his own point of view, a highly enjoyable part — continued throughout October. Cranmer wrote to the Council imploring and urging them to ignore the egregious criticisms of the Scottish Chaplain: Knox did not desist from his fulminations against the cringing and inept attitude of the kneeler, as not truly representative of 'a joyful sharing of the feast'. He added that the communicant should not look on himself as God's slave or servant, but as His child. This hair-splitting deeply distressed Edward: but the influence of the foreign Protestants had been too strong for him to disregard it, as his father would have done. After many long, anxious and exhausting discussions on Reverence, Humility, Joyfulness, Adoration, Idolatry and Sincerity, the whole matter was thrashed out in a debate at Windsor that Edward attended. He made no notes — was he too weary to do so? — merely desiring Cecil to write a précis of the main arguments on either side. Finally, agreement was effected by Cranmer, who composed the Black Rubric of the Second Prayer Book, explaining that the communicant knelt to receive the Sacrament in reverence, not in idolatrous adoration. On November 1st it was so issued; the penalty for not using it was a short term of imprisonment. The Archbishop observed that His Majesty had been 'much alarmed' by the effects of Knox's vociferations. Knox himself was partially appeased by Northumberland's offer of the bishopric of Rochester. There was one repercussion from Calvin, who wrote to Edward warning him of the danger of vanity and self-will; kings, he said, were especially liable to these sins. 'It is a great thing', he concluded, 'to be a king, and especially of such a country; yet I have no doubt that Your Majesty esteems it incomparably better to be a Christian, and the Vice-Regent of Jesus Christ.'[33]

There is no mention of this degraded squabble in Edward's journal, in which he continued to record only foreign and economic affairs until the last day of November 1552. Then he wrote in it no more.

NOTES TO CHAPTER XIV

[1] *Cal. Span. P.*, vol. X, p. 517.
[2] *Lit. Rem.*, vol. II, p. 74.
[3] Ibid., p. 75.
[4] *Cal. Span. P.*, vol. X, p. 517; *Lit. Rem.*, vol. II, p. 400.
[5] Ibid., p. 504.
[6] Burnet, *History of the Reformation*, vol. III, part 2, p. 359.
[7] *Lit. Rem.*, vol. I, p. clxxxi; Trollope, *History of Christ's Hospital*, pp. 30-47.
[8] *Lit. Rem.*, vol. II, p. 87.
[9] Machyn, p. 30; *Cal. Span. P.*, vol. X, p. 519.
[10] *Lit. Rem.*, vol. II, p. 90.
[11] Machyn, p. 18.
[12] *Cal. Span.*, vol. X, p. 518.
[13] Strype, *Life of Sir John Cheke*, p. 87.
[14] Heylyn, p. 150.
[15] *Lit. Rem.*, vol. I, p. clxvi.
[16] *Cal. Span. P.*, vol. X, p. 546.
[17] Ibid.
[18] *Lit. Rem.*, vol. II, p. 433.
[19] Ibid.
[20] Ibid., p. 436.
[21] Ibid., p. 80.
[22] Halliwell-Philipps, vol. II, p. 50.
[23] *Lit. Rem.*, vol. II, p. 81.
[24] Ibid.
[25] Ibid., p. 83; *Cal. Span. P.*, vol. X, p. 560.
[26] *Lit. Rem.*, vol. II, p. 82.
[27] *Cal. Span. P.*, vol. X, p. 566.
[28] Aubrey, *Natural History of Wiltshire*, p. 69.
[29] *Lit. Rem.*, vol. II, p. 86.
[30] Ibid.
[31] *Cal. Span. P.*, vol. X, p. 572.
[32] H. Morley, *Life of Girolamo Cardano*, vol. II, pp. 129-40.
[33] P. Lorimer, *Life of John Knox*, p. 98; J. R. Tanner, *Tudor Constitutional Documents*, pp. 99-113; *Original Letters*, 2nd ser., p. 714; C. Hopf, p. 62; C. H. Smyth, *Cranmer, and the Reformation under Edward VI*, p. 267.

CHAPTER FIFTEEN

THE KING'S DEVICE

THE alliance between Knox and Northumberland came to an end shortly after the publication of the Second Prayer Book. The Scottish preacher's self-righteousness heightened his perception of others' sins; and as his monumental conceit enhanced his delight in public discourtesy, he hastened to defy and abuse the Duke when his campaign against kneeling for the Sacrament failed. His attacks barely scraped the surface of Northumberland's assurance; the orator his patron had hoped would be 'a whetstone to quicken and sharp the Archbishop of Canterbury' was allowed to thunder on about Judases, foxes and crafty councillors. Northumberland was not to be drawn; when it was reported to him that in a sermon preached before Edward at Westminster his former protégé had described him as 'an ungodly, conjured enemy to God's true religion' and a traitor to his innocent prince, he wrote to Cecil that 'poor Knox' was 'neither grateful nor pleasable', and recommended that he should be given the post of King's preacher in the North. (After that, he might perhaps be moved on, back to Scotland.) 'He cannot tell', Northumberland added mildly, 'whether I be a dissembler in religion or not: but I have for twenty years stood to one kind of religion, in the same which I do now profess; and I have, thank the Lord, passed no small dangers for it.' The Duke received Cecil's hints of his increasing unpopularity with Christian patience; it was indeed true that he had endured much obloquy, and he was ready to go on doing so; but it might be as well for the secretary to find out who, besides Knox, was spreading lies about him: not that it really signified – for 'the living God, that knoweth the hearts of all men, shall be my judge at the last day with what zeal, faith and truth I serve my master ... So for my part I will serve without fear, seeking nothing but the true glory of God and His Highness's surety; so shall I most please God and have my conscience upright, and then not fear what man doth to me'.[1]

THE DUKE OF NORTHUMBERLAND

Knox could only retort with further virulence and more effusive praise of Edward, whose godliness, he said, 'passed the measure given to other princes in their greatest perfection', adding that England was not worthy of him; although Somerset, he concluded, had been cold enough in God's word (did he not supervise his new buildings on Sunday mornings instead of going to church?), Northumberland's cunning and greed surpassed the Protector's pride and frivolity, and were infinitely more harmful.[2]

These fulminations did not affect Edward; he was used to the eloquence born of spite and hatred, and he was still to some extent in accord with Northumberland's ideas of government, although he had begun to chafe against his domination. As if to pacify him, Northumberland got the Council to agree that His Majesty should attain his majority at sixteen — two years earlier than the time ordained in his father's Will; the Duke then withdrew from Court, on the plea of ill health, telling Cecil that he had no heart for the Christmas and Twelfth Night festivities. 'Like the faithful servant in the Italian proverb,' he explained, 'I shall become a perpetual ass ... I am pestered by cravers that hangeth now daily at my gate for money.' Longing to retire from the world, he went to bed every night 'with a careful heart and a weary body; and yet abroad no man scarcely hath any good opinion of me ... What should I wish any longer this life, that seeth such frailty in it? I have no great cause to tarry much longer here.' His letters to Sir John Gates were more practical; he 'scribbled his simple mind' to this agent on Parliamentary matters, complaining that the Princess Elizabeth, who had asked for Durham Place as a town residence, was prejudiced against him. Her Grace did not really need an establishment in London, and on the whole it was better she should not stay too long at St James's with the King; but the refusal must be tactfully presented. 'Herein I trust His Highness will defend me unto Her Grace, who indeed I would not offend willingly, knowing her relation, as I do, to His Highness.'[3]

It was some time since Edward and his half-sisters had kept their Christmas and Twelfth Night revels together. Elizabeth's attempts to obtain Durham Place while temporarily moving into St James's, show that she would have liked to re-create the intimacy of the past. Yet although there was no religious division between her and the King, he had become as much estranged from her as from Mary, perhaps because he did not quite believe in the strict Protestantism that she discarded at his death. Her brand of piety seemed genuine to many — 'That were a shame to follow the Lady Mary, who leaveth God's word, and leave my Lady Elizabeth, who followeth God's word', said the naive little Lady Jane Grey — but it could hardly have convinced the brother with whom Elizabeth had been brought up, and whose acuteness equalled her own. [4] The practical separation of Edward and Elizabeth was effected secretly, as were most of Northumberland's manœuvres; as if to compensate for this, and for the absence of Barnaby Fitzpatrick, who had been summoned to Ireland to set his dying father's affairs in order, [5] an unusually elaborate series of masques was planned for the Greenwich festivities by George Ferrers, once more Edward's Lord of Misrule.

Ferrers's schemes were at first held up by the imprisonment of one of his team of writers — John Heywood, a Catholic, who had been in disgrace since his share in the rebellion of 1549. Fortunately Heywood had a friend at Court, who spoke for him to the King. Edward said: 'One who writes such harmless verses cannot have any evil designs', with the result that Heywood was re-admitted, and the preparations set in hand. [6] Ferrers, determined to excel himself, outlined his ideas in a letter to the Master of the Revels, Sir Thomas Cawarden. The first essential was a magnificent blue dress, for, as he had formerly appeared before His Majesty 'out of the moon', now he proposed to 'come out of the great waste or space, where there is neither fire, air nor earth ... How I shall come into the Court, whether under a canopy, or in a chair triumphal, or upon some strange beast — that I reserve to you; but the serpent with seven heads ... is the chief beast of mine arms and the holm-bush is the device of my crest; my motto is *semper ferians*, i.e. always feasting and keeping holydays. Upon Christmas Day I send a solemn ambassade to the King's Majesty by an herald, a trumpet, an orator speaking in a strange language, an interpreter with him'. Ferrers then arranged for drummers to precede him dressed in Turkish costume, sending Cawarden patterns of the white and gold material he needed for their robes, with orders for capes, slippers, hunting coats, fools' coats and a splendid dress for Will Somers, recalled from his retirement for the occasion. [7]

As Ferrers's orders multiplied, his ambitions swelled, and his sense of proportion seems to have disappeared. The King's Master of Horse, he told Cawarden, must meet him at Greenwich pier, where he and his space-men would appear, and where His Majesty and the Court would be waiting to receive him. His ship must be painted — or perhaps even draped? — with blue and white, and, as he disembarked, Sir George Howard, his stage manager, was to come forward with a horse, pages of honour and men-at-arms. Then the performers, having recited some complimentary verses, would lead Edward and his attendants into the Palace. By the time this had been arranged, Ferrers's cast numbered some hundreds, disguised as philosophers, astronomers, poets, physicians, jugglers, tumblers and clowns. He himself appeared in five different fancy dresses during the masques that were written by William Baldwin and Heywood and produced by Howard. The climax was *A Triumph of Cupid*, showing Venus, Mars and the blind god in a torchlight procession, accompanied by dancers dressed as monkeys (Ferrers had ordered grey rabbit-skins for these) on whose backs the musicians were carried in, playing and singing. This masque was supplemented by one of cats, another of 'Greek worthies' and a chorus of satyrs, monsters, soldiers and 'wild Irish savages' carrying clubs, with a few extras on hobby-horses for good measure. The total cost — £717 10s. 9d. — was moderate, considering that the baudkyn for Ferrers's first dress was priced at 16s. a yard and that one pair of gold breeches came to £6 8s.[8]

This catering for Edward's love of pageantry was perhaps a little out of date. He himself marked the New Year with honours of an unusual kind for Cheke. The tutor was granted a patent permitting his household servants 'at all times to shoot with the cross-bow, hacket or demi-hack at certain fowl and deer', notwithstanding Henry VIII's law that such a privilege was reserved for the nobility; a few months later Cheke was made a Councillor, and Edward gave him his own clock to commemorate the occasion.[9]

In the last week of January 1553 Edward returned to Westminster, and a few days later the Princess Mary was summoned to visit him. She was to have stayed at the Palace for some days, and a masque to be acted by children had been written for Candlemas

Night, February 2nd. It was not performed. Mary arrived to find Edward in bed with a chill that turned to congestion of the lungs; she sat with him for a little while, but the doctors were there, and their conversation was brief and formal. Nothing was said about religion, for Edward's fever was high and he had difficulty in breathing. The Spanish Ambassador, who accompanied the Princess, noticed that his right shoulder was now much higher than his left, and thought him seriously ill. Mary left the next day, unaware that it was their last meeting.[10]

For the next three weeks Edward remained in bed, and in March, although he was much better, rumours of his death began to circulate; no punishment, however severe, could stop them.[11] His determination to carry out the unfinished work to which he gave all his remaining strength forced him into a semblance of recovery; he had insisted on interviewing his ministers throughout his illness. At last he reached semi-convalescence, and appeared at a Council Meeting.

Those who had not seen him since Christmas were appalled by the change; he was very weak, white and thin, and the strain of presiding utterly destroyed his habitual courtesy. The session opened smoothly enough with a discussion about the French marriage. Madame Elisabeth was well, and had received His Majesty's token of a diamond ring; every morning, as instructed, she 'wished good-day' to the portrait of Edward that hung in her bedroom. Then some matter arose on which King and Council disagreed. Edward burst out, shaking with rage: 'You pluck out my feathers as if I were but a tame falcon — the day will come when I shall pluck out yours!', and the meeting broke up in gloom and terror.[12]

He then took a turn for the better, and public anxiety was soothed by the news that he walked in the palace gardens every day for a little while; his diet was strictly supervised, and the doctors were always with him. Those nearest him expected the worst, although they could not have guessed how stubbornly he was going to fight death during the next three months.[13]

Northumberland had returned to Court. As soon as he saw Edward he was faced, finally, with the collapse of the structure that had taken him more than a decade to build. Another had to

be made, and it was: not solidly, stone by stone, one plan cement-
ing the next, as in the past, but a hollow, tottering edifice that he
must have known would crumble at a touch. Northumberland was
no longer a gambler; now he was forced to become one; common
sense, perception, intellectual grasp were all submerged in the
frenzied, desperate work of reconstruction, of which a dying boy
was the corner-stone.

While Northumberland made his plans to retain power, what
remained of life for Edward continued almost as usual for a short
time. The range and pace of his work were not perceptibly
diminished; in fact, he seems to have done rather more than less;
now that the outdoor amusements were no longer possible, it was
easier for people to interview him. The retiring Venetian Ambassador obtained his farewell audience without a previous appointment, and was given the right to incorporate the lion of England
in his arms, an honour he had long been angling for; he thought
Edward still looked very handsome, but it was clear that he was
about to die — and in heresy, which made it all the more distressing, because that was not his fault; with the right upbringing his
soul might have been saved.[14]

As long as he was still able to take his place as head of the state,
Edward's chief concern was, as ever, religion: after that came the
currency. His best adviser, Sir Thomas Gresham, was something
of a financial genius, for between 1551 and 1553 he had managed
to raise the national credit abroad by playing the exchange, so
that in Antwerp the value of the pound had risen from 16s. to 22s.
Sir Thomas marked the occasion by sending Edward the first pair
of woven silk hose ever worn in England. During his last audience
they discussed the national debt, and at the end of it Edward told
him that he was to receive grants of land in Norfolk and Wales,
adding: 'Hereafter I will reward you better. You shall know that
you have served a king.'[15]

On March 1st Edward was well enough to open Parliament and,
although the ceremonies were curtailed, the people were reassured when they heard that His Majesty had worn a train of crimson velvet ten yards long and had sat in his chair of state two days
running in order to sign seventeen Acts.[16] It was during this session
that the strain under which Northumberland was working became
apparent: hitherto he had managed to maintain his self-control in

public; when Cranmer rose to read out his measures for the re-formed code of canon law, the Duke started up in a fury. 'You bishops!' he shouted, 'look to it at your peril that you touch not the doings of your peers. Take heed that the like happen not again — or you and your preachers shall suffer for it together!' The Archbishop protested: the clergy, he said, might have spoken of 'vices and abuses', but 'There are vices enough'. Northumberland interrupted fiercely: 'make no doubt of that!', adding with mingled bitterness and sanctimony: 'The fruits of the Gospel in this life are meagre enough.'[17] The wheel of Edward's existence was slowing down every day; and although the Duke's position was not yet quite desperate, he had not made up his mind where to place his last throw. His difficulties were enhanced by the King's increasing obstinacy and rebelliousness. He may not have realized that the change in Edward's attitude was partly caused by the violent irritability that was a concomitant of his disease, and partly the result of a rapidly deepening distrust. The personal autocracy which Northumberland had helped Edward to achieve was turning into a weapon against himself; he had under-rated the boy's capacities and disregarded their effect on his tempera-ment. Edward could be as ruthless as any of his family, and now, having at last taken in the economic and religious chaos to which his kingdom was reduced, he had begun to look for the culprit: if he had lived for another six months he would have called Northumberland to account; as it was, there appeared no one else, except Cranmer, on whom he could rely. So the Duke's power was maintained, although precariously; he set about trying to establish it on a permanent basis.

The first step was obvious. It must be made clear to Edward that he was not likely to live, so that he would fall into line with Northumberland's schemes. By the beginning of April the King realized that he might not attain his majority; he was, therefore, from Northumberland's point of view, in the right frame of mind.

It may have been at about this time that Edward wrote in the fly-leaf of Paleario's *Benefit of Christ's Death* 'Live to die, and die to live again'.[18] Such resignation was neither instinctive nor charac-teristic, but achieved through bitterness and despair. There is no contemporary record of his heart-searchings; but a soliloquy — composed and put into his mouth by Sir John Hayward, his first biographer, writing some fifty years later — may have originated from the remarks that he let fall when he first faced his own death and began to wonder whether he had failed in his trust: to see himself as a creature fated from the womb; to recall the execution of his two uncles; to contemplate the inheritance that he must shortly hand over to the half-sister who would undo all his work and lead England back into the darkness and horror of Catholicism.[19] It is only known that he sank into a fearful sadness; that anxiety haunted and tortured him; and that instinctively he turned to Northumberland who, ill himself from suspense and strain, seldom left his side.[20] The Duke found remedies for lesser problems by organizing a fresh campaign against Anabaptists, enforcing the penalties for recusancy and punishing those who complained. Yet not even the most ardent Catholic could be persuaded to look on Edward as a tyrant or a persecutor. 'Alas poor child!' said one gentleman to Bishop Bale. 'Unknown is it to him what Acts are made nowadays. But when he cometh once of age, he will see another rule, and hang up the heretic knaves and their maintainers.' Bale indignantly replied: 'His Majesty's worthy education declareth him to be no poor child, but a manifest Solomon in princely wisdom. Ye shall find at this day no Christian prince like him ... ' and reported the conversation to the Privy Council.[21]

Edward had no time for these trivialities. After the succession, his chief concerns were the charitable institutions for which he had made himself responsible to Ridley and the City fathers, the re-endowment of the grammar schools that still bear his name and the Catechism, compiled by Alexander Nowell, that he corrected and amplified with injunctions that it should be learnt by every child. He saw to all these matters before he left London for the purer air and greater quiet of Greenwich; meanwhile, he listened to the Lenten sermons as usual, knighted the new Lord Mayor — who gave him a full account of the procession of uniformed orphans, their matrons, physicians and governors marching into Christ's Hospital — and sent Mary 'a table diamond with a pendent pearl', presumably to show that whatever steps he might take against her as a king, he still cared for her as a brother. Northumberland saw to it that they did not meet, although Mary made several attempts to visit him. Elizabeth, too, was kept away and her letters were not delivered; her influence was now more dangerous to Northumberland than that of her sister.[22]

On April 11th, 1553, Edward VI left his capital for the last time. In the state barge he was conveyed from the Palace of Westminster to Greenwich. The guns fired and the flags were flown, as for a triumphant progress.[23] With his departure the omens and portents that precede the death of princes began; that they were not recorded till after he died may explain their concatenation and is also accounted for by the pillorying of those who in taverns and stable-yards and private houses were heard muttering of fatality and disaster. It was noted that on the very day His sacred and blessed Majesty left London two gentlemen going by water to see the bear-baiting at Paris Garden were drowned; and that on Ludgate Hill a dog was seen carrying 'a piece of a dead child in his mouth'. One preacher, bolder than the rest, foretold the holocaust of the city in a sermon at Paul's Cross, crying: 'I summon you all, every mother's child of you, to the judgment of God, for it is at hand.' His prophecy was afterwards associated with news of monstrous births, the appearance of a school of dolphins in the Thames and of a whale at Gravesend.[24]

During the first fortnight of April Edward's condition so improved that there was some justification for Northumberland spreading the news that he was nearly well; what remains of the Duke's official and foreign correspondence shows that he was almost persuaded by the doctors that their cures were having effect, although they themselves did not believe this; one told the Spanish Ambassador that if His Majesty did not get very much better within a month he could not live through the summer, adding that 'the matter he ejects from his mouth is sometimes coloured a greenish-yellow and black, and sometimes the colour of blood'.[25] Edward still walked every day in the gardens; Simon Renard, who had just joined the Spanish Embassy, seeing him for the first time, reported that he was wasting away.[26] Yet the King himself felt a little stronger, and began to revolt against the loathsome, and probably harmful, prescriptions, of which the most popular runs as follows: 'A cure for consumption. Take a sow-pig of nine days old, and flea him and quarter him, and put him in a stillatory, with a handful of spearmint, a handful of red fennel, a handful of liverwort, half a handful of red turnip, a handful of

My devise for the succession.

1 For lakke of ~~issu~~ masle of my body ~~to the issu continuing of~~ . To the L Fran~
~~ceses~~ heires masles, ~~For lakke of~~ ~~if she have any~~ such issu befor my death to the
L Janes and her heires masles, To the L Katerins heires
masles, To the L Maries heires masles, To
the heires masles of the daughters which she
she shal have hereafter. Then to the L Mar
gets heires masles. For lakke of such issu,
To theires masles of the L Janes daughters
To theires masles of the L Katerins daughters
and so furth til you come to the L mar~
gets daughters heires masles.

2 If after my death theire masle be entred into
18 yere old, then he to have the hole rule
and governance therof.

3 But if he be under 18, then his mother to
be governeres til he entre 18. yere old and aggreemet
But to doe nothing about thause of 6
parcel of a counsel to be pointed by my
last will to the nomore of 20.

4 If the mother die befor theire entre into 18
the realme to ~~he~~ be governed by the couce.
Provided that after ~~he~~ he be 14 yere al
great matters of importance be ~~so~~ opened
to him.

5 ~~If i died bore issu, and ther there none~~
~~heire masle, then the L Frannces to be rege~~ governeres
~~for lakke of her the her eldest daughters~~
~~and for lakke of them the L margets to be~~

THE KING'S DEVICE

celery, nine dates clean picked and pared, a handful of great raisins stoned, quarter of an ounce of mace and two sticks of cinammon bruised in a mortar; distil together with a fair fire; put in a glass and set in the sun nine days; drink nine spoonfuls of it at a time when you list.'[27]

Edward did not list. Then, feeling himself helpless, he gave in, and did what he was told, remaining indoors, reading a little with Cheke and Henry Sidney — Barnaby Fitzpatrick was still in Ireland — and going through Tye's *Acts of the Apostles in Rhyme* and Sternhold's *Psalms in Metre*, both recently published and dedicated to him. One of Tye's opening verses must have struck him as ironic:

> The living God grant thee to reign
> In great honour and wealth:
> Thy virtuous life, good Lord, maintain,
> And send thee prosperous health.

Encouraged by Cheke, Edward tried his own hand at verse-making. His penultimate written work was a long and very bad poem on the Eucharist; halting and indeed ludicrous though they are, the very inadequacy of his rhymes has a certain pathos:

> Yet whoso eateth that lively food,
> And hath a perfect faith,
> Receiveth Christ's flesh and blood,
> For Christ himself so saith.
> Not with our teeth His flesh to tear,
> Nor take blood for our drink:
> Too great absurdity it were
> So grossly for to think ... [28]

So April passed away, between faint hope and deadly suspense. By the beginning of May, Northumberland had made up his mind, and began to put his plans in action.

The newly created Duke of Suffolk, formerly Marquis of Dorset, had been Northumberland's most powerful ally since Somerset's execution. His hope of marrying his eldest daughter, Lady Jane Grey, to Edward, having been destroyed by Admiral Seymour's downfall, he had arranged no other alliance for her, trusting to

Northumberland to place her and her sisters for him. Northumberland now announced the betrothal of Suffolk's three daughters: Jane to his fourth son, Lord Guilford Dudley; Katherine to Pembroke, Lord Herbert's heir; and Mary — she was a dwarf — to her cousin, Lord Grey of Wilton. (All these arrangements ended disastrously: Jane and Guilford were executed in 1554; Katherine was forced to divorce Pembroke, and then clandestinely married Lord Hertford, with the result that she died in prison in 1568; Mary's engagement to Grey was broken off, and she secretly married Queen Elizabeth's sergeant-porter, dying penniless and disgraced in 1578.) But in the summer of 1553 the prospects of the three girls were excellent. On their mother's side they were princesses of the blood; she was Lady Frances Brandon, Henry VIII's niece; her two brothers, both Dukes of Suffolk in turn, had died without issue in 1551, and the dukedom of Suffolk was re-created for her husband, Dorset, in the same year, as a reward for his share in the plot against Somerset. Because this Dorset-Suffolk-Grey branch of the Tudor dynasty was Protestant, it had been placed next in the succession, after Edward and his half-sisters, by Henry VIII.[29]

Northumberland's scheme was simple to the point of crudity. He had decided to eliminate Mary and Elizabeth from the succession — the first on the grounds of her Catholicism, and the second because, if she married a foreigner, she might endanger the Protestant faith — and replace them by their cousin, the Lady Jane Grey; before doing this he had to attach his family to hers by marrying her to Guilford. Then he was going to persuade Edward to alter the succession in Jane's favour.

Northumberland and the Suffolks were at once opposed by the Lady Jane; she was fifteen and a half, a girl of strong character and remarkable frankness. She detested Guilford Dudley — he was indeed a spoilt, conceited and disagreeable young man — and she told her father that she would not marry him. Suffolk replied that the King had commanded her to do so. She reminded him of her betrothal to Lord Hertford, Somerset's eldest son, now relegated and disgraced. Her obedience was enforced by a beating, and on May 25th, 1553, her marriage to Guilford Dudley was celebrated at Durham Place. (It was given out that Edward would be present, but he was in no condition to move from

Greenwich.) Guilford Dudley made no secret of his dislike for his bride, nor of the fact that he was marrying her because she was the great-niece of Henry VIII and chosen for him by his father.[30]

Meanwhile, Northumberland, aware that after Edward's death his position, and even his life, would be threatened, did what he could to reinstall himself in the Princess Mary's favour. He restored the Royal Arms of which she had been deprived since her mother's divorce, and sent her regular bulletins about Edward's condition.[31] It now only remained for him to combine with Edward in rescinding the late King's Will, and making another in favour of Lady Jane.

Deeply concerned though Edward was about the consequences of Mary's succession, he could not bring himself, at first, either to go against his father's arrangements or to shelve the Princess Elizabeth. Northumberland pointed out to him that if the Catholic party forced Elizabeth to marry a Spanish or French prince, her succession would be as fatal to the Protestant cause as Mary's. Still Edward hesitated. He may have hoped — as did many others — that Mary, in spite of her own beliefs, was not certain to interfere with those of her subjects; she tolerated the Henricians, and did not seem particularly to favour the Catholics; and her claim was purer than Elizabeth's, whose legitimacy had always been more doubtful. The third claimant, Mary Stuart, had already been passed over by Henry VIII, so it was not difficult to get Edward to consent to exclude her for Lady Jane: his half-sisters' rights could not so easily be set aside.

It was at this point that Northumberland produced his final and most effective reason for a new Will. He said: 'It is the part of a religious and good prince to set apart all respects of blood, where God's glory and the subjects' weal may be endangered. That Your Majesty should do otherwise were, after this life — which is short', he added significantly, 'to expect revenge at God's dreadful tribunal.'[32]

Northumberland was not naturally a cruel man, but — what may come to the same thing — a desperate one. He did not make this attack on the dying boy till everything else had failed.

Edward did not now fear death; his sufferings, physical and mental, were such that he desired it.[33] Faced with the thought of his own eternal damnation and the charge of his people's souls,

275

he gave in. During the first fortnight in June he drew up his 'device for the succession'.

Like everything else he set in hand, Edward's arrangements were methodical, detailed and succinct. He made several drafts for his device, all of which survive. Slightly simplified, the first ran as follows: 'For lack of issue of my body ... the Crown shall come (1) To the Lady Frances' [the Duchess of Suffolk's] heirs males. (2) For lack of such issue before my death, to the Lady Jane's heirs males. (3) To the Lady Katherine's heirs males. (4) To the Lady Mary's heirs males. (5) To the heirs males of the daughters which she [the Duchess of Suffolk] shall have hereafter.' Edward did not forget that the Duchess of Suffolk had had a sister Eleanor, who had married the Earl of Cumberland in 1537 and died in 1547, leaving one daughter, the Lady Margaret Clifford. He therefore continued: 'Then to the Lady Margaret's heirs males. For lack of such issue, to the heirs males of the Lady Jane's daughters. To the heirs males of the Lady Katherine's daughters; and so forth, till you come to the Lady Margaret's daughters' heirs males.' He concluded this first draft with arrangements for the government during a Regency, should the occasion arise.

In his second draft Edward ordained that if he died without issue — as he now knew would be the case — the crown should come, not to 'the Lady Jane's heirs males', but to '*the Lady Jane, and her heirs males*'. In the final draft, Lady Jane's direct succession was further ensured by the declaration that neither Mary nor Elizabeth could succeed because they were both illegitimate.* Throughout the three stages of Edward's device, Northumberland's gradual and insinuating methods can be perceived, but only here did he use his old technique; in all other respects the time for subtlety and deviousness was past, and his difficulties were increased by the apparently uncertain progress of Edward's disease. Now and then he rallied, and whenever he did so it was necessary to give out that he was not mortally ill, because, quite apart from policy, the thought of his death was so terrible that few of those about him could endure to speak or write of it, with the result that the only detailed reports of his condition come from the French and Spanish Ambassadors. They were able to per-

* See also S. T. Bindoff's fascinating article in *History Today* (September 1950) in which he suggests that the final alterations may have been forged.

suade the doctors to confide in them, and, once or twice, to see the King for themselves.

During the first fortnight in May, Edward got slightly better. and it was announced to the public that he was merely 'a little sick and accrased' [run down].[34] The Garter ceremony had been postponed in the hope that he would be well enough to attend it; he himself counted on doing so, and seems to have felt that he might be going to live. On May 12th he wrote to Northumberland, who was then at Durham Place, desiring him to return to Greenwich for the festivities. On the same day the Spanish Ambassador was told by one of the doctors that His Majesty could not possibly last till June. He was suffering from 'a suppurating tumour on the lung', and ulcers were breaking out all over him; his cough was harsh and continuous, his body dry and burning, his stomach swollen, his fever very high, and he would never again leave his bed. No soothing remedies were then used; as his sufferings increased, stimulants were applied, so that it was impossible for him to slip into a merciful unconsciousness.[35] If he had not been what he was, the doctors might have let him die peacefully; they had to keep him alive and aware for as long as they could, irrespective of what he endured. Cecil, who read the reports sent to Northumberland, wrote guardedly to a sick friend: 'God deliver you from the physicians.'[36]

Still, for a little while every day, Edward was able to read with Cheke; through the tutor, he sent a message to one of his foreign protégés to say that he had taken pleasure in his new book, but was not yet well enough to write himself. He insisted on interviewing the French Ambassador; the audience lasted only a few minutes, for he was hardly able to speak.[37] On May 15th there was another rally, and a few days after that he received a letter from Mary congratulating him on his recovery and begging to be allowed to visit him.

At this point the despair and terror of the people became so violent that Northumberland, returning from his son's marriage festivities in London, gave orders that His Majesty was to be lifted out of bed and held up at the window, so that the waiting crowds might see for themselves that he was still alive. The spectacle of that helpless and wasted figure must have enhanced the panic and misery of those who saw it; Northumberland's announcement that the King was now able to walk every day in the gardens was not believed.[38]

On May 20th the sound of cheering and the thunder of cannon reached Edward from the river that ran past his window. He was too weak to be lifted up to see the departure of the three great ships in which he had taken such pride and whose building he had supervised a year ago. Sir Hugh Willoughby was setting out to try to discover the North-West Passage through the Arctic regions; his navigator, Sebastian Cabot, was a pensioner of Edward's; two years before, he had explained the use of the compass to the King, and they had discussed science and mathematics together. The ships, all hung in pale blue damask, their decks thronged with sailors in their new blue uniforms, passed the Palace, dropped down the river and disappeared.[39]

In the first week of June, Edward saw the Duchess of Suffolk for a few minutes. The Spanish Ambassador was told that his condition had become such that he could not last another ten days. Sometimes he was delirious; between the bouts he was so weak that he could not keep down the food they forced on him, and was therefore 'restored' by spirits; he had to lie on his back all the time, and was beginning to suffer agonies from bed-sores.[40]

He clung to Henry Sidney, and to Cheke; indeed, he would hardly allow Sidney to leave his room; in the intervals of his delirium he tried to prepare himself for the death that was so long in coming. 'I am glad to die,' Cheke heard him whisper.[41] Presently those about him became aware that he was murmuring over and over again the prayer that, methodical to the end, he had composed but was too weak to write down. As it was heard it was written out, and, long afterwards, published. 'Lord God,' they heard him say, 'deliver me out of this miserable and wretched life, and take me amongst Thy chosen; howbeit, not my will but Thy will be done. Lord, I commit my spirit to Thee. O! Lord, Thou knowest how happy it were for me to be with Thee: yet, for Thy chosen's sake, send me life and health, that I may truly serve Thee. O! Lord God, bless Thy people and save Thine inheritance. O! my Lord God, defend this realm from papistry, and maintain Thy true religion, that I and my people may praise Thy holy name, for Thy son Jesus Christ's sake. Amen.'[42]

The story of Edward VI should have concluded with the utterance of this prayer; it is that of the child who had commanded the Bible to be carried before him out of Westminster Abbey, and for whom the hearts of his people 'sang up and down', for joy that he was king; it well becomes 'the goodly flower' of his great dynasty, Henry VIII's 'most noble jewel', whose prospects had been so fair, whose reign was to have created a golden world. That his life did not end with this return to innocence and simplicity, but in an agonized, terrible rallying of anger, tyranny and injustice, is his tragedy, perhaps; yet he cannot be entirely exonerated for forcing his will on those who were responsible for the administration of his kingdom. In the last days of June, as he lay in torment, his brain was clear, his mind made up, his resolve crystallized; as in lesser crises, the resultant decision remained secret, hidden from all but the evil genius who stood behind him.

By the middle of June, his state could no longer be concealed. In the chapel at Greenwich Palace the service included a prayer that God should 'look down with pitiful eyes upon Thy servant Edward, our King'.[43] In the Courts of Europe bets were being made about the date of his death.[44] From Brussels, Sir Thomas Hoby wrote to Cecil that the punishment of the national wickedness had 'caused God to turn His face aside, and to plague us with the most gravest and greatest plague that could come to England'.[45] Now the Council met daily in sessions from which clerks and secretaries were excluded; they replied to all inquiries with a bulletin of 'slight improvement', presumably in order to prevent further questioning from the foreign ambassadors.

In the same week this formula was emphasized by the resumption of music during meals, and the French envoy was granted an audience with His Majesty. He and his suite were asked to dine at Greenwich. As they finished eating, they were told that Edward would receive them. They left the banqueting-hall for one of the ante-chambers, where they found Northumberland and some others of the Council. A short discussion ensued, in which the question of their seeing the King did not arise, and they did not press the point. Northumberland said that his policy was wholly French; then he turned to de Theligny du Bois-Daulphin, at whose expense they had all been so merry two years before, and said desperately: 'What would your lordship do in my case?' The Ambassador replied with a formal speech about his master's interests, and the interview ended less than an hour after it had begun.[46]

On June 10th the doctors told the Spanish Ambassador that His Majesty could not live for more than three days; Northumberland's plans depended on the prolongation of the King's existence for a little longer than that time. He ignored the verdict of Wendy, Owen and Butts, who had looked after Edward since his birth, turned them out of the sick-room and called in three other opinions: his own doctor, a professor of medicine from Oxford, and a female quack, whose name has not survived. This woman declared herself perfectly able to cure His Majesty, provided she was left in sole charge. Northumberland gave her a free hand. She began her ministrations with a dose of what she described as 'restringents', and which seem to have included arsenic. The immediate effect was another rally.[47]

Edward was still concerned about the installation of Christ's Hospital for which his grant had not yet been made; when the document was brought to him, he was able to sign it under his promise of four thousand marks a year, thanking God that he was strong enough to do so.[48] He was in fact stronger than he had been for some while: the time had therefore come for Northumberland to make his final arrangements. Edward's 'device for the succession', already drawn up and signed by himself, must now be approved and signed by the whole Council, and by the legal and clerical authorities, so that the crown should pass without dispute to Lady Jane.

On June 11th, the Lord Chief Justice, Sir Edward Montague, with the Solicitor-General and the Attorney-General, received orders to present themselves at Greenwich Palace on the following day. As soon as they arrived they were taken to Edward's bedside. Coughing, gasping for breath, he was nevertheless in control of the situation. Northumberland, Paulet, Sir John Gates and half a dozen other Councillors were standing by the bed. The judges knelt and waited for the King to speak.

'Our long sickness', he began, 'hath caused us heavily to think of the conditions and prospects of our realm. Should the Lady Mary or the Lady Elizabeth succeed, she might marry a stranger, and the laws and liberties of England be sacrificed, and religion changed. We desire, therefore, that the succession be altered, and we call upon your lordships to receive our command upon the drawing up of this deed by letters patent.' At a sign from Northumberland the new Will was read out. Montague was then told by Edward that he and his comrades were at once to make a deed of settlement based on its articles.

The Lord Chief Justice, in terror, as he afterwards declared, of Northumberland's vengeance, was not prepared to betray his trust without a struggle. He said that what His Majesty required was illegal, and could not be drawn up under the heading of an Act of Parliament. Edward said: 'I will hear no objections. I command you to draw the letters patent forthwith.' After a pause, Montague asked if he and the other two judges might be allowed to study the document. Permission was given, and they withdrew, taking the book, as it was now called, back to London with them. After a short conference all three agreed that the King's device was illegal, and that to sign it would be a criminal act. The final clause declared that any person going about to undo the device or interfere with its arrangements for the succession would be found guilty of high treason. Aware that Northumberland had the Council behind him, they felt themselves trapped and in great danger. They decided, nevertheless, to speak the truth.

At this point they were summoned by the Council to Northumberland's palace of Ely Place in Holborn. The Duke was not present. Montague, asked whether he and his fellows had signed the deed, replied: 'I cannot. Such an act would be high treason.'

The door opened, and Northumberland burst in, white and shaking. 'You are a traitor!' he shouted. 'I will fight any man living in my shirt, in this quarrel!' Montague stood silent. Then he was told to go.

Next day the judges were again summoned to Greenwich. Waiting in the ante-chamber to the King's bedroom, they found themselves among a crowd of courtiers, who looked at them coldly and in silence, 'as though they had not known them'. From this Montague concluded the worst, and prepared himself for immediate arrest. As soon as they entered the bedchamber, it became clear that Edward had been told of their refusal. With an angry countenance, he demanded: 'Where are the letters patent? Why have they not been drawn?'

Montague saw that Northumberland and a group of Councillors were standing on the other side of the dais. He fell on his knees, and said: 'To do the same would be to put the Lords and us in danger of high treason — and yet be nothing worth.' 'Why have you refused to obey my order?' Edward exclaimed. 'To refuse were treason ... ' Northumberland added, and there was a mutter of assent from the other Lords.

Sir Edward Montague burst into tears. 'I have served Your Majesty and Your Majesty's most noble father these nineteen years,' he said, 'and loath would I be to disobey Your Grace's commandments.' He added: 'I have seventeen children. I am a weak old man and without comfort.'

Edward ignored this appeal, and Sir Edward went on: 'If these writings were made, they would be of no use after Your Majesty's decease, while the statute of succession remaineth in full force, because it could only be abrogated by the same authority whereof it was established, that of Parliament.' 'We mind to have a Parliament shortly,' Edward replied. 'If that be Your Majesty's intention,' pleaded Montague, 'this matter may be deferred to the Parliament, and all perils and dangers saved.' Edward's answer was rapped out in so fierce and haughty a tone that the judge began to tremble. 'I will have it done now,' he said, 'and afterwards ratified by Parliament. On your allegiance — make quick dispatch!' Glancing at Bromley, the Attorney-General, he went on: 'And what will you do?' 'I will obey Your Majesty.' 'And what say you, Sir John Baker?' Edward pursued, relentlessly turning on the Solicitor-General, 'for you have said never a word this day.' 'I will obey Your Majesty's command.' 'Away with you, then, and make speed,' said the King.

After a moment's pause Montague began timidly: 'If Your Majesty would grant me a licence under the Great Seal — and a pardon for having signed Your Majesty's device — I will obey Your Majesty's command.' Edward agreed to this. 'I will not suffer that licence to be sealed,' Northumberland broke in: 'I will have no man in better case than myself.' It was then decided that a pardon should be issued for all who signed. Montague and the other judges, completely cowed, departed from the Palace 'with sorrowful hearts and weeping eyes, in great fear and dread, to devise the said book, according to such articles, signed with the King's proper hand, above, beneath, on every side'.[49]

Northumberland's task was nearly done. His own faction signed the deed readily enough; only Cecil abstained, sending word that he was ill. The King insisted on his attendance, and his signature, saying: 'It is my pleasure to have it so to pass, which you have no reason to deny ... ' and the secretary obeyed. Afterwards he declared that he had signed simply as a witness.[50]

In this way more than a hundred signatures were subscribed. The most important of all — Cranmer's — was missing. Without the Archbishop's approval Edward's device was, as Montague would have said, nothing worth.

The situation was perhaps the most difficult that Cranmer had ever faced. He stood to lose everything (although it is unlikely that he foresaw his own martyrdom) through Mary's accession, and not only in a personal sense; he knew that she would immediately undo most, if not all, of the work to which he had dedicated his life and his soul. Yet her right seemed unassailable; and, as Edward's godfather and spiritual director, it was Cranmer's duty to prevent him forcing through an illegal act that deprived the Protestant as well as the Catholic Princess of her inheritance. If Northumberland had married Guilford Dudley to Elizabeth (and presumably he did not do so because he realized that he would never be able to dominate her) Cranmer might have signed the device without demur; the substitution of Lady Jane for both her cousins was too much for him.

Clearly Edward's decision to enforce his will had been strengthened by Montague's opposition; apart from his conviction that he was in the right, to feel his authority questioned when he was about to relinquish it must have helped to stimulate him, and it did so to a phenomenal and unexpected degree; he was determined not to die until the Archbishop had signed.

Cranmer was first appealed to by the Council, to whom he said: 'I cannot subscribe without perjury, being foresworn to my Lady Mary by King Henry's Will.' To their protests he replied: 'I am not judge over any man's conscience but mine own only; for, as I will not condemn your fact [action], no more will I stay my fact upon your conscience, seeing that every man shall answer to God for his own deed, and not for other men's.' He then asked to see the King alone; naturally Northumberland was not going to allow this; he and a number of the Council were present at the interview.

When Cranmer had given Edward his reasons for not signing, Northumberland broke in, 'very harshly', before the King could summon strength to reply. 'It doth not become your lordship', he said, 'to speak so to His Majesty.' Edward then pointed out that according to a statute made by his father, it was legal to leave the crown by Will, irrespective of any previous settlement; he added gently: 'Be not more repugnant to my will than the rest of the Council.' Cranmer asked if he might consult with the judges before making up his mind; he never forgot the affectionate look with which his godson granted this request.

Finding that all but one of the principal legal authorities had signed Edward's device, he hesitated; they assured him that he might follow their example without breaking the law. He was not quite convinced, and asked for another audience with the King. 'You alone must not stand out ... ' was all that Edward could say. Cranmer was not proof against such an appeal; if he gave in, the person he loved most in the world would die in peace, and the true faith be maintained. He signed, as he afterwards told Mary, not under pressure, but from conviction, 'unfeignedly, and without dissimulation'. [51]

As a Councillor, Cheke, too, was bound to sign. He said: 'I will never distrust God so far in the preservation of his true religion as to disinherit orphans' — but was persuaded or terrorized into signing. [52] So the succession was settled. Northumberland's last measure was added after Cranmer's signature, during the third week in June, in a clause by which the subscribers swore to maintain the Will 'to the uttermost of their power' and 'never at any time during their lives to swerve from it'. [53] And now Edward had only to die. He suffered for fifteen more days.

The inevitable rumours of his having been poisoned which circulated for nearly a hundred years after his death (it was said by some that Northumberland had brought this about by means of a bunch of flowers) [54] had some foundation. Edward, dying of tuberculosis of the lungs, was, finally, poisoned by the medicine that had at first so stimulated him as to give the impression that he might live for several months, or even entirely recover. This phase lasted until the succession had been settled. Then the reaction began. He had eaten nothing since June 11th. Now his legs and arms swelled up, his skin darkened, and his nails and hair fell off: his fingers and toes became gangrenous. The laundress who washed his shirts lost her nails and the skin of her fingers. Breathless, moaning, too weak to cough, he was still conscious, still praying for death, still clinging to those whom Northumberland allowed to remain with him — Henry Sidney, Sir Thomas Wroth, and a favourite servant, Christopher Salmon, who was there to help the quack doctor and carry out duties that no one else could face. And with this hideous decay of the body, there came a return of the serene and gentle sweetness of spirit that had made him so dear to those who now watched his final agonies. He could not often speak; but he smiled instead of thanking them.[55]

During the week of July 1st, Northumberland dismissed the empiricist and recalled Edward's own physicians — only so could he put himself in the right before the moment of death. She disappeared. Whether he had her murdered or not will never be known; nothing more was heard of her. Northumberland then composed a message as from the King to the Princess Mary, who was in Hertfordshire; he wished to see her for the last time. The Duke intended to kidnap and imprison the Princess as soon as she reached London. She was warned — probably by the Spanish Ambassador, who had already written to her as 'Your Majesty' — and fled to Suffolk.[56]

In the late afternoon of July 6th, the doctors, Sidney, Wroth and Salmon, were watching. Dr Owen, leaning over the ghastly figure on the bed, thought that the end had come. Then, suddenly, Edward began talking to himself; the words were inaudible. Sidney took him in his arms, holding him to his breast.

Edward's murmuring ceased. He turned his head and fixed his eyes on Sidney; then he looked round the room. He said: 'Are you so nigh? I thought you had been further off.' Dr Owen said: 'We heard you speak to yourself — but what you said we know not.' Edward smiled. 'I was praying to God', he said.

There was a long silence. He seemed to have sunk into unconsciousness. Several hours passed. Then he murmured: 'I am faint ... ' and Sir Thomas Wroth came to support him on the other side. Edward said, quite clearly: 'Lord, have mercy upon me — take my spirit.' His eyes opened wide and rolled upwards: the maimed hands moved convulsively. They held him between them until he died.[57]

As dusk fell, a thunderstorm burst over London. Rain came down in cataracts, houses were swept away, trees uprooted: hail, said to be the colour of blood, covered the gardens by the riverside; in the City a church spire, struck by lightning, crashed to the ground.[58]

NOTES TO CHAPTER XV

[1] Tytler, vol. II, pp. 103-12; Lorimer, *Life of John Knox*, p. 170.
[2] Ibid.
[3] Tytler, vol. II, p. 112.
[4] Foxe, vol. VIII, p. 700.
[5] *Lit. Rem.*, vol. I, p. 63.
[6] A. à Wood, *Athenae Oxoniensis*, vol. I, p. 351.
[7] Losely MSS, pp. 83-160.
[8] Ibid.
[9] Strype, *Life of Sir John Cheke*, p. 91.
[10] *Cal. Span. P.*, vol. XV, p. 9; Machyn, p. 30.
[11] *Cal. Span. P.*, vol. XV, p. 17.
[12] Ibid., vol. XI, p. 21.
[13] Ibid.
[14] *Ven. S.P.*, vol. V, p. 933.
[15] Burgon, *Life of Sir Thomas Gresham*, vol. I, pp. 110-11.
[16] *Lit. Rem.*, vol. I, p. clxvi.
[17] *Cal. Span. P.*, vol. XV, p. 12.
[18] *Lit. Rem.*, vol. I, p. cccxxxviii.
[19] Hayward, p. 341.
[20] Ibid., p. 426; Sharon Turner, *History of England*, vol. II, p. 143.
[21] Nichols, *Narratives of the Reformation*, p. 316.
[22] Sharon Turner, vol. II, p. 143.
[23] Machyn, p. 35.
[24] *Lit. Rem.*, vol. I, p. cxcvii.
[25] *Cal. Span. P.*, vol. XI, p. 35.
[26] Ibid.
[27] Tytler, vol. II, p. 170.
[28] *Lit. Rem.*, vol. I, p. 206.
[29] See Genealogical Table.
[30] Strickland, *Lives of the Tudor and Stuart Princesses*, p. 85 (from Badoer, ed. by Luca Cortile).
[31] *Cal. Span. P.*, vol. XI, p. 106.
[32] Godwin, p. 255.
[33] Burnet, *History of the Reformation*, vol. II, part 2, p. 274.
[34] Tytler, vol. II, p. 171.
[35] *Cal. Span. P.*, vol. XI, p. 45.
[36] Tytler, vol. II, p. 170.
[37] *Cal. Span. P.*, vol. XI, p. 46.
[38] Tytler, vol. II, p. 178.
[39] *Lit. Rem.*, vol. I, p. clxxxvi.
[40] *Cal. Span. P.*, vol. XI, p. 45.
[41] *Original Letters*, 1st ser., p. 273.
[42] *Lit. Rem.*, vol. II, p. xx.
[43] W. Baldwin, *Elegy for Edward VI*.
[44] Haynes, pp. 61-153.
[45] Ibid.
[46] *De Noailles*, p. 190.

[47] *Lit. Rem.*, vol. I, p. cxxxviii; Tytler, vol. II, p. 84; Heylyn, p. 139.
[48] *Lit. Rem.*, vol. I, p. clxxxv.
[49] H.M.C. Montague MSS., pp. 4-6.
[50] Haynes, pp. 61-153.
[51] Strype, *Life of Cranmer*, p. 424.
[52] Lloyd, p. 213.
[53] Strype, *Ecclesiastical Memorials*, vol. II, part 1, p. 329.
[54] Godwin, p. 253.
[55] *Lit. Rem.*, vol. I, p. cxcvii.
[56] Ibid., p. cxcviii.
[57] Ibid.
[58] Parker Society, *Zürich Letters*, vol. III, p. 100.

EPILOGUE

MORE than a month went by before Edward VI made his last entry into his capital. There was no lying in state, no reverence, no tribute for the pitiful remains of England's Treasure, 'that young, innocent and blessed King', whom his country, wrote Sir Richard Morrison, was not worthy to keep. 'Which of us is there', he added, 'but sin might draw us to the bar, and prove us guilty of his death?'[1] It is a dramatic simplification: but not a false one. Edward's burden, like the coronation gift of the City of London, had been too heavy for him to carry; it may have intensified the weakness that, created by his attack of measles, developed into the consumption of which he died. That aspect of his story must remain conjectural.

Until July 10th his death was kept secret from the public. On the 8th the Lord Mayor and the aldermen were summoned to the Palace of Greenwich and told of it; it is doubtful whether they were allowed to see the body. The Will was read to them, and their allegiance to the Lady Jane required. On the 11th Ridley declared that Mary and Elizabeth were illegitimate in a sermon that shocked and disgusted his congregation.[2]

Then — while England was jerked into the confusion of an abortive civil war — while Lady Jane, crowned and weeping, wrangled with her husband and his family in the Tower — while the nine days of her reign passed in a storm of dispute and treachery — while Northumberland summoned his sullen and mutinous troops for a last, desperate attack that was never made — while Mary rallied hers to ride into London in triumph — Edward was forgotten; his body was neither embalmed nor coffined; there was a rumour that it had been smuggled out of the Palace and thrust into the ground in a neighbouring paddock outside the gates and another substituted.[3] Cheke, who with the help of William Baldwin, tried to solace his grief with the composition of a long, lame and romanticized elegy for his pupil, gives no information on this point; he merely ascribes his end to 'Crazy Cold', sent by God to attack 'this blessed, guiltless child', after a game of tennis, hiding in a cup of wine to poison his stomach, and so making way for Death with his piercing dart, who, at the last,

288

comforts Edward with the promise of everlasting glory in his Saviour's arms.[4]

With Mary's accession Edward was revenged on Northumberland and his accomplices, specifically at the moment of the Duke's progress to the scaffold, when 'a sprightful dame' ran up to him, and shaking a bloody handkerchief in his face, cried: 'Behold, the blood of that worthy man, that good uncle of that excellent King, which now revenges itself upon thee!'[5] Of those Edward had most loved, Sidney and Barnaby Fitzpatrick prospered, achieving length of days and many honours. Judged by the standards of his own time, Cheke's fate was more terrible than that of Cranmer, Latimer or Ridley. He could not face the fires of martyrdom, and recanted. Miserable and outcast, he retired to the country, where he died — of a broken heart, people said — in 1557.[6]

As her troubled kingdom sank into temporary quiescence, Mary had time to think about her brother's funeral. Her first action was characteristic: she commanded that he should be buried according to the rites of the old faith; when it was pointed out that this would cause public and violent hostility, she compromised by having a private Mass sung for him in the chapel of the Tower.[7]

Edward's sealed coffin had already been conveyed up the river to the Palace of Whitehall. On August 8th the procession set out for the Abbey. The route was artificially extended so that as many of his people as possible could watch the King's last journey. Their cries and sobs were so loud and continuous as to rise above the sound of horse-hooves and drums.

The cortège was headed by the Dean and the choir, singing one of Sternhold's rhyming psalms; then followed a group of bedesmen from Greyfriars, then the heralds carrying twenty-three great banners: among them waved those of the Welsh dragon, St George, the Seymour arms, the Plantagenet greyhound and the Angevin lion; after these came the Gentlemen of the Household in black velvet, and Norroy King of Arms on horseback bearing the King's plumed helmet and sword. He preceded the funeral car, drawn by four horses draped in black and ridden by masked and hooded mourners; the car itself was covered with cloth of gold; on it lay the effigy of the King, crowned, sceptred and robed in a mantle of cloth of gold lined with white satin. The procession closed with four more banners made to represent Tudor roses, and a squadron of men-at-arms led by the Master of the Horse.[8]

Cranmer preached the funeral sermon. The coffin was placed in Henry VII's chapel, at the head of his tomb, beneath the high altar; the splendid and elaborate catafalque erected over it was destroyed during the Civil War, so that there now remains nothing to mark the grave of the last Tudor king — and it is perhaps as well. Edward VI is more fittingly commemorated by his Prayer Books, and by the schools that bear his name.

For many years after his death his library in the Palace of Westminster remained as it was when he left London to die. There were the Prayer Books bound in red velvet, with clasps of silver, pearls and gold; the volumes of Italian poetry; collections of sermons tied with black silk ribbons; the huge bulk of Tyndale's New Testament; illustrated manuscripts of travel; rows of Greek and Latin classics; works on archery, music, hunting, theology; concordances; atlases; histories of countries that he never saw.[9]

And beyond this elegant and impressive array a small door led into the Chair House — his study, where he read by himself or with his tutors, and wrote in his diary. Long, long after he had made his last entry, the black and gold desk in which it was locked lay there, untouched, flanked by the silver-gilt ink-pot, the sand-boxes, the seals, the container for dried ink, the quadrant left him by his father, a set of astronomical instruments, and a scent-burner given him by the fastidious Cheke, his own recipe for scent lying beside it.[10] When the desk was opened, there was the thick red book with its gold clasps; and heaped about it a miscellany of little treasures: a boy's hoard; coins, aglets, four black and white buttons, a gold brooch with an agate centre, a crimson silk purse, some counters — and six red velvet dog-collars with leashes of white leather.

NOTES

[1] Harleian MSS, 353.
[2] Greyfriars, p. 78.
[3] *Original Letters*, 2nd ser., p. 648.
[4] *Elegy for Edward VI*.
[5] Godwin, p. 251.
[6] Strype, *Life of Sir John Cheke*, p. 180.
[7] Machyn, p. 39.
[8] Ibid.
[9] *Lit. Rem.*, vol. I, p. xxb.
[10] Ibid., p. xxb.

BIBLIOGRAPHY

BIBLIOGRAPHY

Acts of the Privy Council, vol. II: 1547-50.
ALLEN, J. W.: *History of Political Thought in the Sixteenth Century*.
Ancaster MSS.
ASCHAM, ROGER: *Toxophilus*; *The Schoolmaster*.
AUBREY, JOHN: *Natural History of Wiltshire*.
AUERBACH, E.: *Tudor Portraits*.
BALDWIN, T. W.: *Shakespeare's Small Latin and Less Greek*.
BALDWIN, W.: *Elegy for Edward VI*.
BALE, JOHN: *Life of Edward VI*.
BECON, THOMAS: *Jewel of Joy*.
BINDOFF, S. T.: *Tudor England*.
BISHOP, E. and CARDINAL GASQUET: *The Prayer Book and Edward VI*.
BREWER, J. S. and GAIRDNER, J.: *Letters and Papers of Henry VIII*.
Burghley MSS (ed. Haynes, 1740).
BURGON, J. W.: *Life and Times of Sir Thomas Gresham*.
BURNET, GILBERT: *History of the Reformation*.
Calendar of Patent Rolls.
Cambridge Modern History (vols. II and III).
CARLOIX, P.: *Mémoires du Sire de Vielleville* (ed. Michaud and Pou-joulat).
CARPENTER, S. C.: *The Church in England*.
CASTLETON, BARON: *A King and His Favourite*.
CAVENDISH, WILLIAM: *Cardinal Wolsey* (ed. Singer).
CHAMBERLAIN, A. B.: *Life of Hans Holbein the Younger*.
CLIFFORD, HENRY: *Life of Jane Dormer*.
COBBETT, T. C.: *State Trials* (vol. I).
COLLINS, A.: *Letters and Memorials of State*; *Peerage of England* (vol. I).
CONSTANT, J.: *The English Reformation*.
DIXON, R. W.: *History of the Church of England*.
Domestic State Papers (1537-53).
ELTON, G. R.: *The Tudor Revolution in Government*; *England Under the Tudors*.
ELYOT, SIR THOMAS: *The Governor*.
EVERETT-GREEN, M. A.: *Letters of Royal and Illustrious Ladies* (vol. II)
FABYAN, ROBERT: *Chronicle*.
FEILING, KEITH: *History of England*.
Foreign State Papers of Edward VI.
FOXE, J.: *Acts and Monuments*.
FROUDE, J. A.: *History of England*; *Life and Letters of Erasmus*.

BIBLIOGRAPHY

FULLER, THOMAS: *Church History*.

FURNIVALL, J. A.: *Early English Poems and Treatises on Manners*.

GAIRDNER, JAMES: *Lollardy and the Reformation in England*; *History of the English Church in the Sixteenth Century*.

GARNER, T. and STRATTON, A.: *Domestic Architecture of England During the Tudor Period*.

GODWIN, F.: *Annals of England*.

GRAFTON, RICHARD: *Chronicle*.

Greyfriars' *Chronicle*.

HALL, EDWARD: *Chronicle*.

HALLIWELL-PHILIPPS, J. O.: *Letters of the Kings of England*.

Harleian MSS, 353.

HARTLEY, D. and E.: *Life and Work of the People of England*.

HAYWARD, SIR JOHN: *Life of Edward VI*.

HERBERT OF CHERBURY, LORD: *Life of Henry VIII*.

HEYLYN, PETER: *History of the Reformation*.

HEYWOOD, THOMAS: *Works*.

HOLINSHED, RAPHAEL: *Chronicle*.

HOPF, C.: *Martin Bucer and the English Reformation*.

HUGHES, P.: *The Reformation in England* (vols. I and II).

HUME, M. A. S. (ed.): *Chronicle of Henry VIII*.

JARDINE, C.: *Criminal Trials* (vol. I).

JONES, C.: *Recollections of Royalty*.

KAULEK, J. (ed.): *Correspondance Politique de MM. de Castillon et de Marillac*.

KNOX, JOHN: *Collected Works* (ed. Laing).

Lansdowne MSS.

LATIMER, HUGH: *Sermons*.

LAW, E.: *Hampton Court Palace* (vol. I).

LEACH, A. F.: *English Schools at the Reformation*.

LEFÈVRE-PONTALIS (ed.): *Correspondance de Odet de Selve*.

LELAND, JOHN: *Itinerary* (ed. Toulmin-Smith).

LESLEY, BISHOP: *History of Scotland* (vol. II).

L'ESTRANGE, A. G.: *Greenwich Palace and Hospital*.

LEWIS, C. S.: *English Literature in the Sixteenth Century*.

LLOYD, D.: *State Worthies*.

LODGE, EDMUND: *Illustrations of British History and Manners*.

Lonsdale MSS.

LORIMER, PETER: *Life of John Knox*.

Losely MSS.

MACHYN, HENRY: *Diary*.

MACKIE, J. D.: *The Earlier Tudors*.

MADDEN, SIR F.: *Expenses of Princess Mary.*

MARKHAM, C. R.: *H.M. King Edward VI.*

MERRIMAN, R. B.: *Life of Thomas Cromwell.*

Montague MSS.

MORLEY, HENRY: *Life of Girolamo Cardano.*

MORRIS, CHRISTOPHER: *Political Thought in England — Tyndale to Hooker; The Tudors.*

MOZLEY, J. F.: *Coverdale and His Bibles.*

MULLER, J. A.: *Stephen Gardiner.*

NAUNTON, SIR ROBERT: *Fragmenta Regalia.*

NICHOLAS, SIR HARRIS: *Life and Times of Lady Jane Grey.*

NICHOLS, J. G. (ed.): *Literary Remains of Edward VI*; *Memoirs of the Duke of Richmond*; *Narratives of the Reformation*; *Queen Jane and Queen Mary.*

NUGENT, E. M.: *Thought and Culture of the English Reformation.*

Parker Society: *Original Letters*; *Zürich Letters.*

PASTOR, L.; *History of the Popes* (vol. XII).

PEGGE, SAMUEL: *Curialia.*

PERLIN, E.: *Antiquarian Repertory* (vol. IV).

PERROT, SIR JOHN: *Life* (Anon., 1728).

POCOCK, N.: *Troubles Connected with the Prayer Book of 1549.*

POLLARD, A. F.: *Henry VIII*; *Thomas Cranmer and the Reformation*; *England Under Protector Somerset*; *History of England*; *Tudor Tracts.*

POLLINI, G.: *Historia Ecclesiastica* (1594).

Portland MSS.

Prayer Books: (*First and Second of Edward VI*).

PRESCOTT, H. F. M.: *Mary Tudor.*

Privy Council Register (vol. II).

RAE, JAMES: *Deaths of the Kings of England.*

RAPIN DE THOYRAS: *History of England* (vol. VII).

RAUMER, C. F. VON: *History of the Sixteenth and Seventeenth Centuries.*

READ, CONYERS: *Bibliography of British History — Tudor Period*; *Mr Secretary Cecil and Queen Elizabeth.*

ROSE-TROUP, F.: *The Western Rising of 1549.*

Rutland MSS.

RYMER, THOMAS: *Foedera* (ed. A. Clarke).

ST MAUR, H.: *Annals of the Seymours.*

SANDFORD, FRANCIS: *Genealogical History of England.*

Scottish State Papers (1537-53).

SMYTH, C. H. E.: *Cranmer and the Reformation Under Edward VI.*

SNEYD, C. A. (ed.): *Italian Relation.*

Spanish State Papers, Calendar of (1537-53).

SPEED, JOHN: *Chronicle.*

State Papers of Henry VIII.

STERNHOLD, THOMAS: *Works.*

STOWE, JOHN: *Chronicle.*

STRICKLAND, AGNES: *The Bachelor Kings of England; Mary Queen of Scots; Queens of England* (vols. II and III); *Tudor and Stuart Princesses; Queens of Scotland* (vols. I and II).˙

STRYPE, JOHN: *Ecclesiastical Memorials; Annals of the Reformation; Life of Sir Thomas Smith; Life of Cranmer; Life of Sir John Cheke.*

TANNER, J. R.: *Tudor Constitutional Documents.*

TAWNEY, R. H.: *Agrarian Problems in the Sixteenth Century.*

THOMAS, WILLIAM: *The Pilgrim.*

Throckmorton MSS.

TREVELYAN, G. M.: *Social History of England.*

TROLLOPE, WILLIAM: *History of Christ's Hospital.*

TURNER, SHARON: *History of England.*

TYE, DR: *Works.*

TYNDALE, W.: *The Obedience of a Christian Man.*

TYTLER, P. F.: *History of Edward VI and Mary I.*

UDALL, NICHOLAS: *Works.*

Venetian State Papers, Calendar of (1537-53).

VERTOT, RENÉ (ed.): *Ambassades de M. de Noailles.*

WILLIAMSON, J. A.: *The Tudor Age.*

Winchester Cathedral MSS.

WOOD, ANTHONY À: *Athenae Oxonienses.*

WRIOTHESLEY, CHARLES: *Chronicle of England.*

WYATT, GEORGE: *Memoir of Queen Anne Boleyn.*

YEARSLEY, MCLEOD: *Le Roye Est Mort.*

INDEX